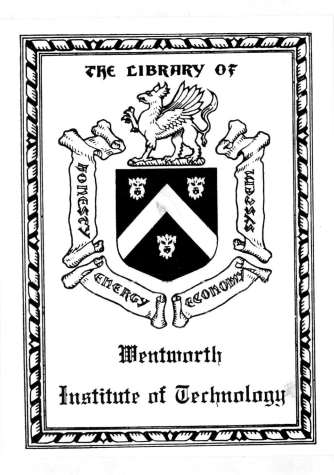

Other McGraw-Hill Books in Software Engineering

ISBN	AUTHOR	TITLE
0-07-040235-3	Marca, McGowan	*Structural Analysis and Design Structures*
0-07-043198-1	Morris, Brandon	*Relational Diagramming: Enhancing the Software Development Process*
0-07-036964-X	Lecarme, Pellissier, Gart	*Software Portability*
0-07-057299-2	Shumate	*Understanding Concurrency in ADA®*
0-07-046536-3	Nielsen, Shumate	*Designing Large Real-Time Systems with ADA®*
0-07-042632-5	Modell	*A Professional's Guide to Systems Analysis*
0-07-001051-X	Alford	*Requirements-Driven Software Design*
0-07-016803-2	Dickinson	*Developing Quality Systems*
0-07-065086-1	Towner, Ranade	*CASE: Concepts and Implementation*
0-07-010661-4	Charette	*Software Engineering Risk Analysis and Management*
0-07-023165-6	General Electric Co. Staff	*Software Engineering Handbook*
0-07-010646-0	Wallace et al.	*A Unified Methodology for Developing Systems*
0-07-010645-2	Charette	*Software Engineering Environments: Concepts and Technologies*
0-07-067922-3	Wallace	*Practitioner's Guide to ADA®*
0-07-044119-7	Musa et al.	*Software Reliability*
0-07-050783-X	Pressman	*Software Engineering: A Practitioner's Approach*
0-07-050790-2	Pressman	*Software Engineering: A Beginner's Guide*
0-07-030550-1	Howden	*Functional Program Testing and Analysis*

Ranade IBM Series

ISBN	AUTHOR	TITLE
0-07-065087-X	Towner	*IDMS®: A Professional's Guide to Concepts, Design, and Programming*
0-07-002673-4	Azevedo	*ISPF: The Strategic Dialog Manager*
0-07-050686-8	Prasad	*IBM Mainframes*
0-07-046263-1	McGrew, McDaniel	*On-Line Text Management*
0-07-039822-4	Malamud	*The Book of DEC Networks and Architectures*
0-07-071136-4	Wipfler	*Distributed Processing in CICS*
0-07-051144-6	Ranade, Sackett	*Introduction to SNA Networking: Using VTAM/NCP*
0-07-051244-2	Ranade, Ranade	*VSAM: Concepts, Programming, and Design*
0-07-051245-0	Ranade	*VSAM: Performance, Design, and Fine Tuning*

Zero
Defect
Software

G. Gordon Schulmeyer

McGraw-Hill, Inc.
New York   St. Louis   San Francisco   Auckland   Bogotá
Caracas   Hamburg   Lisbon   London   Madrid   Mexico
Milan   Montreal   New Delhi   Paris
San Juan   São Paulo   Singapore
Sydney   Tokyo   Toronto

Library of Congress Cataloging-in-Publication Data

Schulmeyer, G. Gordon.
    Zero defect software / G. Gordon Schulmeyer.
       p.   cm.
    Includes bibliographical references and index.
    ISBN 0-07-055663-6
    1. Computer software—Quality control. I. Title.
  QA76.76.Q35S38 1990
  005—dc20   90-6341
                                                                       CIP

1 2 3 4 5 6 7 8 9 0 DOC/DOC 9 6 5 4 3 2 1 0

ISBN 0-07-055663-6

The sponsoring editor for this book was Theron Shreve, and the production supervisor was Suzanne W. Babeuf. It was set in Century Schoolbook by Archetype, Inc.

Printed and bound by R. R. Donnelley & Sons Company.

This book is dedicated to the long-suffering software development professional

---

Subscription information to BYTE Magazine:
Call 1-800-257-9402, or write Circulation Dept.,
One Phoenix Mill Lane, Peterborough, NH 03458.

Contents

Foreword

Every day we read about the quality dilemma of the United States. Management criticizes the seemingly lackadaisical attitude of American workers when it comes to the quality of their work. Workers blame management for their short sightedness, their lack of commitment to quality, and their failure to invest in quality controls. Meanwhile, consumers rush to purchase foreign goods because they believe that those goods will last longer and won't wind up at the dealer for repair week after week. And, more and more executives are turning to Japan to determine how to adapt statistical quality control concepts that were originated in the United States for their own industrial use.[1]

The United States still maintains a world leadership position within the information technologies industries. Its computer, communication, and software industries are growing at a quick rate and account for an increasing percentage of its new jobs and its trade surplus. Yet, the professional journals continue to publish page after page of criticism about the quality problems that plague this industry, for example, any issue of *Software Engineering Notes* published by the Association for Computing Machinery/SIGSOFT. They challenge the industry to do better, especially on major new national projects like the Strategic Defense Initiative and Space Station.

In addition, they describe foreign initiatives, like ESPIRIT in Europe and SIGMA in Japan, where the rest of the world has mounted a challenge to the United State's leadership position in this world of high technology. It appears that the entire fabric of our current industrial infrastructure is being challenged internally and by foreign competitors, whose passion for quality may determine who will win the race for world domination in the information industries in the year 2000.

How will the quality dilemmas described above affect the growth and prosperity of our information technologies industries? Will they impact industry's ability to deliver those high-quality software, computer, and communications products envisioned for the future? Will help become available to deal with these problems and those reported in the recent American Society for Quality Control's Software Quality Survey?[2] This 1988 survey described a sorry state of affairs across most of the American industry in the area of software quality. For example, it reported that fewer than 10 percent of the over 100 firms that responded to the survey were using Pareto and statistical analysis in their state-of-the-practice to identify error-prone methods. It also showed that few tools and few metrics were being used for software quality analysis.

Gordon Schulmeyer's new book, *Zero Defect Software,* is therefore a very timely piece. It fills the void when one looks for help in the battle for high-quality software. It discusses approaches that work and demonstrates how they can work using real examples. It is thought provoking and insightful when it comes to helping us to deal with our quality challenges.

The book did six things that I liked and thought useful. First, it frankly discussed the quality challenges that the software industry is facing and showed how practitioners in other industries and nations are trying to handle them. Second, it took proven quality concepts from such notables as Crosby and Deming and showed how to integrate them together into a total quality framework for software. Third, it illustrated how to make the framework work by discussing tools, metrics, models, and indicators that make software quality, or its absence, evident to all of those involved in development of the product. Fourth, it stressed processes that contribute to quality more than techniques that make it apparent. Fifth, it emphasized that quality is everyone's business and talked to the difficult issues involved in motivating workers to achieve defect-free software goals. Sixth, and finally, it discussed what I believe is the key to success in software quality—the intelligent use of statistical controls over the controlled and certified process of software development.

Probably the most difficult problem facing our industry is figuring out how to get programmers to think quality during each step in the development process. Schulmeyer's book helps us combat this problem by establishing a framework which enables the programmer to weave together the use of automated error detection, error checklists, statistical controls, quality circles, and team approaches. In essence, the book treats every software review, both formal and informal, as a gate where teams can be built; quality can be checked and lessons learned relative to error; and trends can be assessed and fed forward to reduce the chances of their reoccurrence. Teamwork and focus on quality goals are enforced through the use of quality circles and peer reviews. Manual and automated tools that help detect errors are reviewed. Statistical controls and programmer self-checks are emphasized and guidelines for their use are established.

When Gordon asked me to write this Foreword, I was honored. I've known Gordon for many years and have watched him grow throughout his career, as first a quality specialist and then as a manager at Westinghouse. This book should be considered one of the high points in his career because it successfully communicates to the layman who is looking for help the knowledge he has gained through the application of good methods. To summarize my thoughts, good job, good sense, and good timing.

Donald J. Reifer
December 1988

REFERENCES

1. Ouchi, William, *Theory Z,* Addison-Wesley Publishing Co., Inc., Reading, MA, © 1981.
2. Reifer, Donald J., Richard W. Knudson, and Jerry Smith, *Final Report: Software Quality Survey,* prepared for American Society for Quality Control, Milwaukee, WI, 1987.

Preface

Controversial not only describes the subject of this book—*developing zero defect software*—but captures the essence of why such a book needs to be written. Many of us believe that zero defects in software is not achievable in today's software environment. But what about tomorrow? What management philosophy, planning and controls, and state-of-the-art techniques do we need to strive toward to achieve zero defect software?

Even if one achieves zero defects, the controversy continues. How do you prove your claim? What criteria do you establish? What techniques do you use to prove the condition of zero defects, and how acceptable are the results to those "unbiased" believers?

Given the nature of the controversy, given the current state of defects in the industry, and given such compelling notions as actually being able to achieve zero defect software, how could I resist?

Since 1961, I have been involved in every aspect of software development. In 1977, I was introduced to the concepts of standards for software quality. In 1982, I became Manager for Software Quality Assurance. In 1985, I managed a large software development group. In 1986, after reading Philip B. Crosby's books, *Quality is Free* and *Quality Without Tears,* I was further compelled to investigate the nature of zero defect programs. I began to apply these zero defect concepts to the software development process and formed a zero defect software committee which, since that time, has met on a regular basis.

Even though there was no plan for achieving zero defect software, I believed it was my responsibility to "preach" zero defect software and would settle for no less than zero defects as the manager of a software development group. Shigeo Shingo's book, *Zero Quality Control: Source Inspection and the Poka-yoke System,* came to my attention in 1987, and many of the concepts from Shigeo Shingo are used in this book.[1] When I read Shingo's book, I became convinced that his fundamental manufacturing ideal could be applied to software development. That, combined with a course in Value Analysis, established the basis for the zero-defect-software-oriented software development process chart described herein and provided the foundation for this book.

The editor of the *IEEE Spectrum* that published the article "Zero-defect software: the elusive goal" highlighted the following comments in that article:

> Recent software publications make it clear it is not possible to develop tools for detecting logical redundancy; inconsistency, or incompleteness of specifications and that "zero-defect system" is impossible to build today.
>
> Even when software, used to solve numerical problems, reliably follows the specifications of the user and has been checked out on a number of test cases, there always seems to be other cases for which numerical conditioning can obviate the usefulness of the software.
>
> This paper deemphasizes the enormous complexities in the development of very large-scale software systems. It argues that once we get into a difficult problem, we often find that things aren't as bad as they seemed from the outside. While this is often true, it is not always true. I doubt that even with infinite time one could develop a very large-scale software system that was error-free.[2]

These comments could certainly be applied to this book, and the rebuttal could only be to try the methodology in the book because it makes sense to attempt to achieve "the elusive goal."

Many of the ideas in this book come from the general quality field or applications to manufacturing quality. The lessons learned in general or from manufacturing quality are significant and can be applied to software quality as explained in the *Handbook of Software Quality Assurance.*[3]

In the epilogue to the book, *Software Quality Management,* the editors state that hardware quality assurance procedures are only partially applicable to software development. Many software quality evaluation methods, still evolving, are unique to software and foster a reevaluation of some of the traditional hardware quality concepts.[4]

Of particular concerns to the authors of *Software Quality Management* are the application of hardware reliability methods to software reliability and placing software quality personnel in the hardware quality organization, because they both have "quality" in their title and the hardware organization existed before the software one.

In this book, the application of the quality imperative and a process for carrying it out in software development is espoused. The quality principles are applied to a process, and this book focuses on that software development process. At this level, even though it is agreed that "many software quality methods evolving are unique to software" (such as in this book), the general quality principles are applicable. There is little, if any, attempt to apply "hardware quality assurance procedures" to software development.

Dr. Myron Tribus, management consultant, states that successful companies are customer oriented. They work to please customers

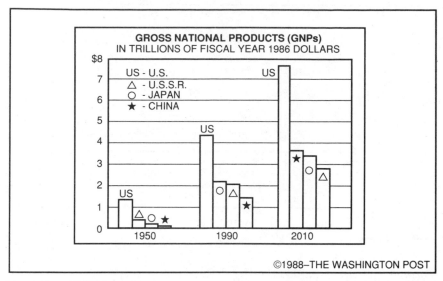

GROSS NATIONAL PRODUCTS (GNPs)
IN TRILLIONS OF FISCAL YEAR 1986 DOLLARS

©1988–THE WASHINGTON POST

Figure P.1   GNP chart.[7]

because only customers can define quality. Most companies in the United States are share price oriented; they work to please the equity markets, not the customer.[5] This book stresses the importance of the customer for the software and extends the customer's role as the next person in the software development process—the internal customer.

It was refreshing to see the author's note in an article by John Guaspari: "It is my intent to be the first living human being to write an entire article about quality without once using the J-word. [JAPAN]"[6]

However, in this book it is clearly necessary to provide much information from the Japanese quality experience. The importance is underlined by the Gross National Product (GNP) chart in Fig. P.1, which projects Japan's GNP (insignificant in 1950) to be more than half the United States GNP in 1990 and in 2010. The Japanese growth in GNP is even more significant when one considers the population and physical size differences between the United States and Japan.

Another view of the situation is illustrated in Fig. P.2 which highlights the erosion of the U.S. companies' share of the domestic American market for six consumer products. The first five listed products were pioneered in the U.S. and the Japanese took significant share of these products by 1987. One final chart (Fig. P.3) shows the targeted software market by the Japanese through 1996, which highlights the potential loss of that market by U.S. software companies, if the Japanese achieve the same type of penetration of market as they

PERCENT

Year						
1970	90	90	40	10	100	88
1975	40	80	10	10	95	82
1980	30	60	10	0	89	70
1987	0	10	0	0	25	70
	Phonographs	Color TV	Audio tape recorders	Video tape recorders	Telephone sets	Ball bearings

Figure P.2   U.S. share of the American market.[8] (*International Trade Administration, Commerce Dept.*)

showed they are capable of in Fig. P.2.

The impact of the quality revolution on Japan's GNP is clear in Fig. P.1, because the worldwide customer buys quality. There is a significant Japanese national project to put software in that global marketplace as illustrated in Fig. P.3. The initial reports coming from Japan are that they are already achieving significantly better defect rates than United States delivered software (Japan 0.2 defects/KLOEC versus United States 10 to 50 defects/KLOEC), where KLOEC is thousand lines of executable code.[10] Once the Japanese decide to produce

Year	Expected sales (billion $)	Growth (%)
1985	4.9	26
1991	14.7	20
1996	31.4	16

Figure P.3   Targeted Japanese software markets.[9] (*Japanese Ministry of International Trade and Industry, Reprinted with permission of "Software Magazine," November extra 1988, Sentry Publishing, Inc., Westborough, MA.*)

software, they are determined to produce it defect free, and as a result, will increase their market share, thereby inflicting losses in market share on U.S. companies.

W. Edwards Deming is the namesake for the important Deming Prize awarded in Japan since 1951. Recently, he was asked what he thinks of U.S. competitiveness. His answer is illuminating.

> What do you mean, competitiveness? Is that what you do? Compete? Why not do better? People talk about keeping up. That's nonsense. Let's get ahead. We do everything except apply knowledge. We have the knowledge but don't know how to use it, don't try. Do you think somebody is going to stand still while we catch up? Someone who hopes to become competitive already has his back to the wall, is admitting defeat. The alternative is to get ahead through innovation of product, innovation of process. That means upper management has to pay attention to business instead of churning money. American management hasn't enough respect for knowledge. Do you think short term thinking and churning money contribute to our balance of trade or reduction of the national debt?[11]

This zero defect software program could be viewed as a response to "innovation of process" in software development.

To return to the question, "How are you going to prove you have zero defects?" requires a few words. What is an error, fault, failure, and defect? An error is a discrepancy which creates faults that cause failures. Failures that occur in the software after delivery are called defects. Therefore, if customer-delivered software performs without a failure, then zero defect software is achieved.

As usual with the software development field, there are many TLAs (three-letter acronyms) used throughout the book. These are listed alphabetically following the Preface. The complete term also is given in the first usage in this book.

This book provides training material for a zero defect software course. It contains the complete story for moving an organization toward zero defect software. Face the challenge now (acronyms and all), and proceed to the goal of achieving zero defect software. It is only through the continuous efforts of those willing to face the challenge that the results will be achieved.

REFERENCES

1. Shingo, Shigeo, *Zero Quality Control: Source Inspection and the Poka-yoke System,* Productivity Press, Cambridge, MA, 1986.
2. Hamilton, Margaret H. "Zero-defect software: the elusive goal," *IEEE Spectrum,* vol. 23, no. 3, March 1986, Copyright © 1986, IEEE, New York, p. 53.
3. Schulmeyer, G. Gordon, "Software Quality Lessons From the Quality Experts" in *Handbook of Software Quality Assurance,* G. Gordon Schulmeyer and James I. McManus, eds., Van Nostrand Reinhold Co., New York, 1987, pp. 25–45.

4. Epilogue in *Software Quality Management,* Matthew J. Fisher and John D. Cooper, eds., Petrocelli Books, Princeton, 1979, p. 276.
5. Tribus, Myron, "The Quality Imperative," *The Bent of Tau Beta Pi,* vol. LXXVIII, no. 2, Spring 1987, Tau Beta Pi Association, Inc., Knoxville, TN, p. 26.
6. Guaspari, John, "The Role of Human Resources in Selling Quality Improvements to Employees," *Management Review,* March 1987, American Management Association, New York, © 1987, p. 22, Reprinted by permission. All Rights Reserved.
7. Oberdorfer, Don, "China could place 2nd, Soviets 4th Economically," *The Washington Post,* January 12, 1988, p. A17.
8. Gladwell, Malcolm, "Scientist Warns of U.S. Reliance on Foreigners," *The Washington Post,* September 8, 1988, source of chart is International Trade Administration, Commerce Dept., p. E1.
9. Hiyoshi, Yoshikata, "Japan, Underdeveloped in Software, May be Changing," *Software Magazine,* vol. 8, no. 14, November extra 1988, Sentry Publishing, Inc., Westborough, MA, Copyright © 1988, p. 74, Reprinted by permission.
10. DeMarco, Tom, *Controlling Software Projects: Management, Measurement, & Estimation,* Yourdon, Inc., New York, © 1982, p. 200. Reprinted by permission of Prentice Hall, Inc., Englewood Cliffs, NJ.
11. Pellerin, Cheryl, "One on One—W. Edwards Deming," *Defense News,* vol. 3, no. 24, June 13, 1988, Copyright © 1988 by Times Journal Publishing Company, Springfield, VA, p. 62, Reprinted courtesy of *Defense News.*

Acknowledgments

I owe thanks to many associates who helped to review the manuscript and provided ideas for improvement. James J. Holden III provided a strong influence to make the Zero defect software program practical as well as produce the important software activities list to go along with the software development process chart. Initial comments and reviews through various drafts were cheerfully provided by Halsey Chenoweth Ph.D, James McManus, Chin-Kuci Cho, Ph.D, Donald J. Reifer, Joel Glazer, and James J. Holden III. I take responsibility for all defects in thought that may be in this book.

I appreciate the rapid turnaround in typing the manuscript by Mary Holden, even though she is busy raising three children. Thanks to my editor at McGraw-Hill Book Company, Theron Shreve, to my associate editor, Kay Magome, and copy editor, Maureen Cook.

Abbreviations and Acronyms

ACAP	Analyst capability
ADSI	Adjusted delivered source instructions (Project size)
AFSCP	Air Force System Command Pamphlet
AI	Artificial Intelligence
AQL	Acceptable Quality Level
ARTCC	Air Route Traffic Control Center
ASQC	American Society for Quality Control
ASQS	Assistant for Specifying the Quality of Software
CASE	Computer Aided Software Engineering
CDR	Critical Design Review
CIDS	Critical Item Development Specification
CMS	Configuration Management System
CPM	Critical Path Method
CRISD	Computer Resources Integrated Support Document*
CSC	Computer Software Component
CSCI	Computer Software Configuration Item
CSOM	Computer System Operator's Manual*
CSU	Computer Software Unit
DACC	Design Assertion Consistency Checker
DBDD	Data Base Design Document
D.C.	Developmental Configuration
DD	Data Dictionary
DFD	Data Flow Diagram
DI	Documentation Index
DID	Data Item Description
Doc.	Documentation
DOD	Department of Defense
DR	Design Review
EASL	Equivalent Assembler Source Lines
ESG	Electronic Systems Group
FAA	Federal Aviation Administration
FCA	Functional Configuration Audit
FDA	Food and Drug Administration
FQT	Formal Qualification Testing
FSM	Firmware Support Manual*

*May be vendor supplied

Funct.	Functional
GNP	Gross National Product
IDD	Interface Design Document
INSP.	Inspection
IPO	Input, Processing, Output
IRS	Interface Requirements Specification
J-word	Japan, Japanese
KLOC	Thousand Lines of Code
KLOEC	Thousand Lines of Executable Code
KSLOC	Thousand Source Lines of Code
LCL	Lower control limit
LOC	Lines of Code
LSL	Lower statistical limit
MCCR	Mission Critical Computer Resources
Mgmt.	Management
MIL	Military
MTTF	Mean time to failures
NASA	National Aeronautics and Space Administration
OMS	Object Management System
PCA	Physical Configuration Audit
PCAP	Programmer capability
PDL	Program Design Language
PDR	Preliminary Design Review
PERT	Program Evaluation and Review Technique
PIDS	Prime Item Development Specification

PMR	Program management review
PMS	Program Management System
ppm	Parts per million
Prelim.	Preliminary
QA	Quality Assurance
QC	Quality Circle; Quality Control
OQC	Zero Quality Control
Qual.	Qualification
RADC	Rome Air Development Center
RFP	Request For Proposal
Rqmts.	Requirements
RSVP	Research Software Validation Package
RVOL	Volatility of requirements
SCCB	Software Configuration Control Board
SCR	Software Cost Reduction
SDD	Software Design Document
SDF	Software Development File
SDIP	Software Development Integrity Program
SDP	Software Development Plan
SDR	System Design Review
SeCS	Self Check System
SLCSE	Software Life-Cycle Support Environment
SMED	Single-Minute Exchange of Die
SOW	Statement of Work
SPC	Statistical Process Control
Spec.	Specification

*May be vendor supplied

SPM	Software Programmer's Manual*	**STP**	Software Test Plan
SPQL	Shipped-product quality level	**STR**	Software Test Report
		SuCS	Successive Check System
SPR	Software Problem Report	**SUM**	Software User's Manual*
SPS	Software Product Specification	**T & S**	Timing and sizing
SQC	Statistical Quality Control	**TC**	Test coverage
		TIP	Transition Improvement Program
SQPP	Software Quality Program Plan	**TLA**	Three letter acronym
SRR	System Requirements Review	**TQC**	Total Quality Control
SRS	Software Requirements Specification	**TQM**	Total Quality Management
SSDD	System/Segment Design Document	**TURN**	Turnaround time on development computer
SSR	Software Specification Review	**TRR**	Test Readiness Review
		UCL	Upper control limit
SSS	System/Segment Specification	**U.S.**	United States
STD	Standard	**USL**	Upper statistical limit
STD	Software Test Description	**VDD**	Version Description Document

---

*May be vendor supplied

Introduction: The Need for Quality Software

"But I am constant as the northern star,
Of who true-fix'd and resting quality
There is no fellow in the firmament."
SHAKESPEARE
Julius Caesar, Act III, Scene 1

Software development is in a crisis. When delivered, computer software is often late, and it fails often because it contains defects. The answer to lateness and failures is quality. Quality activities ensure prevention of defects and a "cleaner" product gets done faster.

Analyzing and removing identified errors in the software area provide the basis for improving software quality. Some organizations spend half their software quality effort on error tracking and analysis. This involves analyzing errors as they are detected, ensuring corrective action, as well as seeking long-range solutions. Some organizations issue "error alert" reports which serve two purposes: avoid repeating the same error, and publicizing a positive quality service.[1]

On the average, 49 percent of the faults inherent in avionics programs are uncovered prior to the use of the software.[2] So, in general, there are 51 percent defects when the avionics software is used. On a fielded avionics software system with which the author is familiar, the defects reported from the field over many years number about 1,500, but the internal errors uncovered are nearly 5,000. During a particular air defense software development project, for example, over 3,000 problems were uncovered by the developers, and about 200 were discovered in the incomplete product sent to the customer. Something must be done about these defects, and it is the objective of quality control to do that something during software development.

Generally, a product can be defective in one of four ways: a design defect, a construction defect, an expressed warranty failure, or a failure to adequately warn the user. For a design or construction defect, a plaintiff in a product liability suit needs to show that "the product deviates from the defendant's own designs or specifications, or that it differs from similar units produced by the defendant."[3]

Customer comments on software quality are freely quoted in the press. A July 1989 *Business Week* article contained the following shocking commentary:

> It seems dBase IV has done poorly because its 450,000 lines of code contain as many as 100 bugs, say outside developers. Ashton-Tate says the glitches number 44. Still, the flaws make functions such as file-sorting worthless. "This program is nothing but a stick-up," says Denis Bellemare, a Monteral immigration lawyer and dBase IV buyer. "It's so bug-ridden I can't use it."[4]

The ultimate result of what software failures may have wrought is death. The Therac 25 machine registered "malfunction 54" which means a dose rate discrepancy, but not a hazard, while providing radiation treatment. But it was allegedly a fatal dose that killed Voyne R. Cox and Verdon Kidd in 1986. Therac's computer software "failed to access the appropriate calibration data" stated a report given to the U.S. Food and Drug Administration (FDA). An attorney in the case thinks the use hinges on the software defect and has requested the name of the Therac 25 programmer.[5]

Of interest to software professionals is whether courts will view software as a service or a product. If a service, those producing the programs are liable for defects only if negligent. The step in the development process, such as design or manufacture, that caused the defect that caused the injury must be determined. Also, it must be shown that the defect was caused by a failure to use sufficient care.

If a product, the manufacturer is held strictly liable for injury caused by defects. It is easier to recover damages under strict liability than under negligence standards.*

Following up on problems of this type, a United States House of Representatives investigations subcommittee study raises concern about the lack of government regulation of software quality. The document reports, "There is no infallible method whereby a regulatory agency can assure that the software embedded in a system will not cause death or injury."[6]

Another reported example of a software defect having national impact occurred two years before the first space shuttle launch. A pro-

---

*Excerpted from *Datamation*, May 15, 1987, Copyright © 1987 by Cahners Publishing Company.

grammer changed shuttle software timing by 1/30th of a second. That minuscule change introduced a 1 in 67 chance that the five on-board shuttle computers would not work in sync. In April 1981, twenty minutes before lift off, the defect appeared and the computers were unable to communicate. Thousands of hours of testing did not uncover this defect, and NASA had to postpone the flight.[7]*

QUALITY PRINCIPLES

To prevent these problems—this crisis—it is necessary for attitudes to change. There are guiding principles for this quality imperative to help attitudes change. The starting point is with management. Dr. Myron Tribus, a management consultant, has contributed these "principles":

First, the *quality principle:* Quality is the driving force for competitiveness. Quality is never the problem; it is the solution to the problem. Quality improvements reduce costs, prevent the propagation of errors, and provide better products and service.

Second, the *intelligent use of statistics:* All systems exhibit variability. Statistics help to determine if the variance is a signal that something is wrong. Learning to remove the causes of variation is the first step in improving the process. Eighty-five percent of the time the system is the cause of the problem (variation), and 15 percent of the time it is the workers. The workers know the system best and so are the best ones to fix the system.

Third, the *quality cost principle:* The producer of highest quality will be the producer of lowest cost for a given set of features. High quality in processes results in both a low cost and a high quality product.

Fourth, *only customers can define quality:* Successful companies are customer-oriented. Most companies in the United States are share-price oriented, driven by the equity market. Sometimes this equity market consciousness is necessary for survival in this age of takeover, but so is customer orientation.

Fifth, *drive out fear* (borrowed from Dr. Deming): Fear paralyzes a company. There is a big fear of telling managers things managers do not want to hear.[8]

The cost of low quality is a tally of such elements as defects, rework, scrap costs, lost sales, and less credibility/reputation/goodwill. Preventive techniques, such as statistical process control (SPC), are used extensively in Japan.

The cost of low quality is thought to be two to three percent of sales

*Excerpted from *Design News*, Feb. 1, 1988, Copyright © 1988 by Cahners Publishing Company.

in Japan, but in the United States, it is believed to be at least 20 percent of sales. A study conducted by Bell Laboratories on one of its projects concluded that a two percent investment in quality-related activities during design (an up-front phase) yielded an 18 percent net cost savings.[9]

THE QUALITY IMPERATIVE

An imperative to being a winner is a quality management system that is the best for producing products and for delivering the finest customer service. Being the best in quality gives an organization its greatest opportunity for survival, growth, and industry leadership. The greatest single aspect of a business that yields more substantive rewards is improvement in quality. Evaluation of the following three criteria will demonstrate the need to improve quality to pursue a company's goals for success:

- the importance of quality to the business must be recognized
- the responsibility for quality must be accepted and met
- quality must be clearly understood by everyone

Since there are many approaches to quality improvement, any one approach or combination thereof can lead to success. One essential element in any approach is that it be responsive to and considerate of the culture of the organization. Another important element is a well understood, repeatable process. Other essential elements relate to basic concepts of quality improvement that are necessary if potential benefits are to be realized.

Management's acceptance of the need to improve quality begins an organization's efforts toward creating a leadership position in quality. Acceptance of the need encourages management to establish a strategy for quality improvement and to make a long-term commitment to success in quality.

To achieve a significant improvement in quality, there must be consistent understanding of quality realities. When people have a common understanding of quality, the stage is set for a cultural change through the company. Understanding will dispel inaccurate beliefs and practices in quality and move behavior toward quality realities.[10]

It is the intention of this book to challenge software developers to pursue a leadership position in quality by providing a framework for achieving zero defect software—the ultimate software quality reality.

To achieve the quality imperative in software development, the principles and steps discussed above must be brought into the software field. Some of these are already happening, such as, defect data collection and analysis, the use of statistical quality control in software, and the continued expansion of software quality auditing personnel to become an integrated part of the process—the prevention mindset. Some are just starting to happen in the software field and are highlighted in this book, such as, attention to quality, the systemic nature of quality problems, the responsibilities of management and the software developers for quality software production, and enhanced definition of who is the customer for software development.

A few words of definition of quality and their implication to software development are appropriate here. Philip Crosby defines quality as conformance to requirements.[11] In the *Handbook of Software Quality Assurance,* software quality is defined as the fitness for use of the total software product.[12]

Consistent with the precepts that quality is conformance to requirements and prevention of defects (fitness for use), a quality evaluation organization should act as an instrument of management in auditing all aspects of software development and procurement. Software quality must be built in by its developers, with the quality organization an independent assurer of compliance with performance and standards.[13] As such, software quality personnel play a key role in the software development process as it is discussed in this book.

THE CRISIS

This introduction concerns the quality imperative and has focused on those principles, but do not forget the opening sentence of this Introduction—"Software development is in a crisis." The complex of problems associated with trying to produce software that operates properly, within budget, on time, and is maintainable is "the software crisis." The Department of Defense, among the largest consumer of software technology, has found that the software crisis is forcing the military to wait for software to be defect free before it can use new systems. Progress in alleviating this crisis has been slow.[14]

Beside the defect crisis, just the number of available software personnel is in crisis. For example, in Japan, despite factories of programmers lined shoulder to shoulder, a sense of crisis is mounting. According to Japan's Ministry of International Trade and Industry, by the year 2000, Japan will face a shortage of a million programmers.[15]

So, of importance to the quality imperative for software development is the understanding of crisis management. First, the stages of a crisis are reviewed as applicable to software development. Then, a model for crisis management in general is provided with guidelines for software development.

The following stages of a crisis, according to Steven Fink in *Crisis*

Management, Planning for the Inevitable, have names rooted in medicine because a crisis is viewed as the turning point in the course of a disease: *prodronal crisis stage, acute crisis stage, chronic crisis stage,* and *crisis resolution stage.**

The prodronal stage of a crisis is the warning stage, such as, when a sailor spots the warning clouds of a storm. Often the prodronal stage is called precrisis, but this happens only after the crisis hits. The prodronal stage of the software development crisis is long since past.

The acute stage of a crisis is the time when the crisis erupts, such as, when a sailor reacts to the storm at sea. Most people think of the acute crisis stage when they speak of a crisis. The acute crisis stage of software development appeared in the early 1960s when checks were miswritten by programs, and space program delays and accidents resulted from defective programs.

The chronic stage of a crisis is the time when the crisis is being cleaned-up or post-mortemed. With the continuing awareness of the software development crisis, it is the responsibility of those in the field to work through the chronic crisis stage to heal the disease.

The crisis resolution stage is the final stage when the crisis is resolved and the "patient" is well again. Clearly, software development has not arrived in the crisis resolution stage yet, as witnessed by the Therac 25 example provided earlier.

Proper crisis management allows the participant to achieve more control by suggesting certain proactive behaviors. One can exert a degree of influence over a potential crisis or see what can be done to alter the currently forecasted event. In the software development crisis, action must be taken now to alter this chronic crisis. A consideration important to this proactive chance is the cost of intervention. It is clearly cost-efficient to intervene proactively in the software development crisis.[16]

The crisis management model (Fig. IN.1) is a guide to approaching crisis management. There follows a brief review of each step along the way.

Step one is the design of the organizational structure that is a lean, cost-effective structure that has minimum economic burden to the organization. A crisis management matrix design is ideal for flexibility, adaptability, and cost-effectivity.

The next step of selecting the crisis team should follow the normal job assignment process in the company. It should identify the functional divisions from which to assign people, and from which level of management they should come.

---

*Reprinted by permission of publisher, from *Crisis Management, Planning for the Inevitable,* pp. 1, 20–26, 47–53, © 1986, Steven Fink. Published by AMACON, a division of American Management Association, New York. All Rights Reserved.

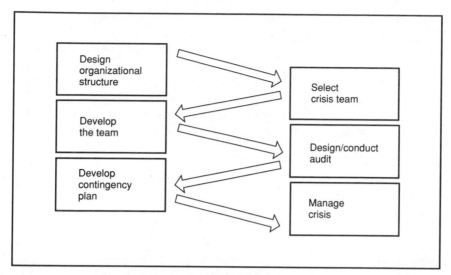

Figure IN.1   Crisis management model.[17] (*Reprinted by permission of publisher, from "Crisis Management—A Team Approach," p. 14, Copyright © 1983, Robert F. Littlejohn. Published by AMACOM, a division of American Management Association, New York, All rights reserved.*)

The third step is to develop the team, which is the responsibility of the crisis team manager. The team manager sets up team development, which is accomplished by analyzing goals (where the team is going), roles (who will be doing what), and processes (how members will function as a team).

Step four is to design and conduct a crisis audit. The audit is a data-gathering process which considers both probability of an event (threat) actually occurring and the impact if it did occur.

The development of a five-part contingency plan, consisting of introduction, objectives, assumptions, trigger mechanism, and the action steps is the next step.

Finally, step six is the management of the crisis where each issue is carefully evaluated for its potential impact. After issue evaluation, the team must formulate its crisis policy.[18]

This crisis management model is a map for protection against a forthcoming crisis, but we are dealing with an existing, acute crisis in software development. So the crisis management model must treat the forthcoming crisis in software development as the present crisis. Therefore all six steps need to be applied now in our software industry, but of prime emphasis are the action steps from the plan and the management crisis policy. The concepts provided in this book serve some of these purposes in ameliorating the software development crisis.

Two general social-psychological observations about group behavior are especially relevant to the crisis-ridden programming team, says Gerald Weinberg in *The Psychology of Computer Programming*. First, it has been observed that in a crisis, group members are more accepting of relatively strong leadership. But, the group quickly loses patience if the provided direction does not produce quick, effective solutions. Thus, a programming team in which leadership may be constantly changing is in a continual crisis. Once the team has an effective leader, it will follow that leader to successfully accomplish its tasks.[19]

It may be said that we are not doing well after almost twenty-some years of battling the software crisis. *Business Week,* in July 1989, reports on the defects released with dBase IV causing substantial loss to its producer, Ashton-Tate Inc.[20] Others may say we have done well when consideration is given to the greatly increasing complexities surrounding all aspects of software development. The software crisis is more an attitude than a turning point because the profession includes people born after the term "software crisis" became popular.

There has been progress, but not concomitant with software technology. The rate of progress is lagging behind the rate of public dependence on computer systems. Programs today must be more than correct; they must be reliable, safe, and trustworthy.[21] So, for today's complex software crisis, the process of software development must be more structured to manage that complexity.

It has been said that to move people and organizations to change goals, managers must identify a crisis.[22] Developing zero defect software is a new goal for structured software development, and the crisis (defect-ridden software) has already been identified. A final important point to remember from Watts S. Humphrey is that crisis prevention is more important than crisis recovery.[23] Keep that point in mind as you undertake your next project. Zero defect software development is the better way to proceed.

The reader is invited to follow the development of zero defect software through the three parts of this book: Part 1—Current Practice, Part 2—Current Methods, and Part 3—Improvements.

Part 1 gives an overview of software development processes and models. What is involved in the development of zero defect software is introduced. The types of software defects are given some exposure. Existing software quality indicators are illustrated to show how to track the quality of software during its development. This part concludes with a discussion of the problems with current software development practice.

Part 2 starts with some statistical considerations as applied to software development. These statistical measures, though not directly an aid to zero defect software, do provide a way of moving toward zero defects. Manual and automated ways to detect errors in software are reviewed. Some of the newer trends of writing correct software are exposed. This part concludes with some of the problems encountered with using current software development methods.

There is a brief, reflective Interlude to focus attention on the Total Quality concept because of the renewed interest by the U.S. government on Total Quality Management (TQM) and the press coverage given the Malcolm Baldridge National Quality Award.

Part 3 delves into the people role in achieving development of zero defect software. A review of the meetings that provide the background concepts to a zero defect software program and details about its implementation are given in this part. The benefits derived from the development of zero defect software close out the book.

REFERENCES

1. Perry, William E., *Effective Methods of EDP Quality Assurance,* Q.E.D. Information Science, Inc., Wellesley, MA, 1988, p. 21.
2. Shepard, John, "A Method of Designing Fault Tolerant Software," presented at the Royal Aeronautical Society's Symposium on "Certification of Avionics Systems," April 1982, p. 1.
3. Bequai, August, "Law Says Vendors Are Liable For Defects," Reprinted from *Digital Review,* vol. 5, no. 8, April 18, 1988, Ziff Communications Company, New York, Copyright © 1988, p. 87.
4. Cole, Patrick E., "dBUGS in dBase IV Spread to the Bottom Line," *Business Week,* no. 3115, July 17, 1989, McGraw-Hill, Inc., New York, p. 135.
5. Joyce, Ed, "Software Bugs: A Matter of Life and Liability," *Datamation,* vol. 33, no. 10, May 15, 1987, Cahners Publishing Company, Des Plaines, IL, © 1987, pp. 89–91, Reprinted by permission.
6. Richards, Evelyn, "Study: Software Bugs Costing U.S. Billions," *The Washington Post,* October 16, 1989, p. D5.
7. Davis, Phillip M., "Software: A Pandora's Box for Legal Liability," Excerpted from *Design News,* vol. 44, February 1, 1988, Cahners Publishing Company, Des Plaines, IL, © 1988, p. 118.
8. Tribus, Myron, "The Quality Imperative," *The Bent of Tau Beta Pi,* vol. LXXVIII, no. 2, Spring 1987, Tau Beta Pi Association, Inc., Knoxville, TN, pp. 24–27.
9. Skrzycki, Cindy, "Making Quality a Priority," *The Washington Post,* October 11, 1987, p. k4.
10. Cooper, Alan D., *The Journey Toward Managing Quality Improvement,* Westinghouse Electric Corp., Orlando, 1987, pp. 1, 5–6.
11. Crosby, Philip B., *Quality is Free,* New American Library, Inc., New York, 1979, p. 15.
12. Schulmeyer, G. Gordon, "Software Quality Assurance—Coming to Terms," in *Handbook of Software Quality Assurance,* G. Gordon Schulmeyer and James I. McManus, eds., Van Nostrand Reinhold Co. Inc., New York, 1987, p. 5.
13. Dunn, Robert and Richard Ullman, *Quality Assurance for Computer Software,* McGraw-Hill Book Company, New York, 1983, pp. 10–11.
14. U.S. Congress, Office of Technology Assessment, *SDI: Technology, Survivability, and Software,* OTA-ISC-353, U.S. Government Printing Office, Washington, D.C., May 1988, p. 225.
15. "The Software Trap: Automate—or Else," *Business Week,* no. 3051, May 9, 1988, McGraw-Hill, Inc., New York, p. 145.
16. Fink, Steven, *Crisis Management, Planning for the Inevitable,* AMACOM, New York, 1986, pp. 20–26, 47–53.

17. Littlejohn, Robert F., *Crisis Management—A Team Approach,* American Management Association, New York, Copyright © 1983, p. 14.
18. *Ibid.*
19. Weinberg, Gerald M., *The Psychology of Computing Programming,* Van Nostrand Reinhold Co. Inc., New York, 1971, p. 90.
20. Cole, Patrick E., *op. cit.,* pp. 135, 136.
21. Shore, John, "Why I Never Met A Programmer I Could Trust," *Communication of the ACM,* vol. 31, no. 4, April 1988, Copyright © 1988, Association for Computing Machinery, Inc., New York, p. 372.
22. Miller, Donald Britton, *Managing Professionals in Research and Development,* Jossey-Bass Publishers, San Francisco, 1986, p. 165.
23. Humphrey, Watts S., "Statistically Managing the Software Process," *Chance: New Directions for Statistics and Computing,* vol. 2, no. 2, 1989, Springer-Verlag, Berlin, Copyright © 1989, p. 34.

Current Practices

How is Software Built Today?

"O! what a world of vile, ill-favour'd faults"
SHAKESPEARE
The Merry Wives of Windsor, Act III,
Scene 4

The concept of what a process is and its importance is initially discussed in this chapter. The important aspects of process considerations as related to software development are then given exposure.

It is interesting to note the shift from the first age of *writing* computer programs to the second age of *building* software. The term "software engineering" has become the rallying cry to champion that paradigm shift. "Software architecture" is a term clear in the building imagery. Specification of requirements and design elements have even been viewed as blueprints and material lists.[1]

Process concepts are followed by a brief examination of various development processes in use for software. Phil Babel's Software Development Integrity Program emphasizes that propagation of errors during software development must be eliminated. The "V" diagram of software development points out that each step must be accommodated by a three-pronged attack of negotiation, compliance, and regression. An approach is discussed that recognizes that software developers try to optimize what they are asked for or directed to accomplish;

that is, if the software development schedule is minimized, would life-cycle costs suffer?

Various software development models are explored and a discussion about their relationship to the development of zero defect software is given. The systemic model is the hierarchial decomposition or successive transformations of the system. The faulty model emphasizes that the process needs correction, not just continual correction of the products produced by the process. The software factory model stresses many intermediate reviews and inspections before hand-off in the software factory. The DOD-STD-2167A model brings the system elements into focus with the software development and highlights products, reviews, and configuration control. The inspection models of Michael Fagan and Shigeo Shingo stress that inspections are essential to progressive elimination of errors. The spiral model provides the opportunity for prototyping critical software elements. The software defect model is an approach to capture software reliability during software development.

What is needed to improve the software development process? A discussion of inspection methods that allow software developers to act as sensors is given. With all this emphasis on the process, is the product forgotten? That issue concludes this chapter.

THE PROCESS

Michael Fagan has defined a process as "a set of operations occurring in a definite sequence that operates on a given input and converts it to some desired output."[2] A truly effective process is predictable, i.e., cost estimates and schedule commitments would be met with reasonable consistency and the quality of the resulting product would generally meet the users' needs. Such a process, according to a Software Engineering Institute document on processes, has five levels of maturity:

1. Initial. Until the process is under statistical control, no orderly progress in process improvement is possible.
2. Repeatable. A stable process with a repeatable level of statistical control is achieved by initiating rigorous project management of commitments, cost, schedule, and change.
3. Defined. Definition of the process is necessary to assure consistent implementation and to provide a basis for better understanding of the process. Advanced technology can be usefully introduced at this stage.
4. Managed. Following the defined process, it is possible to initiate

process measurements. This is where the most significant quality improvements begin to appear.

5. Optimized. With a measured process, the foundation is in place for continuing improvement and continuous optimization of the process.[3]

It is because Statistical Process Control (SPC) has been successful in improving manufacturing processes that such an emphasis is placed in items 1 and 2. There are advantages to SPC, but they do not have a zero defect objective; they have an objective of minimizing defects.

Items 3, 4, and 5 have not been achieved by many involved in software development. Companies may posture themselves for their software development process to be defined and managed by following the zero defect software agenda. They may be able to optimize the process of software development once it settles in place.

Mr. M. Matsushita, chairman of Matsushita Electric, has made the following comments about how Americans manage: "We are going to win and the industrial West is going to lose out; there's not much you can do about it because the reasons for your failure are within yourselves. Your firms are built on the Taylor model (Frederick W. Taylor started the scientific management movement emphasizing centralized management techniques 85 years ago). Even worse, so are your heads. With your bosses doing the thinking while the workers wield the screwdrivers, you're convinced deep down that this is the right way to run a business. For you, the essence of management is getting the ideas out of the heads of the bosses into the hands of labor. We are beyond the Taylor model."

With mastery of process improvement, not just mastery of the process, the Japanese are now in a strong position to invent and innovate more rapidly than we are. Our management is wedded to the idea of a "steady state," not "continuous improvement" as a way of life. American managers want to know how to make a system better; the Japanese want to know how to be better at improvement.[4]

Again, harkening to another Japanese, Genichi Taguchi, Ph.D., who, as the chief architect of "robust quality," says that instead of constantly fiddling with the production equipment to assure consistent quality, design the product to be robust enough to achieve high quality despite fluctuations on the production line. He came to realize that the major hang-up and expense in new product development is designing the manufacturing process, not the product. There is a parallel to new software product development where the software development process is the major hang-up and expense.

Edward Fuchs, director of the Quality Assurance Center, agrees, "What we're focusing on is an entire product-realization process that views everything—from design and systems engineering through manufacturing and marketing—as totally integrated." He goes on to relate that the primary key to better quality hinges on fixing the manufacturing system, not its products.[5]

It is appropriate here to state a significant point: that is that 85 percent of the time the system is the cause of the problem (variation), and 15 percent of the time it is the worker.[6]

Therefore, the focus on the process and its continual improvement are the keys to the achievement of a better product. Such focus on process and its continual improvement is what this book is about. One such process step for the software developer is the development of zero defect software. The software product flows from a disciplined development method with checkpoints tightly integrated along the way in order to concentrate on the 85 percent of the time when the development system is the cause of the variation.

SOFTWARE DEVELOPMENT PROCESSES

The quality solution to software development then is based on a systematic approach. To be systematic, the approach must incorporate measurable milestones at which one can verify that the work completed thus far is consistent with the satisfaction of the purpose of the program and the constraints of the development environment. Without a systematic approach, milestones are meaningless, and without milestones there can be no control.[7]

Software development integrity program

This milestone emphasis is picked up in the MIL-STD-1803(USAF) draft where it calls for "inchstones". This *Software Development Integrity Program* (SDIP) Military Standard has the following direction concerning the software engineering process:

> The contractor shall implement internal reviews in addition to the reviews required by DOD-STD-2167. The internal reviews to be conducted between the major program milestones shall be defined as "inchstones", (i.e. lower level milestones). Associated with each inchstone shall be a verifiable product, a responsible organization, a scheduled date, predefined completion criteria, and a responsible verification organization.[8]

For quality software development, explicit requirement statements are mandatory as input. The series of processing operations that act on this input must be placed in the correct sequence with one another; the output of each operation satisfying the input needs of the next operation. The output of the final operation is the explicitly required output in the form of a verified program. Thus, the objective of each

TABLE 1.1 Software Development Integrity Program (SDIP)[10]

CHALLENGE	APPROACH
Develop systematic process to minimize number of errors in the software design	Specific error reduction analysis and procedures implemented by contractor
• Preclude introduction of errors	• Tasking contained in the integrity standard
• Prevent errors in requirements and design phases	• Multiple techniques required
• Eliminate propagation of errors	* Requirements & design reviews
• Process must be integral to the system design process	* Design analyses
	* Simulation & modeling
	* Rapid prototyping
	• Use of improved productivity tools
	• Process documented in the integrity master plan

processing operation is to receive a defined input and to produce a definite output that satisfies a specific set of exit criteria. A well-formed process can be thought of as a continuum of processing during which sequential sets of exit criteria are satisfied, the last set in the entire series requiring a well-defined end product.[9]

The Software Development Integrity Program (SDIP) was presented by Philip Babel of the U.S. Air Force System Command, Aeronautical Systems Division as a major thrust to minimizing software errors. Table 1.1 shows the major challenges and solution approaches—there is a marked similarity of the challenges to those in the zero defect software program. The approaches presented in the table lead to the error reduction process (Fig. 1.1). On the left of the figure is the constant reminder to minimize errors at each step. On the right are the improved productivity tools. The center of the figure highlights the SDIP initiatives which include prototyping and various analyses and reviews during the process.

The "V" diagram

Two broad concerns of software management and developers are the quality of the actual process and the quality of the final software product. Process control is a technique for enforcing a limited form of control at specific application points in the development cycle. In the case of software, the "V" diagram (Fig. 1.2) defines all of the up-front phases which require process control. Each phase of the requirements side and the validation side of the "V" diagram should undergo process control.

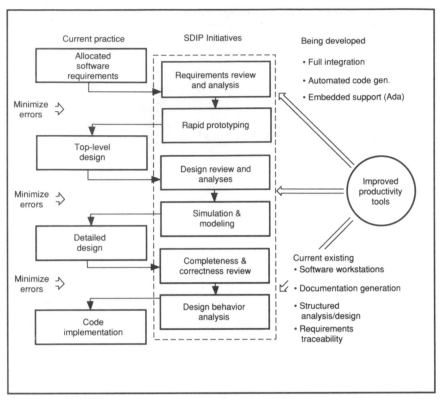

Figure 1.1   Error reduction process.[11]

A key element of process control as related to software development is the quality management (QM) diagram (Table 1.2). Three stages of QM are defined as: (1) *negotiation,* (2) *compliance,* and (3) *regression.* All three are critical to effective management for achieving quality software. Similar to the way analysis, design, coding, and testing are the phases of the development cycle, so too, negotiation, compliance, and regression are necessary to the quality process of software development.[12]

The "V" diagram provides a strong argument for handling software development as an engineering discipline from beginning to end. Too often, the critical front-end activities are treated casually. The requirements *must* be defined formally before implementation of the system begins, so that software tools may be used to determine whether a set of requirements is logically consistent and complete.[15]

For successful software development, it is important to develop a series of small tasks, with each series resulting in a tangible product

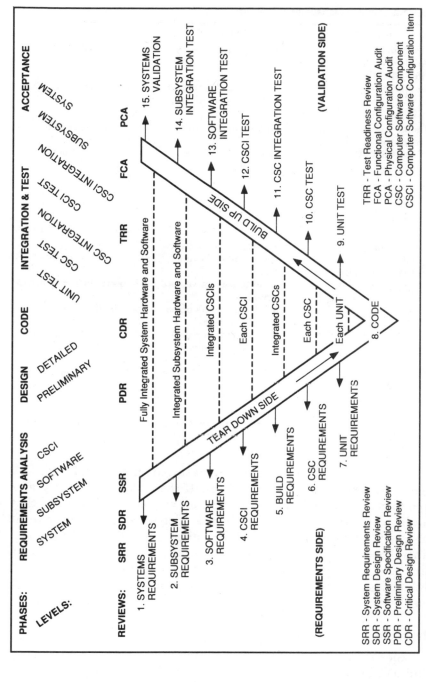

Figure 1.2 "V" Diagram.[13]

TABLE 1.2   Quality Management Diagram[14]

Negotiation	Compliance	Regression
— Apply to life cycle. — Apply to each phase of life cycle. — Define objectives, goals.	— Apply to life cycle. — Apply to each phase of life cycle. — Monitor, audit, inspect practices, procedures, progress.	— Apply to life cycle. — Apply to each phase of life cycle. — Update records.
— Define how to achieve. — Define role of SQA: — Where does SQA fit in? — How does SQA fit in?	— Review, inspect software.* — Review, inspect documentation.* — Witness verification tests.*	— Support regression techniques. — Peer inspections of design.* — Peer inspections of requirements.* — Peer inspections of code.* — Perform trend analysis.
— Tailor plans to requirements. — Select tools, metrics, etc.	— Participate at software configuration review board.* — Monitor corrective action. — Write up reports on noncompliant items. — Prepare status report for upper management.	— Certify verification processes, test results.* — Assure follow-up activities. — Validate software.* — Validate documentation.* — Enforce regression of noncompliant items before proceeding to next phase.

*as applicable per phase

as shown in the "V" diagram and detailed in DOD-STD-2167A, *Defense System Software Development.* If the tasks are properly allocated to personnel and executed within a controlled environment, they should result in a system that works. Software managers can no longer say "software is different", but must apply basic management principles from other disciplines. Maintaining current versions of plans and products used during the development process is not a methodology to aid development, but a requirement to get the job done.[16]

Total approach process

An experiment in software development conducted by Weinberg-Schulman in 1974 has the following results: Programmers work hard to produce what they are asked for, and so have a very high achievement motivation. It appears that concentration on minimizing software development budget and schedule will have a deleterious effect on software life-cycle budget, schedules, and effectiveness. So, different software objectives do conflict with each other. Successful life-cycle software engineering requires continuing resolution of a variety of important but conflicting goals during the development process.[17]

Since many errors usually escape detection during testing, it is sensible to adopt a programming approach which reduces their number prior to testing. This approach, a total approach, not only reduces the time spent on testing, but also increases confidence in the software released to the customer.[18] Another argument to have strong process control comes from industry quality experts' claim that 80 percent of a product's defects get "designed-in" or come from low-priced marginal parts.[19]*

A major consideration, then, is the quality of the process, not just the product. A reason that quality and productivity are seen as conflicting is that process quality is often ignored. If a high quality development process is used, it is believed that productivity automatically increases. So checks should be made not just of the software product, but also of the methods and tools used to produce those products.[20]

SOFTWARE DEVELOPMENT MODELS

There is a variety of software development models, and some of these are presented here. An attempt is made to point out the influence of these models on the development of zero defect software.

Systemic model

At the highest level an overall system is represented by a descriptive model, which is transformed into a model of problems and needs, which is transformed into requirements specifications, which is transformed into a conceptual design, which is transformed into programmed code. This programmed code is part of the developed software system, which finally becomes a new component of the original, but now transformed, system.[21]

These successive transformations (Fig. 1.3) are essential to the successful implementation of computer software. They are inherent in the DOD-STD-2167A *Defense System Software Development* method and flows directly into the zero defect software methodology.

Faulty model

If you have a program that is continuously producing output listings filled with thousands of errors (Fig. 1.4), you would not continually hand-correct each listing; you would correct the program.

---

*Excerpted from *Mini-Micro Systems*, December 1985, copyright © 1985 by Cahners Publishing Company.

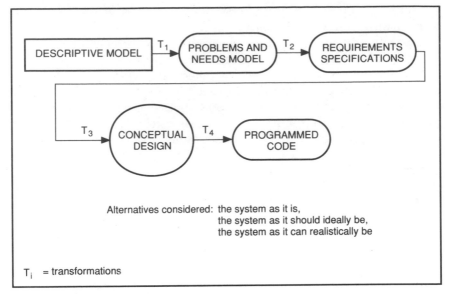

Figure 1.3 Systemic model.

Correspondingly, if you have defective coded systems (Fig. 1.5), you do not hand-correct the code to remove defects one by one; you correct the faulty procedures used in building the system.

When software developers say, "This is the problem," while pointing to their listing, they are really only pointing out the symptom, not the problem. The real problem is a defective development procedure that allows defective code to be put there. Faulty codes in the system result

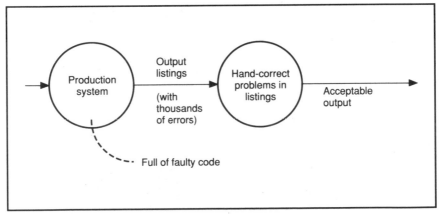

Figure 1.4 Correct the program.[22]

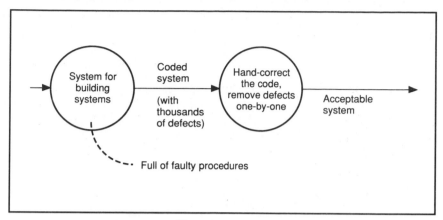

Figure 1.5   Correct the system.[23]

in output listings filled with errors. Faulty procedures used in building the system result in defective systems.[24]

The purpose of the zero defect software program is to improve the software development system. By moving the improvement into the software development process, it is clear that a better software product can be developed.

Software factory model

Yoshihiro Matsumoto in his IEEE article about a software factory presents the life cycle model shown in Fig. 1.6. Notice the incidence of design reviews (DR) and inspections (INSP.) at just about every step. This life cycle model is influenced by the incorporation of many inspections into the zero defect software methodology. By using source and successive inspections (explained later) throughout the process, progressive elimination of errors is achieved, which leads to zero defect software.

DOD-STD-2167A model

The *Defense System Software Development* standard DOD-STD-2167A provides a process chart for software development (Fig. 1.7). It has products (documents) flowing from each phase. It has reviews and audits regularly spaced. And it stresses the importance of configuration control by defining baselines along the way.

This process is the basis for the software development process chart which lies at the center of development for zero defect software. The eight phases for software development are system requirements analysis and design, software requirements analysis, preliminary design,

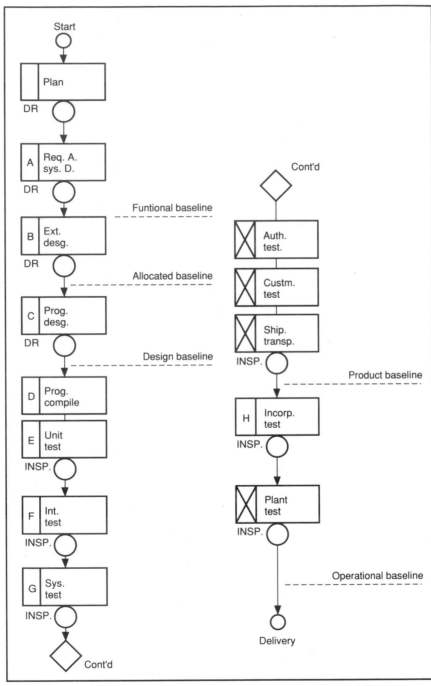

Figure 1.6   Life cycle model and baselines in the Software Factory.[25] (*Copyright © 1987, IEEE. Reprinted by permission.*)

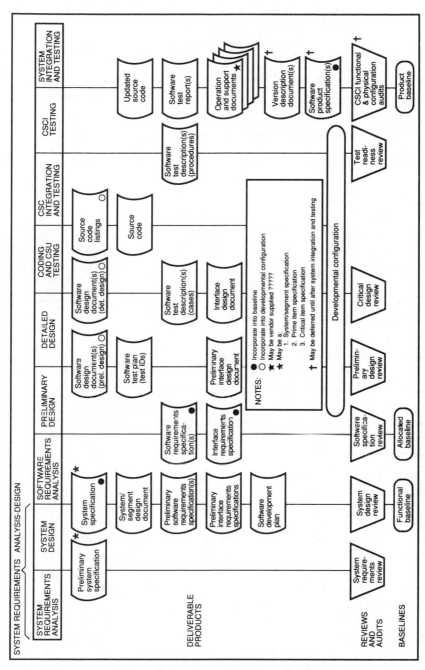

Figure 1.7 DOD-STD-2167A Software Development Process. 26

15

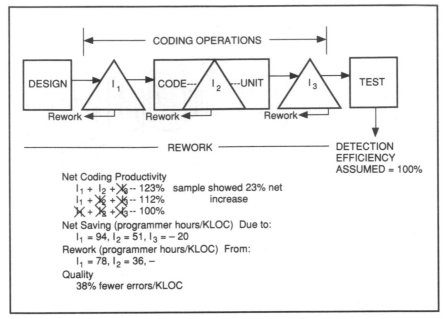

Figure 1.8   Inspection model from sample problems.[27]

detailed design, code and CSU (computer software unit) testing, CSC (computer software component) integration and testing, CSCI (computer software configuration item) testing, and system integration and testing. Notice the emphasis on the system and the fact that the software must be a subsystem and then integrated back into the system.

Inspection model

Michael Fagan's landmark work on software development using inspections to improve quality has charts showing that the closer to the worker the inspection is held, the fewer the errors. Figure 1.8 shows an example of how design inspections, I_1, code inspections, I_2, and test inspections, I_3, result in 38 percent fewer errors per thousand lines of code (KLOC). Figure 1.9 compares Fagan's model with a similar model that does not include inspections at the points Fagan proposes. The effect of using requirement inspections I_0, and I_1, and I_2 is a reduction in the overall schedule.

Fagan did this work in 1976 and since then many examples have been given proving the efficacy of the inspection model. The method for development of zero defect software hinges critically upon the use of inspections throughout the process. A major difference with the software development process method for zero defect software and the

Fagan inspection method is in the zero defect software method, *every* element is inspected by its originator(s), and when passed to the next person in the development process, it is reinspected by that *internal* customer.

Shigeo Shingo has devised a process cycle for the managing of errors and defects (Fig. 1.10). The check and feedback portion is analogous to inspections (I_0, I_1, I_2, and I_3) shown in Figs. 1.8 and 1.9.

A major point of Shingo's process cycle is that the internal short route of "action—errors—check and feedback" occurs frequently during software development. Whereas, if the long route is being used, defects will be delivered to the ultimate customer as the check-and-feedback stage is too late in the cycle for timely corrections to be made. The zero defect software process focuses on the short route to progres-

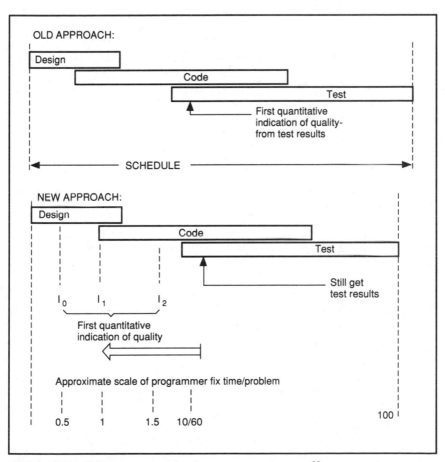

Figure 1.9   Effect of inspection on process management.[28]

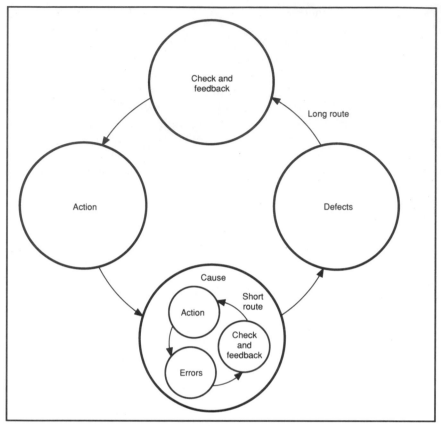

Figure 1.10   Cycle for managing errors and defects.[29]

sively eliminate errors before they drift to the *ultimate* customer as defects.

The spiral model

The spiral model of Dr. Barry Boehm is illustrated in Fig. 1.11. The radial dimension in Fig. 1.11 represents the cumulative cost incurred in accomplishing the steps to date; the angular dimension represents the progress made in completing each cycle of the spiral. The spiral model holds that each cycle involves a progression through the same sequence of steps, for each portion of the products and for each of its levels of elaboration, from an overall concept-of-operation document down to the coding of each individual program.

Each cycle of the spiral begins with the identification of:

- The *objectives* for the portion of the product being elaborated (performance, functionality, ability to accommodate change, etc.)

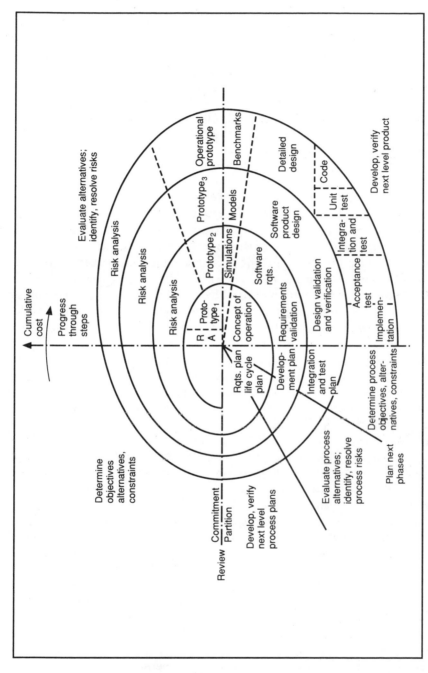

Figure 1.11 Spiral model of the software process (not to scale).[30] *(Reprinted with permission from Barry W. Boehm.)*

- The *alternative* means of implementing this portion of the product (design A, design B, reuse, buy, etc.)
- The *constraints* imposed on the application of the alternatives (cost, schedule, interface, etc.)

The next step is to *evaluate* the alternatives with respect to the objectives and constraints. Frequently, this process will identify areas of uncertainty which are significant sources of project risk. If so, the next step should involve the formulation of a cost-effective strategy for resolving the sources of risk. This may involve prototypal, simulation, administering user questionnaires, analytic modeling, or combinations of these and other risk-resolution techniques.

Once the risks are evaluated, the next step is determined by the relative risks remaining. If performance or user-interface risks strongly dominate program development or internal interface-control risks, the next step may be an evolutionary development step: a minimal effort to specify the overall nature of the product, a plan for the next level of prototypal, and the development of a more detailed prototype to continue to resolve the major risk issues. On the other hand, if previous prototypal efforts have already resolved all of the performance or user-interface risks, and program development or interface-control risks dominate, the next step follows the basic waterfall approach, modified as appropriate to incorporate incremental development.

The spiral model also accommodates any appropriate mixture of specification-oriented, prototype-oriented, simulation-oriented, automatic-transformation-oriented, or other approaches to software development, where the appropriate mixed strategy is chosen by considering the relative magnitude of the program risks and the relative effectiveness of the various techniques in resolving the risk. (In a similar way, risk-management considerations determine the amount of time and effort which should be devoted to such other project activities as planning, configuration management, quality assurance, formal verification, or testing.)

An important feature of the spiral model is that each cycle is completed by a review involving the primary people or organizations concerned with the products. This review covers all of the products developed during the previous cycle, including the plans for the next cycle and the resources required to carry them out. The major objective of the review is to ensure that all concerned parties are mutually committed to the approach to be taken for the next phase.

The plans for succeeding phases may also include a partition of the product into increments for successive development, or components to be developed by individual organizations or persons. Thus, the review and commitment step may range from an individual walkthrough of the design of a single programmer component to a major requirements review involving developer, customer, user, and maintenance organization.[31]

The spiral model imbeds the more traditional software development methods within the spiral, but allows for the production of a prototype prior to full implementation. The development method for zero defect software follows the more traditional methodologies, but may be imbedded within the spiral model. Often, it is desirable and even necessary to reproduce a prototype of the software subsystem, so that aspect is a major benefit to software development.

Software defect model

A new methodology, pioneered by D. L. Wood, is combining error/defects occurrence mechanics during the structured development hierarchy. This is accomplished by establishing a hierarchical description of the software development process. Then, the mechanics of error/defect propagation along the hierarchy are modeled using a profile concept. The profile model concept utilizes the following types of parameters or model descriptors at each level in the hierarchy:

- defect/fault type
- number
- defect size and category
- correction size and category
- detection phase
- detection activity variables
- other parameters/variables as required

A given defect is tracked and traced from the software development specification, down through the software product specifications, and on through detail design documentation and source coding. This process is continued throughout production and operation/deployment. The defect is modeled using the kinds of concepts listed above. This characterization Wood calls the "Software Defect Model."

For example, defect sizes are measured in terms of the number of registers which comprise the software item as though it were translated to a magnetic disk with specific characteristics. Then, a specific defect size can be characterized as affecting a finite number of registers. Defect detection times, sizes, and types are then measured using this formalization of the problems. A typical characterization of defect type, category, and propagation descriptors is presented in Fig. 1.12.

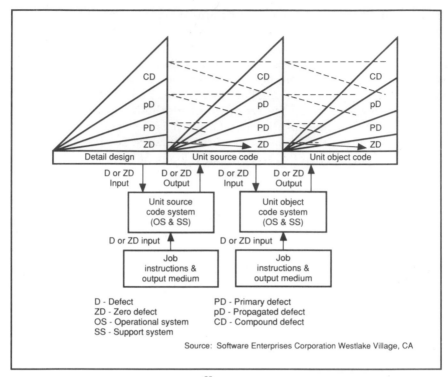

Figure 1.12 Software defect model.[33]

Once the defect characterization and concept is formalized, the defects in a specified "software item" are tagged by number and then tracked through time. Typical tracking benchmarks are program-oriented milestones: *Preliminary Design Review, Critical Design Review, Software Configuration Reviews,* etc. Time-between-failures by defect number and category is established and histograms are constructed. Each histogram of time-to-failure occurrences then appears to represent a probability density distribution conditioned on its specific characterization and defect parameterization. These probability density distributions can then be integrated (or convoluted by formulating derivate moments, conditional expectation, characteristic functions, or spectral compositions) at each program milestone. Subsequently, the resultant time-to-failure curves can be integrated along the entire software item development time line. Although Wood's concepts appear to be in their formative stages, they have been applied to a number of software development efforts and, given their potential promise, are expected to yield significant insights to the "software reliability problem."[32]

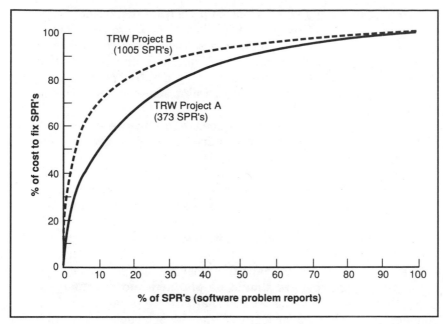

Figure 1.13 Rework costs.[37]

PROCESS IMPROVEMENTS

Prevention means eliminating the potential for error. Prevention involves identifying opportunities for error and taking actions to eliminate those opportunities before a problem occurs. Appraisal, however, requires that errors be found, evaluated, dispositioned, and corrected. Since prevention is more cost effective, it is preferable to appraisal.

Too often prevention is not a planned activity. Traditionally, problems were found and fixed after the fact. Prevention involves analyzing processes to determine where the opportunities for error are, and then taking action to assure that errors do not happen.

Prevention must be related to individual jobs, such as, coding a unit. Jobs are composed of processes. To understand quality improvement opportunities on a specific job, it is necessary to look at the job from a process standpoint. This approach provides insight in positioning prevention steps logically into the process to enhance their acceptance as the best way to perform activities.[34]

For instance, one may put prevention steps into the process of test planning. If a program looks difficult to verify, it is the program that should be revised, *not* the verification,[35] because that step was not done with its testability in mind. Dr. Barry Boehm points out that rework instances tend to follow a Pareto distribution: 80 percent of the rework costs typically result from 20 percent of the problems, such as shown in Fig. 1.13 from recent TRW software projects. The major implication of this distribution is that software verification and validation activities should focus on identifying and eliminating the specific *high-risk* problems to be encountered by a software project, rather than spreading their early-problem elimination effort uniformly across all problems.[36]

Quality in design assures that proper requirements are set and completely met. Reviews of design requirements are essential to assure agreement on all the requirements.

There are three basic outputs of the design process: (1) configuration—defines what the products look like and sets requirements for making them, (2) verification—proof that the products can be made and that they will do what they are supposed to do, (3) concerns—issues not completely satisfied by verification and require further work.

The design review is perhaps the most useful verification tool. The timing of design reviews should be planned and documented. The usual three design reviews occur: (1) after conceptual design has been completed, (2) when major features have been completed, and (3) after the design is completed, but prior to production.

The design checklist is another tool with high potential for improving design quality. It serves as a reminder to assure that the designers do not overlook or forget to address aspects of the design tasks. A checklist must be used on a continuing basis. People tend to rely on memory once they are familiar with a checklist. Then the value of the checklist is lost. To instill discipline, require check-off, signature, and date on any checklist.[38] Where possible, an automation of checklists would fit well, which is a distinct aid to software developers during the development process.

Robert Poston and Mark Bruen in "Counting Down to Zero Software Failures" highlight five techniques of a methodology which are in concert with the development process for zero defect software: (1) defining requirements for testability, (2) designing software for testability, (3) designing tests for most-probable errors, (4) designing tests before code is written, and (5) performing reviews (inspections and walkthroughs).[39]

The inspections and reviews that are integral features of zero defect software development provide a way for software developers to act as sensors. A sensor is a detecting device which recognizes certain stimuli and converts sensed knowledge into information. All forms of sensing serve a useful purpose, but each fits different circumstances. Table 1.3 shows the relationship of the option of sensing events before, during, or after they happen.

TABLE 1.3.   Time of Sensing versus Activities Sensed[40]

	Before	During	After
Type of situation most appropriate	Prior to embarking on major programs; to defend against major disasters	For regulation of the "trivial many"	For review of effectiveness of long-range program
Type of sensor	Specially expensive, early warning, or predictable sensors	Simple. Often done direct from deeds without creating any data	Information systems based on data, which are mainly a by-product of operations
Who collects the sensed information	Specialized personnel or departments	Mainly the regular operating forces	Regular statistical departments
Who acts on the summarized information	The upper and middle managers	Middle managers and people on the firing line	The upper and middle managers

In the software development cycle, the sensing done before the development would include the planning, scheduling, and estimating. This is usually done by management and lead software developers.

The sensing done during software development is the focus of most of the software development process chart (App. A) and this book. During the development process, the software developers are in the best position to sense errors and to do something about them. Continually sensing through reviews and inspections allows reduction of errors while moving through the software development process to achieve the progressive elimination of errors which leads to zero defect software.

After software development is completed, a count of defects is made which may have been delivered to the customer. This is usually collected on a field trouble report form which is sent back to the developing organization. In this way, the users of the system sense and provide feedback about the status of the delivered software system. The goal of a zero defect software program is to have no field trouble reports sent in because there are no defects.

THE PRODUCT

What about the product? All the emphasis in this chapter is on the process, except for an occasional word pointing out that the product is good if the process is good. Is that too simplistic?

A number of management personnel have brought to my attention the fact that software developers put emphasis on the process (the means) and forget the product (the end). The product is important. One should not lose sight of the "end objective" of the process (or why have the process?).

Dr. Barry Boehm in *Software Engineering Economics*[41] has presented a balanced picture in his goals approach to software engineering. This is a hierarchical goals approach for successful software engineering (Fig. 1.14). There are two primary subgoals that need attention:

1. Achieving a successful software *product*
2. Conducting a successful software development *process*

Each of these has three components:

a. Human relations
b. Resource engineering
c. Program engineering

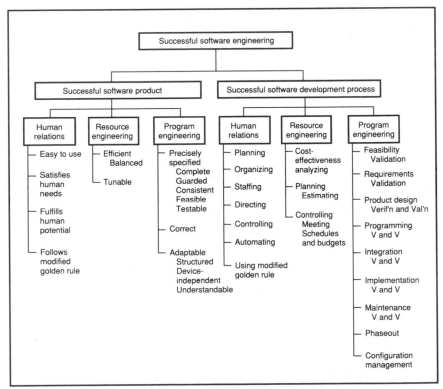

Figure 1.14 Software engineering goal structure.[42]

As shown in the figure, these components have specific elements associated with each. Here the traditional Ms of Men, Machines, and Money has the added element of program engineering. So, for a successful software product, there exists a successful software process.

In summary, from the *Business Week* issue devoted to quality, the point is made that fixing the manufacturing system, not its products, is seen as the key to better quality.[43] This extends to fixing the software development process, which will then result in a quality software product.

The software development processes and models are covered in this chapter as a groundwork for what techniques are available. Each has some benefit to help the software developer, and yet each has proved inadequate to solve the software crisis.

A point of primary emphasis made in this chapter which bears repetition for remembrance here at the conclusion is this: Software managers can no longer say "software is different"; they must apply basic management principles from other disciplines. A requirement to get the job done is maintaining current versions of plans and products used during the software development process.

REFERENCES

1. Daughtrey, Taz, "The Search for Software Quality," *Quality Progress,* vol. XXI, no. 11, November 1988, American Society for Quality Control, Inc., Milwaukee, WI, Copyright © 1988, p. 30, Reprinted by permission.
2. Fagan, Michael E., "Design and Code Inspections and Process Control in the Development of Programs," *IBM-TR-00.73,* June 1976, p. 125.
3. Humphrey, Watts S., "Characterizing the Software Process: A Maturity Framework," *Software Engineering Institute Technical Report CMU/SEI-87-TR-11,* ESD-TR-87-112, Software Engineering Institute, Pittsburgh, PA, June 1987, pp. 2, 3.
4. Tribus, Myron, "The Quality Imperative," *The Bent of Tau Beta Pi,* vol. LXXVIII, no. 2, Spring 1987, Tau Beta Pi Association, Inc., Knoxville, TN, p. 25.
5. "The Push for Quality," *Business Week,* no. 3002, June 8, 1987, McGraw-Hill Publications Company, New York, pp. 132, 142, 143.
6. Tribus, Myron, *op. cit.,* p. 26.
7. Dunn, Robert and Richard Ullman, *Quality Assurance for Computer Software,* McGraw-Hill Book Company, New York, 1982, pp. 81, 82.
8. U. S. Dept. of Defense, MIL-STD-1803(USAF), *Military Standard—Software Development Integrity Program (SDIP)* draft, NAVMAT 09Y, Washington, DC, June 8, 1988, p. 17.
9. Fagan, Michael E., *op. cit.,* p. 125.
10. Babel, Philip S., "Software Development Integrity Program," presentation for Aeronautical Systems Division made at Westinghouse Electric Corp., June 14, 1988, Baltimore, p. 4.
11. *Ibid.,* p. 3.
12. McManus, James I., "The Heart of SQA Management: Negotiation, Compliance, Regression," in *Handbook of Software Quality Assurance,* G. Gordon Schulmeyer and James I. McManus, eds., Van Nostrand Reinhold Co. Inc., New York, 1987, pp. 60–78.
13. *Ibid.,* p. 65.
14. *Ibid.,* p. 69.

15. Hamilton, Margaret H. "Zero-defect software: the elusive goal," *IEEE Spectrum*, vol. 23, no. 3, March 1986, IEEE, New York, Copyright © 1986, p. 53.
16. Evans, Michael W., Pamela Piazza, and James B. Dolkas, *Principles of Productive Software Management*, John Wiley & Sons, Inc., New York, Copyright © 1983, p. 4.
17. Boehm, Barry W., *Software Engineering Economics*, Prentice Hall, Inc., Englewood Cliffs, Copyright © 1981, p. 21. Adapted by permission.
18. Downs, T., "A Review of Some of the Reliability Issues in Software Engineering," *Journal of Electrical and Electronics Engineering, Australia*, vol. 5, no. 1, March 1985, p. 42.
19. Kotelly, George V., "Competitiveness = Quality," Excerpted from *Mini-Micro Systems*, vol. XX, no. 12, December 1985, Copyright © 1985 by Cahners Publishing Co., Div. of Reed Publishing, Denver, CO, p. 9.
20. Basili, Victor R. and H. Dieter Rombach, "Implementing Quantitative SQA: A Practical Model," *IEEE Software*, September 1987, IEEE, New York, Copyright © 1987, pp. 7, 8.
21. Shemer, Itzhak, "Systems Analysis: A Systemic Analysis of a Conceptual Model," *Communications of the ACM*, vol. 30, no. 6, June 1987, Association for Computing Machinery, Inc., New York, Copyright © 1987, p. 509.
22. DeMarco, Tom, *Controlling Software Projects*, Yourdon, Inc., New York, 1982, p. 206, Adapted by permission of Prentice Hall, Inc., Englewood Cliffs, NJ.
23. *Ibid.*, p. 206.
24. *Ibid.*, pp. 205–207.
25. Matsumoto, Yoshihiro, "A Software Factory: An Overall Approach to Software Production," *IEEE, IEEE*, New York, Copyright © 1987, p. 157.
26. U.S. Dept. of Defense, DOD-STD-2167A, *Military Standard—Defense System Software Development*, NAVMAT 09Y, Feb. 29, 1988, Washington, DC, pp. 12, 13.
27. Fagan, Michael E., *op. cit.*, p. 127.
28. *Ibid.*, p. 144.
29. Shingo, Shigeo, *Zero Quality Control: Source Inspection and the Poka-yoke System*, Andrew P. Dillon, trans., Productivity Press, Cambridge, MA, 1986, p. 53. Published with permission.
30. U. S. Dept. of Defense, DOD-HDBK-287 (DRAFT), *A Tailoring Guide for DOD-STD-2167A, Defense System Software Development* draft, NAVMAT O9Y, Nov. 14, 1988, Washington, DC, p. 12.
31. Boehm, Barry W., "Understanding and Controlling Software Costs," private paper, 1987, pp. 17, 19.
32. Chenoweth, Halsey B., Ph.D. and G. Gordon Schulmeyer, "New Directions in Software Reliability Analysis," *IEEE COMPSAC Proceedings*, IEEE Press, Oct. 8–10, 1986, Copyright © 1986, IEEE, New York, pp. 263, 264, Reprinted by permission.
33. *Ibid.*, p. 263.
34. Cooper, Alan D., *The Journey Toward Managing Quality Improvement*, Westinghouse Electric Corp., Orlando, 1987, pp. 22, 23.
35. Mills, Harlan D., Michael Dyer, and Richard C. Linger, "Cleanroom Software Engineering," *IEEE Software*, September 1987, Copyright © 1987, IEEE, New York, p. 21, Reprinted by permission.
36. Boehm, Barry W., "Understanding and Controlling Software Costs," private paper, 1987, pp. 17, 19.
37. *Ibid.*, p. 18.
38. Cooper, Alan D., *op. cit.*, pp. 33–35.
39. Poston, Robert M. and Mark W. Bruen, "Counting Down to Zero Software Failures," *IEEE Software*, September 1987, Copyright © 1987, IEEE, New York, p. 54, Reprinted by permission.
40. Juran, J. M., *Managerial Breakthrough*, McGraw-Hill Book Company, New York, 1964, p. 259.
41. Boehm, Barry W., *Software Engineering Economics*, Prentice Hall, Inc., Englewood Cliffs, 1981, p. 24. Reprinted by permission.
42. *Ibid.*, p. 24.
43. "The Push for Quality," *Business Week, op. cit.*, p. 132.

What is a Zero Defect
Software Program?

*"...urge them while their souls are capable of
this ambition,
Lest zeal, now melted by the windy breath of
soft petitions, pity and remorse,
Cool and congeal again to what it was."*
SHAKESPEARE
King John, Act II, Scene 1

This chapter introduces the basic concepts of the zero defect software program. A thought for the software developer is that this job of software development is creating a deliverable entity, not just writing code.

There are certain analogies between the manufacturing process and the software development process which are explored. Also, certain contrary positions to this analogy are presented with appropriate commentary.

A definition of the zero defect software program is then given, where the distinction between an error and a defect is drawn, and the importance of error prevention and corrective action to the zero defect software program is explained. What the software development process chart is and its relationship to the software activities checklist is introduced.

Next, the concepts of source and successive inspections in relationship to the zero defect software program are discussed. What is poka-yoke and how it is part of the zero defect software program is explained. The chapter concludes with a discussion of the importance of the customer to the zero defect software program.

MANUFACTURING ANALOGIES

Figure 2.1 is a simplified production process block diagram. It portrays what most of us think about when we talk about the factory. It has the added "poka-yoke" feature which will be discussed later in this chapter and throughout the book.

There are questions that need to be answered when planning for process control and inspections for the manufacturing process selected:

1. What quality characteristics of the intermediate and final products can be measured to control the process?

2. Are these measurements properly organized with respect to the process?

3. Is it possible to take these measurements?

4. What is the most effective way to control the process; that is, are adjustments to be made by people or automated mechanisms?

5. Given quality measurements throughout the process, when does management react to poor quality performance, and what action should be taken?

The goal of process control and inspection planning is to develop means of assuring product quality during the manufacturing process.

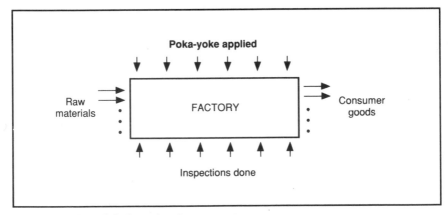

Figure 2.1   Simplified production process.

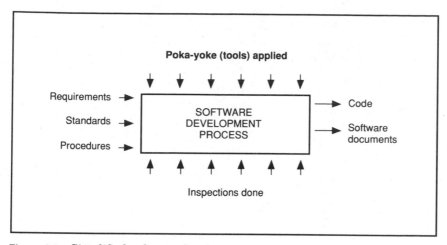

Figure 2.2   Simplified software development process.

Problems are not allowed to grow worse, undetected until the final steps of the process, thus wasting numerous resources. When the process control and inspection system is effective, a poor (error-ridden) process can be modified before many defective product units are manufactured.[1]

Poka-yoke (from Shigeo Shingo) is an automated or mechanized way to prevent mistakes in a production process. It answers question 4 posed on p. 30. Look at this example of a drop device that only drops four rubber feet into a tray for a production worker to affix to a television base. If the television moves forward and all the rubber feet are not used, a warning buzzer sounds to warn the worker to inspect what is wrong.

A simplified software development process (Fig. 2.2) has a look that is analogous to the simplified production process. The raw materials to this process include requirements, standards, and procedures. The analogy to the consumer goods as output from the factory is the customer products of code and software documents.

However, it has been proffered that software development is not like a manufacturing plant, where many "standard-design" products are made. Each development task is done only once for software because the duplication of the developed software is simple and virtually error-free. The software development challenge is to custom design and make one good system.[2] Even though the development task produces one-of-a-kind, how each one-of-a-kind software system is produced is similar. So, the process of software development, like a manufacturing plant, can be described and must be made repeatable.

Process improvement (Fig. 2.3) contains four steps. First, one must

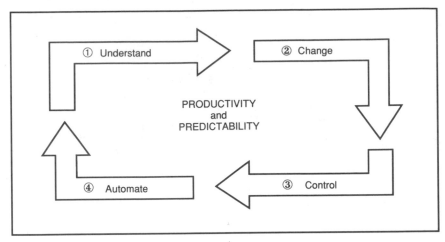

Figure 2.3   Process improvement steps.[4]

① understand how things are done. With such an understanding, ② changes can be made which lead to process improvements and a ③ controlled, repeatable process. Once the process is repeatable, it is easier to identify the parts most susceptible to ④ automation.[3] Through these steps, a movement is made from the software development process to the zero defect software process. Detailed later in the book are the control and automation techniques incorporated into the zero defect software process.

The method of viewing the software code itself as a factory (Fig. 2.4) has been suggested by C. K. Cho. Dr. Cho says that the customer is buying the output of the code, and that the key is to concentrate on the code as the factory producing that output. With that perspective, statistical techniques can be applied to the input streams to be able to give confidence that the software is usable. More about this is explained in Chap. 6.

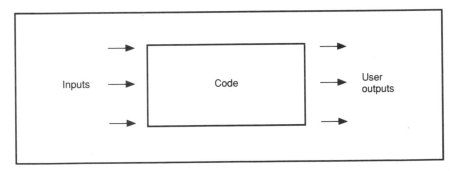

Figure 2.4   Software as a factory.

Because of this perspective, Dr. Cho believes defect-free software may not be usable to the user (customer). It is equivalent, he believes, to a defect-free door-making machine in a automobile plant. The user is looking for a defect-free door when he or she buys an automobile, not an error-free factory (the door-making machine).

A response to this position is that defect-free software meets the requirements which describe what makes the product usable. If the software does not follow the customer's requirements, it is not considered defect free. By following a zero defect software development process, one will meet the requirements, thereby achieving usable software.

ZERO DEFECT SOFTWARE DEFINED

The zero defect software program follows many of the ideas presented by Shigeo Shingo in his book, *Zero Quality Control: Source Inspection and the Poka-yoke System,* about factory control. The primary elements, which are introduced here, are the software development process chart (App. A) and its associated software activities checklist (App. B), inspections and the zero defect software checklists, poka-yoke (software tools) methods, and the importance of the concept of an internal and external customer.

The basic concept of the zero defect software program is a software methodology which invokes error prevention and detection techniques at predefined checkpoints, where "errors" are most likely to occur within the software development cycle, such that, as a goal, zero "defects" are delivered to customers.

In defining a zero defect software program, it is important to distinguish between an "error" and a "defect".

> An "error" is an unwanted condition or occurrence which arises during a software development process and deviates from its specified requirement. It may be detected immediately or go undetected until some corrective action process finds it, but it is always eliminated prior to delivery to the customer.

> A "defect" on the other hand is that specific kind of unwanted condition or occurrence which has defied all attempts (inspections, reviews, walkthroughs, tests, and corrective action measures) to be eliminated during development and, in essence, is delivered to the customer. Either the "defect" was never detected, or it may not have been subjected to adequate corrective action/follow-up measures.

As a result of the above discussion, errors which are prevented and eliminated from software products prior to delivery to the customer, by definition, never become defects.

This distinction has the following significance:

> First, given the condition that people are prone to commit errors, the above distinction implicitly permits errors to occur during the development process. At the same time however, it stresses the importance of committing a dedicated staff with adequate resources to eliminate these errors throughout the development process to prevent delivery of defective software products to the customer.
>
> Second, this distinction makes a strong statement as to where anti-error measures must be focused. Since testing in and of itself does not prevent but rather finds errors, significant preventive measures must be practiced on the front end of software development—prior to testing.

The approach to a successful zero defect software program must consist of two primary interactive functions: error prevention and corrective action.

Error Prevention: Error prevention is designed to stop errors from occurring. This requires engineers, analysts, designers, programmers, test engineers, managers, and supervisors to maintain an awareness of how and where errors originate in the day-to-day tasks they perform and to utilize adequate resources to either:

- prevent the error from occurring or to
- detect the error at its source and eliminate it before continuing other tasks.

For the sake of definition, error prevention is characterized by two aspects:

- true prevention where errors are prevented from occurring, and
- pseudo prevention where an error occurs but is immediately detected, eliminated, and hence "prevented" from transitioning anywhere.

Corrective Action: Corrective action is designed to detect and eliminate errors after the fact; that is, to detect and eliminate errors which were not prevented at their source. These errors have transitioned to another person, task, or activity.

In an effort to detect errors which have transitioned away from their source, several inspections will be conducted as part of the zero defect software program, particularly on the front end of software development prior to test. These inspections are significant for their placement within the software development cycle. Each inspection is designed and placed to find the kinds of errors most likely to occur at a given time in the development cycle.

With these major concepts defined, it is appropriate to next highlight the key elements of the zero defect software process.

SOFTWARE DEVELOPMENT PROCESS CHART

The Software Development Process chart (App. A) is a pictorial representation of the zero defect software program. It highlights the source inspections that a software developer performs 100 percent of the time on the product or activity that he or she performs. Also, highlighted is the successive inspection wherein the next person in the chain who receives a hand-off performs a second, independent inspection.

The Software Development Process chart also provides a pictorial overview of the developmental steps to be made. Associated with the Software Development Process chart is the Software Activities Checklist (App. B) that provides many details of the activities that support the software development process chart. Used together, these aids provide enough detail that no necessary step should be missed in the zero defect software program.

INSPECTIONS

It is interesting to note that Genichi Taguchi, Ph.D. recommends either no inspection or 100 percent inspections. His view of inspections

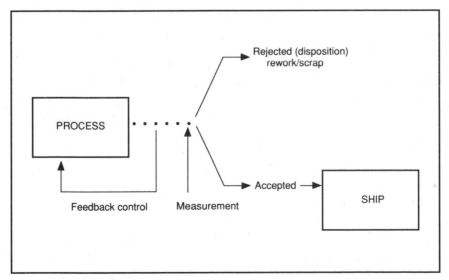

Figure 2.5 Inspection process.[6]

is that they are a decision regarding shipment of a product (Fig. 2.5).[5] The application of this idea to the zero defect software program is that shipment is interpreted as "shipment" to the next person in the process.

The zero defect software program proposes 100 percent inspections all along the process. This means every product and activity a software developer performs is inspected both by himself or herself and by the next person in the process with a successive inspection. This does not mean that a unit of code as shown in Fig. 2.4 will be 100 percent tested, since with today's technology that is virtually impossible.

There are various types of inspections that require some up-front clarification. These include source, peer, successive, quality, and customer inspections. The first four are considered informal, with the customer inspections being formal. Peer inspections are covered in detail later. The design and code inspections of Michael Fagan are described well by him in "Design and Code Inspections and Process Control in the Development of Programs." The customer inspections for software development usually result in a formal qualification test (FQT) of the software.

It is the source, successive, and quality inspections that apply to the zero defect software program. The source inspection is represented by the ⌐ □⁵ in the software development process chart. It means review the product or activity yourself if you produce it. The successive inspection is performed by the user of the product, as is represented by □⁰ᴷ→ in the software development process chart. In the case during software development where the user is the same as the producer of the product, then the successive inspection is performed by a software quality person, in order to insert a different person to look at the product.

The source inspection is a 100 percent self-check (by the originator) of a product or process during and at the end of the time period the product or process is being generated.

- For products, this requires the author or originator of the software, associated documentation, and specification to inspect his/her own work. The inspection process checklist (covered later in the book) for the appropriate inspection is designed to prevent errors. Additionally, DOD-STD-2167A documentation templates (Figs. 7.2 through 7.9) are available which conform to format requirements and prompt for content. Errors which occur have a very high probability of being detected and are immediately "prevented."

- For processes, this requires the originator or first user (as applicable) of a procedure to inspect the written procedure and process for applicability, consistency, and adequacy for use on the program.

Again, checklists will be used to prevent errors by flagging conditions which give rise to errors. Errors detected are to be corrected either by tailoring the procedure to the needs of the program with approvals as necessary, obtaining waivers as necessary, or referring the procedure (if under control) to the appropriate committee or board for immediate change approval and corrective action.

The successive inspection is a 100 percent follow-up check of a product or process, conducted by an approved successive inspector immediately upon completion of the source inspection.

The successive inspector must be someone other than the originator, preferably the person next in line (representing the "internal customer"), who receives the product from the source inspector or who executes the process. Note: When the successive inspector would be the same person as the source inspector, the successive inspection should be conducted by software quality personnel.

By definition, the successive inspection will always occur after completion of the source inspection. In this way, a check and balance system is established which permits a GO/NO GO situation, whereby the product or process is accepted (if approved by the successive inspector) or returned to the originator for rework and preventive/corrective action (if disapproved).

- For products, this requires the successive inspector (acting as the internal customer) to use the appropriate checklist to review the software, associated documentation, specification, etc., developed by someone else on the project.

- For processes, this requires the successive inspector or alternate user (other than the originator) of a procedure to reinspect the written procedure for ease of implementation and for applicability to the program.

Also, for the overall zero defect software program, the independent quality person's inspection ensures the integrity of the entire inspection process throughout. Software quality personnel make sure that source and successive inspections have occurred in accordance with the zero defect software checklists.

Directly connected with the zero defect software inspection process is the zero defect software checklists. These checklists (covered later) provide the "meat" of the source and successive inspections. They lead the software developer to all the points that must be covered before moving on to the next step. There are generic checklists that apply to elements of the software development process, and there are checklists of specifics.

POKA-YOKE

How is poka-yoke (mistake-proofing) applied to the zero defect software program? Throughout the process, software tools need to be incorporated to automate the process and the inspection thereof. These software tools will make the process more "mistake proof".

Inherent in the zero defect software program is the need for consistency. Checklists, as applied to products and processes, will reveal where consistency can be or (more importantly) needs to be stressed. Where such consistency is desirable, new tools can be automated and integrated into the process to reinforce the "expected" level of achievement.

THE CUSTOMER

In *In Search of Excellence,* one of the major facets of excellence is being close to the customer. "In excellent companies, customers intrude into every nook and cranny of the business. Since all business success rests on a sale, that at least momentarily weds company and customer. The excellent companies are really close to the customer, other companies talk about it."[7]

It may seem silly to think that a quote from Ann Lander's column is appropriate in a book such as this one, but this excerpt has caught the essence of the customer as viewed by excellent companies:

What Is a Customer?

A customer is the most important person in any business.

A customer is not dependent on us. We are dependent on him.

A customer is not an interruption of our work. He is the purpose of it.

A customer does us a favor when he comes in. We aren't doing him a favor by waiting on him.

A customer is an essential part of our business—not an outsider. A customer is not just money in the cash register. He is a human being with feelings and deserves to be treated with respect.

A customer is a person who comes to us with his needs and his wants. It is our job to fill them.

A customer deserves the most courteous attention we can give him. He is the lifeblood of this and every business. He pays your salary. Without him we would have to close our doors. Don't ever forget it.[8]

People get paid to produce quality. When customers buy products, aren't they buying more than "the absence of problems"? If the customer only *wanted* absence of problems, the best way to ensure that is not to buy from one with "the absence of problems" mindset. You do not want your customers following that logic.

People do business for positive, not negative, reasons. People do business not to avoid problems, but to receive value. So quality should not be proferred as "the absence of problems as defined by us", but "the presence of value as defined by our customer."[9]

Quality is not what management says it is, but what a customer wants. A 1988 Gallup poll shows that perception of quality by the customer can influence the corporate profitability. Several examples from the poll show that Americans are willing to pay for high quality versus average quality: automobiles $14,518 vs $12,000 (21%), television $501 vs $300 (67%), dishwashers $567 vs $400 (42%), sofas $862 vs $500 (72%), and shoes $50 vs $30 (67%).[10]

Since there is a discrepancy between the price the customer will pay for average versus high quality, there should be a way to recognize the financial loss to the customer because of a defect. Dr. Genichi Taguchi has provided a quality loss function borrowed from the economics arena. Figure 2.6 shows that as the product deviates from the target value, the cost to the customer, shown as the "loss function," starts rising.

To achieve quality requires hard, rigorous quality activity. But while we talk and manage "quality", what the customer *feels* is "value". If

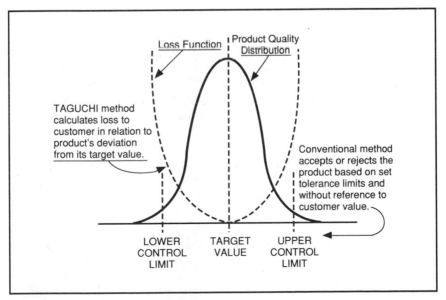

Figure 2.6   Quality loss function.[11]

there is no value, there will be no customers, and without customers, the discussions of quality will be irrelevant.

The value provided to a customer in the software field is a warranty of "fitness for use" by the customer for the software. The warranty will provide assurances for the customer that the software will work as advertised—that is, zero defect software. A full discussion of software warranty is provided in C. K. Cho's book, *Quality Programming: Developing and Testing Software with Statistical Quality Control.*[12]

Make the customer come alive for all employees. It is one thing to produce a quality product for an abstraction called the "customer", and a very different thing to do a job for the customer who is a real person—someone with whom you can identify.

The customer should be made to come alive for all employees, especially those who do not normally come into contact with customers. To accomplish this, several methods can be used: Distribute stories of how customers use the product, allow customers to address employees, let customers explain what it is like to do business with them, and have employees visit customer sites on field trips to see the product being used.

Where direct contact with the customer does not exist, explicitly identify and strengthen all customer connections for the employee. Specifically show the employee how his or her job has an effect on the customer.

The quality professionals in an organization have the know-how to preach the quality gospel. The employees must truly get into church to hear it and respond to it. The focus of the sermon is on one simple question: "What can I do to deliver more value to our customers?"[13]

A new evaluation of that value given to the customer is the National Quality Awards, which is to give six awards yearly commencing in 1988. A *Business Week* editorial focused on the quality of the awards given in 1988 by relating that 10,000 application forms were requested, sixty-six were returned, thirteen detailed audits were performed, and only three companies (Motorola, Westinghouse Electric's Commercial Nuclear Fuel Division, and Globe Metallurgical) received the award. Three of the six awards were not bestowed, these were two for the services sector and one for small manufacturers.[14]

One of the elements of the zero defect software program is its emphasis on the customer. Most industries are aware of and focused to the customer. They want satisfied customers. The zero defect software program is acutely attuned to customer satisfaction.

A unique aspect to this program is the recognition that *everyone* in the software development process has a customer. This internal customer is the next person in line to receive a hand-off of a preliminary item. It could even be the same individual that is considered his or her own internal customer.

When one is trying to please the customer (internal or ultimate), one is on the right road to zero defect software.

REFERENCES

1. Cho, Chin-Kuei, *Quality Programming: Developing and Testing Software with Statistical Quality Control,* John Wiley & Sons, Inc., New York, Copyright © 1987, p. 124.
2. Zultner, Richard, "The Deming Approach to Software Quality Engineering," *Quality Progress,* vol. XXI, no. 11, November 1988, Copyright © 1988 American Society for Quality Control, Inc., Milwaukee, p. 63, Reprinted by permission.
3. Grady, Robert B., and Deborah L. Caswell, *Software Metrics: Establishing a Company-wide Program,* Prentice-Hall Inc., Englewood Cliffs, NJ, Copyright © 1987, pp. 8, 9. Reprinted by permission.
4. *Ibid,* p. 9.
5. *On-line Quality Control: A Cost Driven System of Production Control, developed by Dr. Genichi Taguchi,* American Supplier Institute, Inc., Dearborn, MI, 1988, pp. 2–6.
6. *Ibid,* p. 2–6.
7. Peters, Thomas J. and Robert H. Waterman, Jr., *In Search of Excellence,* Harper & Row, Publishers, New York, Copyright © 1982 by Thomas Peters and Robert H. Waterman, Jr., p. 156, Reprinted by permission of Harper & Row, Publishers, Inc.
8. Landers, Ann, "Ann Landers," *The Washington Post,* November 26, 1988, Copyright © 1988 Los Angeles Times Syndicate and Creators Syndicate, p. C11.
9. Guaspari, John, "You Want to Buy into Quality? Then You've Got to Sell It," *Management Review,* January 1988, Copyright © 1988 American Management Association, New York, p. 25, Reprinted by permission.
10. Skrzycki, Cindy, "The Quest for the Best: U.S. Firms Turn to Quality as Competitive Tool," *The Washington Post,* October 2, 1988, p. H2.
11. Stuelpnagel, Thomas R. "Total Quality Management," *National Defense,* vol. LXXIII, no. 442, November 1988, Copyright © 1988 American Defense Preparedness Association, Arlington, VA, p. 59, Reprinted by permission.
12. Cho, Chin-Kuei, *op. cit.,* pp. 3, 4, 25, 27, 384.
13. Guaspari, John, "The Role of Human Resources in 'Selling' Quality Improvements to Employees," *Management Review,* March 1987, Copyright © 1987 American Management Association, New York, pp. 23, 24, Reprinted by permission.
14. "Three Cheers for Product Quality," editorial in *Business Week,* no. 3083, December 12, 1988, McGraw-Hill Publications Company, New York, p. 136.

What Kinds of Software Defects are There?

"I have no way, and therefore want no eyes;
I stumbled when I saw. Full oft't is seen,
Our means secure us, and our mere defects
Prove our commodities.
                    SHAKESPEARE
            King Lear, Act IV, Scene 1

Terms associated with defects and their distribution within the soft-ware development process are addressed in this chapter. Various types of errors and defects are examined to give the software developers an idea of what confronts them.

By viewing statistics about defects one can do a Pareto analysis con-cerning the type of defect and the defect frequency of occurrence in a particular software development phase. This Pareto analysis permits focusing on the most frequent problems first.

TERMINOLOGY

The term "bug" in relation to software mistakes needs to be stamped out. Ed Yourdon, the software lecturer and author, has stated the case for this the best: "An example ...is the fact that Americans refer to mistakes in their software as 'bugs'. Referring to a bug implies that it's an independent life form that somehow crawled into your computer all by itself, and it's not your fault. The Japanese refer to the same things as 'spoilage', which has connotations of personal guilt and all sorts of things that we don't have as American programmers."[1]*

Having disposed of "bugs", what then are the differences between *error* and *defect*. An *error* is a conceptual, syntactic, or clerical discrepancy which results in one or more faults in the software. A fault is a specific manifestation of an error; a discrepancy in the software which can impair its ability to function as intended. An error may be the cause of several faults. "A software failure occurs when a fault in the computer program is evoked by some input data, resulting in the computer program not correctly computing the required function in an exact manner."[2] In short, errors create faults that cause failures.

A defect is either a fault or a discrepancy between code and documentation that compromises testing or produces adverse effects in installation, modification, maintenance, or testing.[3] Defects will be specifically limited to the delivered software product for the zero defect software program.

DEFECT TYPES

There are three distinct viewpoints for every defect and, because of this, there is often confusion in the attempts to simply describe them. The first viewpoint is that of the product support staff and occurs after a product is released. This view weights the relative importance of different defects and identifies the availability of the staff to address them. This viewpoint must consider fix priority, unit(s) impacted, responsible software developer, and the estimated fix date.

The second viewpoint is from the project manager. The project manager looks at the information provided by the defect fixer and tries to characterize the root causes for defects, the overall product health, and the organization's effectiveness in dealing with defects. The data gathered for this view includes date fixed, hours to fix, the symptoms of the problem, who fixed the software unit, and the development phase in which the defect was introduced, found, and fixed.

The third viewpoint is from the customer's perspective. This view deals with necessary data concerning the customer's profile, the symptoms seen by the customer, and the severity of the defects from their points of view. The important items in this view include the submitter, severity code, criticality, attached documentation of problem, defect description, symptoms of the problem, and required fix date.[4]

---

*Reprinted with the permission of *Software Magazine,* February 1988, Sentry Publishing Company Inc., Westborough, MA 01550.

Besides making sense from the confusion caused by the differing viewpoints for defects, there is much defect data that needs to be introduced.

Tables 3.1 through 3.6 present a variety of ways in which software defects can be categorized. For example, Table 3.1 groups defects according to their cause (fault type), while Table 3.2 uses error categories within the system development process to group defects. No one categorization scheme can fully explain a defect.

First, the types of defects are described below with appropriate statistical information concerning frequency of these types of defects provided in Table 3.1.

Computational. Include incorrect equations or grouping of parentheses, mixing data of different unit values, or performing correct computation on the wrong data.

Logic. Improper order of processing steps, insufficient branch conditions, incorrect branch conditions, incorrectly nested loops, infinite loops, incorrectly nested IF statements.

Input and output. Input from or output to the wrong file or device, defining too much data for a record size, formatting faults, and incorrect input-output protocols.

Data handling. Failure to initialize data before use, improper use or designation of indices, mixing up the names of two or more data and improper control of external file devices.

Interface. Mismatching the parameter list of a procedure call with that internal to the procedure, using procedures as functions, failure to override inadequate default parameters, and incorrect scheduling of other program units.

Data definition. Incorrect type definitions, improper dimensioned arrays, and using subscript constants outside array bounds.

Database. Incorrect data units and anomalies in database initialization.[5]

TABLE 3.1   Distribution of defects by generic faults[6]

Fault type	Lipow (%)	Mendis/Gollis (%)	Craig et al (%)
Computational	9	24	19
Logic	26	38	16
I/O	14	4	19
Data handling	18	10	16
Interface	16	20	16
Database/data definition	10	0	10
Other	7	4	4

TABLE 3.2   Basic Cause Error Categories for Software[7]

ERROR CATEGORY	TOTAL NO.	%	SERIOUS NO.	%	MODERATE NO.	%	MINOR NO.	%
Incomplete or Erroneous Specification								
Dimensional Error	41	—	7	—	17	—	17	—
Insufficient Precision Specified	15	—	0	—	11	—	4	—
Missing Symbols or Labels	4	—	0	—	0	—	4	—
Typographical Error	51	—	0	—	0	—	51	—
Incorrect Hardware Description	7	—	3	—	3	—	1	—
Design Consideration Incomplete or Incorrect	177	—	8	—	47	—	122	—
Ambiguity in Specification or Design	45	—	1	—	4	—	40	—
Subtotals	340	28	19	11	82	17	239	43
Intentional Deviation from Specification	145	12	9	5	61	13	75	14
Violation of Programming Standards	118	10	2	1	22	5	94	17
Erroneous Data Accessing								
Fetch or Store Wrong Data Word	79	—	17	—	52	—	10	—
Fetch or Store Wrong Portion of Data Word	10	—	10	—	0	—	0	—
Variable Equated to Wrong Location	10	—	4	—	6	—	0	—
Overwrite of Data Word	10	—	4	—	4	—	2	—
Register Loaded with Wrong Data	11	—	1	—	10	—	0	—
Subtotals	120	10	36	21	72	15	12	2
Erroneous Decision Logic or Sequencing								
Label Placed on Wrong Instruction/Statement	2	—	2	—	0	—	0	—
Branch Test Incorrect	28	—	10	—	15	—	3	—
Branch Test Set-up Incorrect	2	—	1	—	1	—	0	—
Computations Performed in Wrong Sequence	9	—	1	—	2	—	6	—
Logic Sequence Incorrect	98	—	27	—	65	—	6	—
Subtotals	139	12	41	24	83	17	15	3
Erroneous Arithmetic Computations								
Wrong Arithmetic Operations Performed	69	—	12	—	47	—	10	—
Loss of Precision	9	—	1	—	6	—	2	—
Overflow	8	—	3	—	3	—	2	—
Poor Scaling of Intermediate Results	22	—	4	—	15	—	3	—
Incompatible Scaling	5	—	2	—	2	—	1	—
Subtotals	113	9	22	13	73	15	18	3
Invalid Testing	44	4	14	8	25	5	5	1
Improper Handling of Interrupts	46	4	14	8	31	6	1	0
Wrong Constants and Data Values	41	3	14	8	19	4	8	1
Inaccurate Documentation	96	8	0	0	10	2	86	16
Totals	1202	—	171	14	478	40	553	46

(Copyright © 1975, IEEE. Reprinted by permission.)

Table 3.2 reduces the fault type chart of Table 3.1 to a lower level of basic error categories for software, which indicates the detail of statistics that is available for collection to lead an attack on defects.

A slightly different approach to defect types or classifications emphasizing logic, interface, and documentation categories where the defect was found by the execution of a test case (or operation of a feature) is of interest. Figure 3.1 presents defect-type distribution for logic, interface, and documentation categories similar to what is shown in Table 3.1. It is apparent that logic errors again are the major contributors to those ultimate defects in software.

Switching to the software development phases of error production gives a different perspective on errors in software. Six major error occurrences by development phase are:

Concept errors

- Selected computer(s) inadequate for the task
- Inadequate number of or speed of peripherals
- Use of computer too general—amount of setup for each application inappropriate
- Use of computer too specific—with small amount of additional effort, a better return on investment can be realized

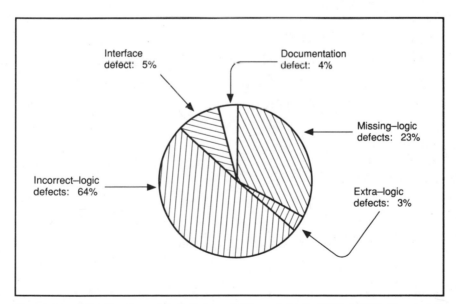

Figure 3.1 Distribution of defect type.[8] (*Copyright © 1987, IEEE. Reprinted by permission.*)

Errors in requirements definition
- Accuracies specified do not conform to need
- Data environment inadequately described
- Erroneous interface definitions
- Training of users poorly considered
- Initial system state not considered
- Functions to be preferred are vague

Errors in top-level design
- Requirements incorrectly understood
- Database compatible with data environments
- Modular decomposition reflects high intermodular dependency
- Major algorithms not evaluated for accuracy or speed
- Control structure inexpansible
- Control structure ignores processing priorities
- Incorrect interface protocols
- No validity checks for input data

Errors in detailed design
- Failure to convert data formats
- Incorrect logic in implementing algorithms
- No consideration given to effects of round-off or truncation
- Indexes not checked for validity
- Logic permits infinite loops
- Incorrectly understood module spec
- Violations of database rules

Errors in code
- Confusion of addressing schemes
- Undefined loop terminations
- Input-output arguments incorrectly defined
- Improper use of registers
- Undefined variables
- Violation of language rules
- Violation of programming standards

Errors in data entry

- Wrong key struck
- Character transpositions

  Records repeated or omitted

  Records not delimited[9]

The value of having a classification of defects (Table 3.3 for example) by when they occurred is that a Pareto analysis may be done to attack the greatest "problem" area. With the highest percent of defects for requirements definition, such as shown in col. A, it is clear that work must be done in the requirements definition phase. Assuming there is a concentrated effort, then the situation should result in a lower percent of defects for requirements definition (such as shown in col. B). It then is time to attack the coding phase because the highest percent of defects is now in the coding phase. This type of Pareto analysis applied to software is covered in Chap. 10 of the *Handbook of Software Quality Assurance.*[10]

Another study from IBM, TRW, and two small projects shown in *Software Engineering Economics* produced approximately the following defects distribution: Requirements 8%, Design 42%, Implementation 30%, and Documentation 25%. The highlight here is that documentation is a significant contributor to defects and must not be ignored.[12]

Table 3.4 shows actual defects data collected by IBM in various projects organized by the phase at which the defects were corrected. The sizes of the programs appear not to substantially contribute to when the corrections were made, with the exception of the "large program", which shows a definite tendency to have more defects corrected in a later phase than an earlier one.

The "large program" in Table 3.4 would lie between a 64k- and a 512k-size program based upon the defect numbers. This is because 663

TABLE 3.3   Defects Classified by Time of Introduction[11]

	Percent of all defects	
Phase	Before Correction Effort	After Correction Effort
Inadequate or incorrect requirements definition	45	15
Inadequate or noncompletion top-level design	20	30
Errors in detailed design	10	15
Coding errors	20	35
Other	5	5

TABLE 3.4   Defects Corrected by Phase[13]

Phase	8K program	64K program	512K program	Large program
Requirements	6*(48)	8 (512)	12 (6144)	(663)
Design	4 (32)	7 (448)	13 (6656)	(993)
Code	5 (40)	6 (384)	10 (5120)	(2526)

*Numbers standing alone are per thousand lines of code.

is between 512 and 6144, 993 is between 448 and 6656, and 2526 is between 384 and 5120.

The number of defects per line of code increases with the number of lines of code in the program based upon Halstead's software science. This result has been available by direct calculations using the software science relationships and is shown in Table 3.5. Also of note in the table is that modularization of the code reduces the defect count.

The Fuchu Software Factory of Toshiba Corporation in Tokyo was founded in 1977 to manufacture application software for industrial process control systems, factory automation, and traffic control. In 1985, there were approximately 2,300 people in the Fuchu Software Factory which shipped about 7.2 million equivalent assembler source lines (EASL) per month. The average size of application software which is manufactured by a project is 4 million EASL (the range is 1 to 21 million EASL). The software manufactured by a project consists of 150–300 real-time tasks associated with common data, common routines, and functions.

The Fuchu Software Factory has captured defect statistics both by category of defect and where the defect was uncovered. The average program quality level at delivery for the Fuchu Software Factory over the past ten years is quoted as two to three defects per 1,000 source

TABLE 3.5   Effect of Modularizing on Number of Defects[14]

Number of Subprograms*	One	Two	Three
Number of Executable Lines of Code		Number of Faults	
100	1.8	1.6	1.3
200	3.9	3.5	3.0
500	11.1	10.1	8.7
1000	24.3	22.2	19.5
2000	53.0	48.7	43.1
5000	147	136	122
10000	317	294	265

*Assumed to be of equal size in order to simplify the comparison.
Copyright © 1982, IEEE, Reprinted by permission.

TABLE 3.6   Software Factory Defect Categories[16]

DEFECT CATEGORY	FACTORY TESTS (%)	PLANT SITE TESTS (%)
Design	35	45
Program	20	10
Data	30	20
Hardware (Interface)	15	25

Copyright © 1987, IEEE, Reprinted by permission.

lines.[15] The percent of defects found in the factory (internal) and in the plant (external—customer site) is shown in Table 3.6.

Finally, once the product is in the customer's control and software maintenance occurs, there are various distributions of defects based upon the maintenance activities (Fig. 3.2). These distributions include: (1) Verifying a feature added to the product, (2) Verifying a feature that existed in a previous version, (3) Verifying a feature determined to be previously functioning properly on the product version being tested (introduced as a result of another correction), and (4) Verifying a feature that exists in the base version of the product where the test case was never before tested—called a *residual defect.*[17]

A question of what does all this data mean is relevant as the defect type section is concluded. First, the type or classification of defects and the frequency of their occurrence provides insight into the most likely

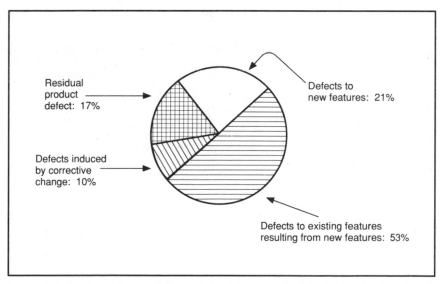

Figure 3.2   Distribution of defect origin.[18] (*Copyright © 1987, IEEE. Reprinted by permission.*)

areas to look for defects. Next, to have statistics on which software development phase or portion of documentation contains errors gives insight into where efforts must be concentrated to control errors.

Also, it is indicated that there are fewer errors when the software is better (more frequently) modularized. The transition from developer control to customer control is shown by the Fuchu defect statistics where the most defects uncovered after delivery are hardware interface problems. Lastly, once in maintenance, the greatest amount of defects occur in existing software due to new software (features) being added to the existing software.

REFERENCES

1. Desmond, John, "The Friendly Master," *Software Magazine,* vol. 8, no. 2, February 1988, Westborough, MA, p. 43.
2. Lloyd, D. K. and M. Lepow, *Reliability, Management, Methods and Mathematics,* 2nd ed., published by the authors, 1977, p. 489.
3. Dunn, Robert, *Software Defect Removal,* McGraw-Hill Book Company, New York, 1984, p. 6.
4. Grady, Robert B., and Deborah L. Caswell, *Software Metrics: Establishing a Company-wide Program,* Prentice Hall Inc., Englewood Cliffs, NJ, Copyright © 1987, pp. 102–104. Adapted by permission.
5. Dunn, Robert, *op. cit.,* pp. 16, 17.
6. Dunn, Robert and Richard Ullman, *Quality Assurance for Computer Software,* McGraw-Hill Book Company, New York, 1982, p. 243.
7. Rubey, R. J., J. A. Dana, and P. W. Biche, "Quantitative Aspects of Software Validation," *IEEE Transactions on Software Engineering,* SE-1(2), June 1975, IEEE, New York, pp. 150–155.
8. Collofello, James S. and Jeffrey J. Buck, "Software Quality Assurance for Maintenance," *IEEE Software,* September 1987, Copyright © 1987, IEEE, New York, p. 50.
9. Dunn, Robert and Richard Ullman, *op. cit.,* pp. 219–221.
10. McCabe, Thomas J. and G. Gordon Schulmeyer, "The Pareto Principle Applied to Software Quality Assurance," in *Handbook of Software Quality Assurance,* G. Gordon Schulmeyer and James I. McManus, eds., Van Nostrand Reinhold Co., Inc., New York, 1987, pp. 195–197.
11. Dunn, Robert and Richard Ullman, *op. cit.,* pp. 241, 242.
12. Boehm, Barry W., *Software Engineering Economics,* Prentice Hall, Inc., Englewood Cliffs, Copyright © 1981, p. 383. Reprinted by permission.
13. Dunn, Robert and Richard Ullman, *op. cit.,* p. 242.
14. Lipow, M., "Number of Faults per Line of Code," *IEEE Transactions on Software Engineering,* vol. SE-8, no. 4, July 1982, IEEE, New York, p. 439.
15. Matsumoto, Yoshihiro, "A Software Factory: An Overall Approach to Software Production," *IEEE,* New York, Copyright © 1987, pp. 155, 156, 163. Reprinted by permission.
16. *Ibid.,* p. 163.
17. Collofello, James S. and Jeffrey J. Buck, *op. cit.,* p. 48.
18. *Ibid.,* p. 49.

Software Quality Indicators

"Our dreadful marches to delightful measures."

SHAKESPEARE
The Tragedy of King Richard the Third
Act I, Scene 1

Much of this chapter is excerpted from an United States Air Force pamphlet entitled *Software Quality Indicators.*[1] To aid readability, the detailed parameters for some of the indicators are given in App. C. The purposes of the software quality indicators are:

1. The *completeness indicator* provides visibility into how well system-level requirements have been translated into software requirements specifications. This indicator is the most complex of the quality indicators. It lays the foundation for quality software and is crucial to obtaining a reliable and maintainable system.

2. The *design structure indicator* recognizes that all software development efforts will have an inherent degree of complexity. The key question it addresses is, "Is the software design as supportable as it can be, consistent with the complexity of the implemented functions?" This indicator can be used to identify the potential for hidden or missing linkages in the software.

3. The defect density indicator addresses the quality of the translation of requirements into design. It provides a quick way of identifying those requirements or functions that may require redesign or additional test emphasis. It is a transitory indicator that leads into the fault density indicator during integration and system test.

4. The fault density indicator performs a function similar to that of defect density indicator. The emphasis is now on how well the requirements have been implemented in testable software products. This indicator can be used with the test coverage indicator to assess software reliability and maturity quantitatively.

5. The test coverage indicator measures the completeness of the test process. It looks at both the percentage of requirements tested and the percentage of software structure tested against the planned test coverage objectives. This indicator provides insight into how well the software has been stressed during testing.

6. The test sufficiency indicator addresses how successful the test processes have been in detecting software errors before fielding the system. The defect and fault density indicators are directly related to this indicator. When used together, the number of errors remaining in developed software can be estimated.

7. The documentation indicator is used to assess how well the software documentation meets the needs of support and user activities in maintaining delivered software.

These quality indicators are not to be interpreted as software quality metrics. The software quality metrics have not yet reached a state of maturity that allows consistent interpretation of each metric. These indicators, however, will support the software quality metrics when the metrics have matured and then can be implemented.

These quality indicators, when related to the goal of zero defect software, are of some help because they measure the trends of quality (conformance to requirements) software development. Each indicator provides the software developer and/or manager with an insight as to how well the development is proceeding toward the goal of zero defect software.

COMPLETENESS

The completeness indicator provides insight into the adequacy of the software specifications beginning during the requirements analysis phase of the software development process. This indicator can be used effectively throughout the software development life cycle. It lays the foundation for quality software and is crucial to obtaining a reliable and maintainable system. The values determined from the compo-

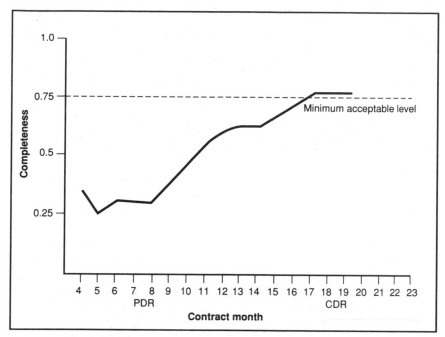

Figure 4.1   Completeness.

nents of the completeness indicator can be used to identify problem areas within software specifications and design.

The inputs for this indicator (App. C) come directly from the requirements analysis and the design and code inspection process. The inspections may be requirements, design, or code walkthroughs; separate inspections; or formal reviews (SSR, SDR, PDR, or CDR). For systems with multiple CSCIs (Computer Software Configuration Items), separate trend data should be maintained for each CSCI. The indicator can also be used for tracking major software modifications and block builds (Fig. 4.1).

The value of the completeness indicator is scaled between 0 and 1. A score near 1 should be considered better than a score near 0. Low values should be investigated to determine where improvements or changes to the specifications may be necessary.

During development of zero defect software when source and successive inspections permeate the entire development process, a possible extension of this indicator would be the measurement of all these "low-level" inspections. However, this would require enlarging an already complex set of input parameters making the completeness indicator ineffective. In its present state, it is just too difficult to collect the inputs required for the extension.

DESIGN STRUCTURE

The design structure indicator is used to determine the simplicity of a CSCI detailed design. Simplicity should not be confused with complexity. Several different ways of determining complexity of the software design have been published. This indicator looks at the "simplicity" or clarity of design, independent of the overall complexity of the implemented functions. The values associated with the inputs and components of the indicator can also be used to identify problem areas within the design that could affect the future maintainability of the software. This indicator can also be used to identify the potential for hidden or missing linkages in the CSCI.

The inputs for this indicator (App. C) come primarily from design and code inspections. These inspections may be design or code walkthroughs or formal reviews, such as PDR and CDR. The indicator can also be used to ensure that the level of simplicity and maintainability is not degraded during major software modification efforts or block builds (Fig. 4.2).

The value of the design structure indicator is scaled between 0 and 1, with 1 representing the simplest and most maintainable design that would meet the software requirements. This indicator should be used

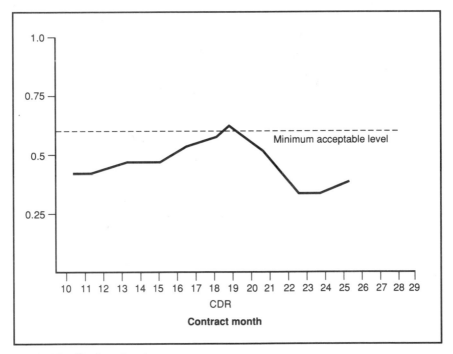

Figure 4.2   Design structure.

in conjunction with the completeness indicator to ensure requirements and design consistency.

As with the completeness indicator, this design structure indicator would benefit the development of zero defect software through incremental collection and exposition of the source and successive inspections in the earlier phases of the software development cycle. Although this indicator has six functions of seven inputs, it is not as complex as the completeness indicator, but needs modification to make it more useful.

DEFECT DENSITY

The defect density indicator provides early insight into the quality of the software design and implementation into code. It is a transitional indicator that leads into the fault density indicator during integration and system test. The defect density indicator's primary thrust is to provide insight into the results of the design and code inspections. If, after these inspections, the defect density is outside the norm for a particular software development effort (the norm can be determined from lessons learned on similar, previous software development efforts), depending upon complexity, application, and so on, it is an indication that the development and/or inspection process may require further scrutiny. In an environment for zero defect software development, this indicator would be renamed Design and Code Error Density because it is not considered a defect until the ultimate customer sees the error.

The inputs for this indicator come directly from the design and code inspection process. These inspections may be design or code walkthroughs; separate inspections; or formal design reviews, such as SSR, PDR, or CDR. The defects reported are composed of requirements errors, design errors, and coding errors. Again, this indicator would benefit from the development of zero defect software by including the results of the source and successive inspections.

The metrics used to support this indicator are the cumulative defects encountered divided by the total number of units in the CSCI, and the cumulative defects corrected divided by the total number of units per CSCI. It has been the author's experience that it is better to represent number of units as a percentage rather than an absolute number because the count changes often during development.

A company's quality reporting system should be considered as a possible means of collecting the data. The data should be updated at least monthly. For systems with CSCIs, separate trend data should be maintained for each CSCI (Fig. 4.3).

This indicator is not absolute and should be used in conjunction

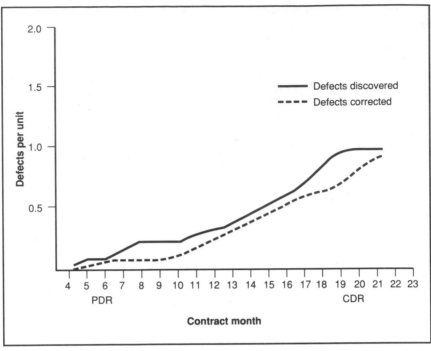

Figure 4.3   Defect density.

with other indicators (for example, the completeness and documentation indicators) in order to better interpret the results of the defect density indicator.

One must be careful of the interpretation from this indicator because a low value may be indicative either of a good product and process or a poor inspection or development process. If the process is found to be adequate through analysis of other indicators, a low value should be indicative of a high quality product. A high value, however, may indicate that adherence to sound software engineering practices may be lacking or that requirement instability is significantly contributing to the introduction of defects. Breaking the defects by type (design, logic, standards, interface, requirements, and so on) can be useful in establishing the true cause and identifying specific areas where further management attention may be needed.

FAULT DENSITY

The fault density indicator is very similar to the defect density indicator. The primary differences are the application phases and an emphasis on test instead of inspection data. This indicator can be used in conjunction with the test coverage indicator to assess software reliability and maturity qualitatively. It can also be used to determine if sufficient software testing has been accomplished. In an environment for zero defect software development, this indicator would be renamed Integration and Test Error Density because the ultimate customer has not seen yet these errors.

The inputs used by this indicator come directly from test results. As software problems are encountered during testing, the severity and class of the failures, as well as the software faults that caused the failure, are documented and used as the basis for this indicator. Table 4.1 (from the Air Force pamphlet 800-14) provides some interesting insight into when software errors are introduced and subsequently discovered, which tells us that too many errors are made in development and not discovered until late in development. This problem is what the zero defect software development process remedies.

The metrics used by this indicator are the cumulative faults (causes of the failures, not the failures themselves) divided by the total number of units in the CSCI, and the cumulative faults corrected divided by the total number of units per CSCI. Again, the recommendation is to stay away from absolute number of units because they vary during development.

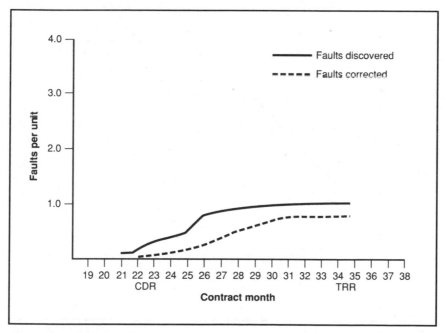

Figure 4.4   Fault density.

TABLE 4.1   Software Error Introduction and Discovery

Life Cycle Phase	Errors Introduced (%)	Errors Detected (%)
Analysis	55	18
Design	30	10
Coding and Test	10	50
Operations & Maintenance	5	22

Reprinted from Air Force pamphlet 800-14.

A company's test and quality reporting system should be used to collect the data. For systems with multiple CSCIs, separate trend data should be maintained for each CSCI. This enables management to focus on those CSCIs that are encountering severe test problems and to provide visibility to each CSCI. The indicator can also be used for major software modification efforts and block builds (Fig. 4.4).

Data analysis is similar to that used for the defect density indicator. A low fault density does not necessarily mean a high degree of software reliability and it can emphasize the need to temper the fault indicator trends with those obtained from other indicators (for example, the test coverage and test sufficiency indicators).

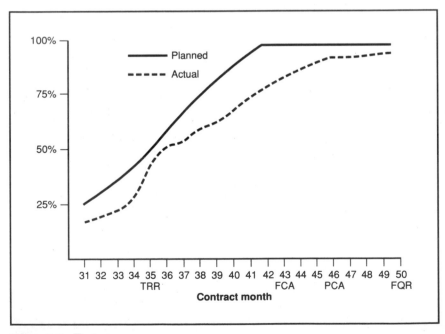

Figure 4.5   Test coverage.

TEST COVERAGE

This indicator presents a measure of the completeness of the testing progress from both a developer's and a user's perspective. It can also be used to quantify a test coverage index for a software delivery. The indicator relates directly to development (including unit, CSC, CSCI, system, and acceptance) testing. It is also beneficial in assessing the readiness of the software under test to proceed to the next test level.

The inputs for the test coverage indicator are in two categories, software structure and requirements. Depending on the level and depth of testing, the software structure inputs may be units, segments, statements, branches (nodes or decision points), or path-test results. The requirements inputs may take the form of either defined test cases or functional capabilities. The planned test coverage from the software test plan can be used as a baseline for tracking coverage deviations.

The combination of the software program and requirements (capabilities) produces the test coverage indicator. The metric used is the percentage of requirements implemented multiplied by the percentage of software structure tested, expressed by:

$$TC = \frac{\text{Number Implemented Capabilities Tested}}{\text{Total Required Capability}}$$

$$\times \frac{\text{Software Structure Tested}}{\text{Total Software Structure}} \times 100\%$$

This indicator should be used in conjunction with the software functional test correlation matrix from the system and CSCI top-level design documents. The test correlation matrix will need to be updated if the requirements and implementation structure are changed during testing. For systems with multiple CSCIs, separate trend data should be maintained for each CSCI in addition to the system trends. This indicator can also be used to assess the test coverage of major software modification efforts and block builds. Data for this indicator are obtained directly from software test plans and reports and a company's quality control system (Fig. 4.5).

The test coverage indicator is a measure of the testing made in two categories of the software product, the software structure and the implemented requirements. Sets of coded instruction make up the design structure and the requirements are a set of capabilities intended for the end user. The intersection of these categories, TC, is the set of implemented capabilities that have been tested.

TEST SUFFICIENCY

This indicator is a useful tool in assessing the sufficiency of software integration and system testing, based on prediction of the remaining software faults. This prediction is, in turn, based on the experienced fault density. Currently, there are insufficient data to make this an absolute indicator. However, many software developers do use this type of indicator as a rule of thumb for making a first approximation for test sufficiency, hence the need for a wide tolerance band at this time. If the indicator falls outside of a tolerance band, the software under test may need further testing before entering the next stage of test, or the software design and test processes may require further scrutiny. The defect density and fault density indicators are directly related to this indicator and can be used, in conjunction with the test sufficiency indicator, to estimate the number of faults remaining in the CSCIs under development.

This indicator, when used with the test coverage indicator, forms a basis for product acceptance at both the CSCI and system level. Although the test sufficiency indicator is primarily focused on CSCI integration testing, combining the data obtained from the individual CSCIs gives the users insight into the acceptability of the software system under development. The inputs for the indicator (App. C) should be obtained from a company's test and quality systems (Fig. 4.6).

The total faults predicted (PF) can be estimated using various techniques. One method would be to calculate the predicted faults using a microquantitative software reliability model based on path structure, or using a software science measure based on path structure. Results obtained from previous developments of similar software development efforts can be used but with caution. Although the usefulness of the indicator is highly dependent on the accuracy of the predicted faults, the use of the test sufficiency indicator as a measure to assess software-to-software integration testing by comparing actual faults remains valid.

The indicator assumes that faults are evenly distributed across units. Consequently, caution should be exercised in applying the indicator during the early stages of the integration test (less than 10 percent of the units have been integrated) and when analysis of the defect density or fault density indicators indicates that an even distribution may be invalid.

The tolerance coefficients (c_1 and c_2) may be tailored to support experience gained on other software development efforts of the same size and complexity. Reliability requirements and confidence in the accuracy of the total predicted faults can also affect these coefficients.

Taken together, the test sufficiency and test coverage indicators help

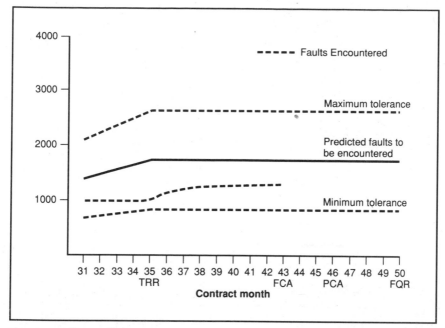

Figure 4.6   Test sufficiency.

the developer gain an insight into the software testing process that is too often lacking. Testing represents significant phases of software development and must be closely monitored to ensure the development of zero defect software.

DOCUMENTATION

The primary objective of this indicator is to gain insight into the sufficiency and adequacy of the software documentation products that are necessary in the operational and postdeployment software support environments. The documentation indicator also provides for the identification of potential problems in the deliverable software documentation and source listings that may affect the usability and maintainability of the operational and support software.

The inputs for this indicator (App. C) are the assessment of the modularity, descriptiveness, consistency, simplicity, expandability, and testability or instrumentation characteristics as reflected in the individual software documentation products (D_i) and source listings (S_i), made on a 6-point scale, with 6 the highest possible score and 1 the lowest (1 represents documentation and source listings that are not suitable for operational and supportable software).

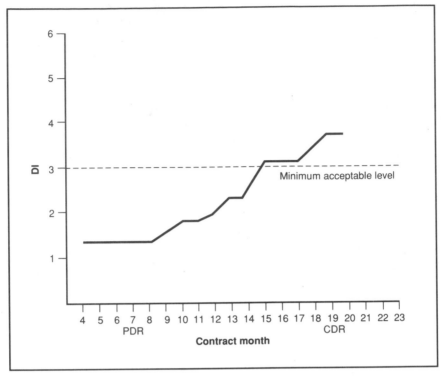

Figure 4.7   Documentation index.

Independent assessments of delivered documentation and source listings can also be used to verify the developer's assessments (Fig. 4.7). For systems with multiple CSCIs, separate trend data should be maintained for each CSCI.

The documentation index is not absolute due to the inherent subjectivity associated with the assessment process. By using evaluation teams from the program's software developers and managers, higher confidence levels of the assessments can be obtained. It is the author's belief that the subjectivity of the Documentation Index is so great as to nullify its validity.

Minimum acceptability thresholds for the documentation and source listings need to be predetermined for both the assessment categories and the delivered documentation. As important as the thresholds are, the numeric indicator is only a pointer to possible problems.

DATA COLLECTION

A summary of when the various quality indicators should be collected in relation to the software development life cycle is given in Fig. 4.8.

SOFTWARE DEVELOPMENT LIFE CYCLE									
Concept expl.	Dem / val	Full scale development							Prod.
SRR	SDR	SSR	PDR	CDR	TRR	FCA/PCA		FQR	
Quality indicator									
Completeness	Periodic		Monthly					As Required	
Design structure					Monthly		As Required		
Defect density			Periodic		Monthly		As Required		
Fault density					Monthly				
Test coverage					Monthly		As Required		
Test sufficiency					Monthly		As Required		
Documentation				As Required					

Figure 4.8   Data collection periods and frequencies.

The emphasis throughout this book is on full-scale development and so it is for the quality indicators.

Also shown in the figure are the frequencies of data collection for each quality indicator. Most are recommended monthly, however, later in the development process they can occur less frequently. The emphasis is where it belongs, i.e., on the front end when something can still be done to improve the product.

These software quality indicators provide a means to monitor the quality of the product as it is ongoing. Of particular interest to the zero defect software program are the defect density and fault density indicators. They provide visibility into how error free the software is and, with that knowledge, allow software management to react.

REFERENCES

1. United States Air Force, AFSCP-800-14, *Software Quality Indicators*, NAVMAT 09Y, Washington, DC, 1987.

Problems with Current Practices

"...my fault is past ..."

Shakespeare
Hamlet, Prince of Denmark
Act III, Scene 3

The main problem with a zero defect software program is that most software-knowledgeable people do not believe it possible. This lack of belief extents to general manufacturing almost as strongly as to software development. The author subscribes to at least one of Bertrand Russell's precepts—*Do not fear to be eccentric in opinion, for every opinion now accepted was once eccentric.*[1]* This chapter covers problems associated with current software development practice in attempting to achieve a zero defect program.

The opinions of Dr. Kaoru Ishikawa concerning why the Zero Defects movement has failed because of various reasons in the United States of America are covered in this chapter. This is followed by discussions of similar problems in software development that have thus far precluded a successful zero defect software program. It is noted

---

*Reprinted by permission of publisher, from *Practical Ethics*, Gordon F. Shea, p. 69, Copyright © 1988, AMACON, a division of American Management Association, New York. All rights reserved.

that with proper attitude and attention, the movement for zero defects can make a comeback.

Turning to software specific problems, the reliability issues and problems endemic throughout software development are covered in this chapter. It is pointed out that estimating the number of defects in a program does not necessarily allow one to accurately compute the program's reliability. The effect of schedule pressures on software development is explored, highlighting poor estimating and outside schedule dictates.

Next, attention is focused on the point that "programs always contain errors". Some statistics are given supporting this view concerning errors, and that is followed up with an analysis of error types. Then, there is a discussion of some of the defect density measures and charts from IEEE *Measures for Reliable Software*. The chapter concludes with why the ideas behind software dependability may conflict with a zero defect software program.

ZERO DEFECTS PROGRAM

"Nothing that's built ever works the first time, no matter how simple its design," says William Howden, professor of computer science at the University of California (San Diego, CA). "Even items as mundane as bicycles and wheelbarrows have design flaws." He believes it is ridiculous to imagine that software will have no flaws. The goal is to get it to run as long as possible, and the way he thinks this can be done is to get rid of the most commonly occurring faults.[2]

The observation of Professor Howden agrees with most of our life experiences, but the pressure to achieve perfection in all we do should never leave us to despair of achieving that perfection. In software development, though difficult, we should never admit defeat in the attempt to achieve zero defect software.

Most commonly, quality is not anything in itself; it is merely what you have left when you remove undesirable things. It is specifically what is left over after the elimination of all defects or problems. It is often made explicit: "Quality means zero defects." Or it is implicit: "Quality is conformance to specifications. We'll define some specifications, make some measurements, compare the measurement to the specifications. If there are no deviations—if there are no problems—then we have quality."

All this makes quality sound very negative. So quality management positioned that way does not sell. Since quality is constantly associated with *problems*—identification, isolation, and removal—the workers perceive that "quality means fewer problems." "We're keeping close tabs on you. So don't 'screw up' as much as you have been!" Even though that is not what is said, it is what is heard or perceived. So, if you really try to sell quality rather than manage a program, you will wind up with a NO SALE.[3]

These quality professionals who believe zero defect products can be built are very often active in helping to reduce the effort of establishing programs. Too often, however, programs are established for workers while top management is being told that zero defect software cannot be built.[4]

Many do not care for the goal of zero defects, which is a tough standard, even though it is nothing more than exactly what we have promised our customers. There has always been pressure to do less. For instance, "continuous improvement" can be utilized as a program to avoid heading for defect-free performance. As we get better each day, our comfort zone is entered and we can be satisfied. Surely and eventually we will hit zero defects, right? If we move 10 percent nearer the target each week, we will never get there.[5]

There are a number of reasons why the Zero Defect movement in the United States of America fails. One is that the movement was made into a mere mental exercise that used people as machines and ignored that people are human. Two is the belief that if standards are strictly adhered to, the number of defects will equal zero. Standards and regulations are always inadequate and, even if strictly followed, defects will appear. Experience and skill make up for inadequacies in standards and regulations.

Giving a command to force a subordinate to implement work almost will never go over smoothly. Commands given by superiors can never catch up with changing conditions, therefore, voluntaryism is essential in quality control.[6]

Dr. Kaoru Ishikawa enumerates in succinct detail why the Zero Defects movement has failed in the United States of America:

1. The Zero Defects movement became a mere movement of will. It emphasized that if everyone did his best, there would be no defects.

2. Since it became a mere movement of will, it failed to teach participants the quality control method of implementation. It was without tools and not scientific.

3. It decreed that if operation standards were closely followed, good products would result. Standards are imperfect; what they lack, experience covers.

4. The United States of America has been strongly influenced by the Taylor method (see NOTE below reason number 8). Workers merely follow work standards and specifications. This ignores workers' humanity and treats them like machines.

5. The word "kickoff" sounded fine for the zero defect movement, but it commanded and forced the workers to start a campaign for which they had very little enthusiasm.

6. All responsibilities for defects were borne by the workers. Managers

and their staff should bear most of the responsibility, workers one-fourth or one-fifth. In the Zero Defect movement, mistakes which the workers were not responsible for were considered to be theirs. Dr. J. M. Juran criticized the Zero Defect movement because of the tendency to shift all blame on the workers whose real responsibility should not exceed one-fifth.

7. The movement became a big show. The Department of Defense encouraged paper compliance by giving no procurement orders to nonparticipants in zero defects.

8. There was no national headquarters like the QC (Quality Circle) Conference to allow mutual development.[7]

Note: The Taylor method of scientific management, introduced around 1911, consists of the discovery, through use of the scientific method, of basic elements of a person's work to replace rules of thumb: The identification of management's function of planning work, instead of allowing workers to choose their own methods. The selection and training of workers and the development of cooperation, instead of encouraging individualistic efforts by employees. The division of work between management and the workers, so that each would perform those duties for which he or she was best fitted, with the resultant increase in efficiency.[8]

Similarly, in the software development arena, there are problems evident throughout software development and they are enumerated below:

1. Inability of development personnel to understand development requirements and organization responsibilities.

2. Inability of design personnel to design a technically acceptable system responsive to the user's needs and requirements.

3. Inability of program management to control the development within schedule or cost constraints.

4. Inability of implementers to build an executable system and successfully complete predefined test cases.[9]

This list highlights the difficulties in the achievement of zero defect software during software development similar to the difficulties listed above for the zero defect movement.

SOFTWARE RELIABILITY

It seems reasonable that the reliability of a computer program is an inverse function of the number of defects within the program.

However, estimating the number of defects in a program does not allow one to accurately compute the program's reliability. A system could have one defect and be totally unreliable. Consider an operating system that crashes anytime an illegal password is used to log in. The same operating system could have multiple defects in functions that no one has used, and these defects would not affect the reliability.

To model reliability from a user's perception, one must model the history of *failure*, not the number of defects. This principle is not compromised by incorporating defect counts within the models, since the defects tallied are exactly those that resulted in failure; somewhat simplistically, at one defect per failure. There are inherent defects of interest with regard to reliability.[10] There should be no confusion between a zero defect software program method for measurement of errors during development and defects (none) after delivery with this methodology for measurement of software reliability.

Software critics should not ask what methods can be found to produce defect-free software, but when will existing methods become widely used. The feasibility of developing complex systems need not be dependent upon the inherent reliability or unreliability of software. Software can no longer become a convenient scapegoat when a problem is not well understood. The real problem with large systems (and many smaller systems) is that the user needs to understand the specific application problem before it becomes a "software problem."[11] In this situation, the question of reliability is begged between system reliability and software reliability.

A point needs to be made here about fault tolerant software. System designers see a need for "resilient" software, which is software that is not error-free at the outset—for this is most likely unachievable early in development—but software that can tolerate faults.[12] The point made here concerning the unachievability of error-free software is another perceived strong statement against the possible reality of zero defect software.

SCHEDULE CONSTRAINTS

A critical challenge in the achievement of zero defect software is the schedule problem. More software projects have gone awry for lack of calendar time than all other causes. Some of the reasons for this are that estimating techniques are poorly developed and assume all will go well, as well as confuse effort with progress. Software managers lack necessary assertiveness needed to control the estimates. Schedule progress is poorly monitored. More people are added when schedule slippage is recognized.[13] Developers have resisted formal testing procedures often because they are under pressure to get new programs or upgrades out the door and do not want to admit there may be problems.[14]* Schedules are dictated by events not under the control of software personnel.

To help resolve the schedule problem in software development, the reasons for the cause of the problem must be addressed. First, the software schedule estimating must be tightened-up; i.e., the estimating models need more than the number of lines of code as the primary driver, and they must be devised to be better predicators of actual schedule. Proof must be confirmed based on actual accomplishment versus model estimate.

Testing cannot be sidestepped to get an upgrade of the software into the hands of the user. The author has seen situations where user organizations directed the delivery of inadequately tested software which has resulted in greater schedule, performance, and cost risk.

Working with the ultimate customer, the software development organization has a responsibility to make that customer understand what realistically is required from a schedule to get the job done. Again, drawing on personal experience, too often very experienced software developers and managers have agreed to unrealistic schedules because that is "what the customer wants".

A contrary point to be made here is that many or most experienced software managers do not know any better than the demand schedule, so it is agreed to because something better or more realistic is not known.

SOFTWARE ERRORS

Following scheduling difficulties, another immediate problem in software development is a mind-set concerning the presence of errors.

A software developer is never certain his/her program is error-free until he or she tries every combination of error data. There is always the possibility that some previously untried combination of input data will lead to program failure, no matter how much testing is applied to a reasonably complex program. It is basically impossible to try every possible input dataset (exhaustive testing) because of the excessive amount of time it takes for all but the most trivial programs.[15] But the zero defect software program proposed in this book does not depend on exhaustive testing as is discussed later. This testing is not to be confused with the 100 percent inspections that are an integral facet of the zero defect software program.

In any case, neither formal verification techniques nor extensive

---

TABLE 5.1   Effectiveness of Test Strategies[17]

Strategy	Faults found	
	Total	Percent
Path testing	18	64
Branch testing	6	21
Functional testing	12	43
Special values testing	17	61
Anomaly analysis	4	14
Interface analysis	2	7

testing can be depended upon to provide sufficient reliability required for critical software, particularly in real-time control systems. The effectiveness of test strategies on six practical programs that contained twenty-eight known errors is shown in Table 5.1. Interestingly, there was at least one error that could not be found by any technique or combinations of these techniques.[16]

This table shows us that test strategies are not good enough to get us to zero defect software. Some similar statistics follow. The indication that software faults will always be with us is found in fault density (faults per KLOC); for good software, it typically ranges from 10 to 50, and after intensive testing with automated tools, is often reduced to 1 to 5. Also, it has been estimated that code that has gone through several iterations of peer reviews, code and design walkthroughs, formal code audits, and independent verification and validation, approximately 0.5 to 3 defects per KLOC still remain. The defects only become known after the system is operational.[18]

To delve even deeper into overcoming additional software development problems, research is needed for the comprehension of errors using analysis of *causes* and *contexts*. This supposes that errors are systematically generated. So there are analogies between an erroneous program—which implements an algorithm different from that of a correct program but always produces the same result from a given argument—and an erroneous understanding of previously learned procedures for problem solving.[19] Results of such research should help in the resolution of some of these software development problems.

SOFTWARE DEFECT DENSITY

Another major problem with software development is that many companies collect no defect data for their software, even though there is a high defect rate. Correcting software defects in the United States accounts for more than $7.5 billion. Measurement of defect rates raises workers' consciousness of the problem and that alone helps to

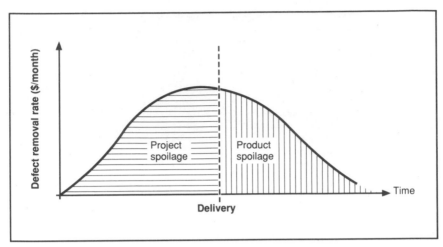

Figure 5.1   Simplified quality metric.[22]

reduce defects.[20] Several suggested ways to collect defect-related data follow. The first is from Tom DeMarco, and others are suggested in the IEEE P982, *Measures for Reliable Software.*

Figure 5.1 represents a way of portraying defect-data collected suggested by Tom DeMarco. The curve shows total spoilage and is composed of project spoilage, which depicts defect removal rate prior to delivery on the left and product spoilage, which depicts defect removal rate after delivery on the right. The final measure of product spoilage may take up to ten years. Since humans are short-term thinkers, ten years or so is too long to wait for an evaluation of quality of work. A quick indicator is the six-month spoilage rate for the total product spoilage provided total defect density is small (~ 2 defects/KLOEC).[21]

Following is a list of data collection for faults, failures, and defects suggested in IEEE P982, *Measures for Reliable Software*[23]:

1. Fault density calculates total faults per KSLOC. It can be used to predict remaining faults by comparison with expected fault density. Based upon predetermined goals for severity class, it can indicate if sufficient testing has been completed. It can establish fault densities for code type and programming organization to use for comparison and prediction.

2. The defect density measure can be used after design and code inspections. If the defect density is outside the norm after several inspections, it indicates that the inspection process requires further scrutiny. This measure is a variation of the fault density measure,

but is considered separate because it focuses on the inspection process rather than the software product.

3. Cumulative failure profile is a graphical method used to predict reliability through the use of failure profiles. It estimates additional testing time to reach an acceptably reliable system. It identifies modules that require additional testing.

4. Defect indexes provide a continuing, relative index of how correct the software is as it proceeds through development. It is generated as a sum of calculations taken throughout development involving number and weighting of defects.

5. Error distribution charts search for the causes of software errors during each software development phase. The results of this analysis can best be depicted by plotting error information to provide the distribution of errors according to different criteria.

These IEEE P982, *Measures for Reliable Software* help to keep track of errors and, thereby, allow improvement during the development process. The early identified errors allow corrective action to be done quickly. It is important, however, to carefully distinguish between errors (made during software development) and defects (those the customer sees), which is not done by these "measures".

SOFTWARE DEPENDABILITY

When mission critical military systems use software, our lives may depend upon successful software implementation, so this issue is most serious. In the Strategic Defense Initiative, a central issue in the debate over the software is whether it can be produced so that it can be trusted to work properly the first time it is used. This is despite the probable presence of software defects that may cause catastrophic failures. A critical point is how would one judge whether or not the software is trustworthy.[24]

There have been posited a variety of ways to evaluate software dependability: *Correctness,* which tells whether or not the software satisfies its specification; *Trustworthiness,* which is the probability that there are no errors in the software that will cause the system to fail catastrophically; *Fault tolerance* which is either failure prevention, i.e., capability of the software to prevent a failure despite the occurrence of an abnormal or undesired event, or failure recovery, i.e., capability of the software to recover from a failure when one occurs; *Availability,* which is the probability that the system will be available for use; *Security,* which is the resistance of the software to unauthorized use, theft of data, and modification of programs; *Error incidence,* which is the number of errors in the software, normalized to some measure of size; and *Safety,* which is the preservation of human life and property under specified operating conditions.

For critical software, correctness and trustworthiness are important indicators of dependability. Fault tolerance assumes importance when the system must continue to perform—as in the midst of a battle—even if performance degrades. Security is important when valuable data or services may be stolen, damaged, or used in unauthorized ways. Safety is important in applications involving risk to human life or property. Error incidence is important in assessing whether or not a piece of software should stay in use."[25]

So with such a life critical system, every precaution is needed. Zero defect software cannot be assumed, the presence of defects must be assumed. With that assumption, the complete utilization or application of the seven items for software dependability are needed to "trust" the software. Of particular interest to a zero defect software program is the error incidence metric. It is not contrary to zero defect software, but allows a sensible measure of error incidence during the development process.

REFERENCES

1. Shea, Gordon F., *Practical Ethics,* American Management Association, New York, Copyright © 1988, p. 69.
2. Falk, Howard, "New Tools Help Exterminate Software Bugs," *Computer Design,* vol. 26, no. 18, October 1, 1987, Westford, MA, p. 52.
3. Guaspari, John, "You Want to Buy into Quality? Then You've Got to Sell It," *Management Review,* January 1988, Copyright © 1988 American Management Association, pp. 24, 25, Reprinted by permission.
4. Crosby, Philip B., *Quality Without Tears,* McGraw-Hill Book Company, New York, 1984, p. 119.
5. Crosby, Philip B., "Editorial," *Quality Update,* Nov., Dec. 1989, The Creative Factory, Inc., Orlando, 1989, p. 38.
6. Ishikawa, Kaoru, *What Is Total Quality Control? The Japanese Way,* trans. by David J. Lu, Prentice Hall Inc., Englewood Cliffs, NJ, Copyright © 1985, p. 66. Reprinted by permission.
7. *Ibid,* pp. 151, 152.
8. Massie, Joseph L., *Essentials of Management,* Prentice Hall Inc., Englewood Cliffs, NJ, 1964, p. 14.
9. Evans, Michael W., Pamela Piazza, and James B. Dolkas, *Principles of Productive Software Management,* Copyright © 1983, John Wiley & Sons, Inc., New York, p. 1, Reprinted by permission of John Wiley & Sons, Inc.
10. Dunn, Robert, *Software Defect Removal,* McGraw-Hill Book Company, New York, 1984, p. 263, 264.
11. Hamilton, Margaret H. "Zero-defect software: the elusive goal," *IEEE Spectrum,* vol. 23, no. 3, March 1986, Copyright © 1986, IEEE, p. 53.
12. Grey, Baron O. A., "Making SDI Software Reliable Through Fault-Tolerant Techniques," *Defense Electronics,* vol. 19, no. 8, August 1987, Englewood, CO, 1987, p. 80.
13. Brooks, Jr., Frederick P., *The Mythical Man-Month,* Copyright © 1979, Addison-Wesley Publishing Co., Inc., Reading, MA, p. 11.
14. Rubin, Charles, "To Get Quality Code, Admit Bugs are a Reality," *Software*

Magazine, vol. 7, no. 11, October 1987, Copyright © 1987, Sentry Publishing Company, Inc., Westborough, MA, p. 61.

15. Downs, T., "A Review of Some of the Reliability Issues in Software Engineering," *Journal of Electrical and Electronics Engineering, Australia,* vol. 5, no. 1, March 1985, p. 36.
16. Hecht, Herbert and Myron Hecht, "Fault Tolerant Software", *Fault-Tolerant Computing: Theory and Techniques,* vol. II, D.K. Pradham, ed., Prentice Hall, Englewood Cliffs, NJ, Copyright © 1986, p. 662. Reprinted by permission.
17. *Ibid.,* p. 662.
18. Grey, Baron O. A., *op. cit.,* p. 79.
19. Wertz, H., *Automatic Correction and Improvement of Programs,* John Wiley & Sons, New York, 1987, p. 14.
20. DeMarco, Tom, *Controlling Software Projects,* Yourdon, Inc., New York, Copyright © 1982, p. 200.
21. *Ibid.,* p. 203.
22. *Ibid.,* p. 203.
23. Dobbins, James H., "Software Reliability Management", in *Handbook of Software Quality Assurance,* G. Gordon Schulmeyer and James I. McManus, eds., Van Nostrand Reinhold Co., Inc., New York, 1987, pp. 398–400, 402–404.
24. U.S. Congress, Office of Technology Assessment, *SDI: Technology, Survivability, and Software,* OTA-ISC-353, U.S. Government Printing Office, Washington, DC, May 1988, p. 222.
25. *Ibid.,* p. 228.

2

Current Methods

Statistical Methods for Error Prediction

"And I another
So weary with disasters, tugg'd with fortune,
That I would set my life on any chance,
To mend it or be rid of it."
                                          SHAKESPEARE
                    Macbeth, Act III, Scene 1

In the Westinghouse No Major Defects program, statistical techniques are used to control all of the manufacturing processes.[1] This chapter looks at statistical techniques. First, since reliability measurement is statistically based, the hardware reliability methods and their adaptation to software reliability are discussed. Some particular software reliability techniques are highlighted to show some statistical application to software quality. The statistical quality control applied to software is highlighted by an example of the technique for a random number generator.

Next, the interplay of statistics and inspections as conceived by Shigeo Shingo are covered. It is through the various inspection methods that Shingo reached his zero quality control concepts.

A section is devoted to the statistics necessary for a zero defects program to achieve zero defects at the process stage. Two statistical techniques, a control chart and a sampling procedure, help to accomplish the goal of making it right the first time—zero defects.

This chapter concludes with some brief comments about Acceptable Quality Levels (AQL) and some lengthier ones about statistical process control (SPC). SPC is important because it helps to make continual improvements to processes.

RELIABILITY

It is tempting to apply hardware reliability, maintainability, and availability techniques to software due to the large body of literature and techniques which have been developed in this area. It is especially attractive because the hardware reliability concepts have been successful, for instance, in the space program. Hardware reliability concepts and methods, however, are not applicable to software reliability. New analytical techniques and concepts are needed to accurately represent the unique characteristics of software.[2]

Time is critical to hardware reliability, but is of little or no (per Dr. C. K. Cho) importance to software reliability. There are time-based models which do achieve some measure of prediction. Burn-in, constant failure rate, and wear-out are characteristics of hardware reliability, but not applicable to software reliability. Operational testing, when tailored to the characteristics of software, has validity for software as well as for hardware.

The inability to express software functions in the form of Boolean equations prevents the use of fault isolation techniques as used in hardware maintenance. The more appropriate technique for software is partitioning of programs into paths and/or branches for testing and error analysis.[3] Layouts based on branches can be subjected to Boolean truth table/action form. The difficulty is that the model resulting is as complicated (almost) as the software and, thus, generally requires a computer program to calculate results.

C. K. Cho's definition of software reliability is:

$$1 - \sigma$$

the probability that the software performs successfully according to software requirements independent of time, where σ is the defective rate of the software product population. The application of this definition (discussed further in this chapter) provides the answers to two questions in software development:

1. When to stop testing?
2. How good is the software after testing?[4]

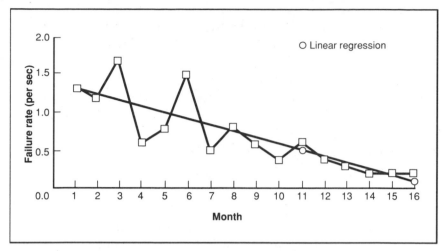

Figure 6.1   Failure rate during software development.[7]

To sum up this position, Fisher and Cooper said, "Software is perfectly reliable. It works the same way each and every time. It never wears out or deteriorates; spare parts for software are inconsequential."[5]

To provide some balance to this issue, it is necessary to provide a contrary opinion that has been posited by Myron Hecht and Herbert Hecht. Execution-time-based measurements are suitable for assessing software reliability because (1) they show consistency in time for a given program, and (2) they show consistency among different programs that are approximately the same magnitude and at the same life-cycle phase. Figure 6.1 shows consistency in time; i.e., the failure rate of a 20,000 statement FORTRAN program during development. Although during the first eight months there were significant variations during the test phase, the failure rate stayed very close to the trend line. Consistency among different programs is given in Table 6.1 abstracted from data compiled by Musa.[6]

Further fuel is provided to the time-based side of software reliability by the IEEE definition that it is the ability of a program to perform a required function under stated conditions for *a stated period of time.*[9]

Sometimes there is confusion between software reliability and software correctness. To help eliminate confusion some definitions of correctness from the draft *Glossary of Software Quality Terms,* by Rome Air Development Center are provided below:

1. The extent to which a program satisfies its specifications and fulfills the user's mission objective.

TABLE 6.1   Summary of Program Failure Rate Data[8]

Number of Programs	Life-Cycle Phase	Size (Kilowords)	Range of Failures/Hour
4	Test	60 - 2500	0.02 - 0.2
6	Operations	100 ->200	0.01 - 0.04

2. The extent to which the software conforms to its specifications and standards.

3. The degree to which the software satisfies its specified requirements.

4. (a) The extent to which software is free from design defects and from coding defects, that is, fault free. (b) The extent to which software meets its specified requirements. (c) The extent to which software meets user expectations.[10]

Software is typically measured in errors per executable thousand lines of code. Current post-delivery levels are one to ten errors per thousand lines, but good methodology produces software with under one error per thousand lines. The numbers are misleading when talking of software reliability because users do not see errors in software, but failures in execution, so the measurement of times between failures is more relevant for continuously running software. If each error had a similar failure rate, efforts to reduce errors would automatically increase reliability. Another misleading aspect is that this only sets the goal after a completed design and test discipline is implemented that still leaves errors/faults/defects.

Every major IBM software product has an extremely high-error-to-failure rate variation. In stable released products, the failure rates run from eighteen months to more than 5,000 years. (Caution: combining all fielded machines could be misleading.) More than half the errors have failure rates of more than 1,500 years between failures. Fixing these errors will reduce the number of errors by more than half, but the decrease in the product failure rate will be imperceptible. A decrease in more than 60 percent of the errors would only decrease the failure rate by less than 3 percent.[11]

Dr. C. K. Cho, in his book, *Quality Programming: Developing and Testing Software with Statistical Quality Control,* says that software acceptance can be determined statistically if the number of defective units in the sample is less than the acceptable number of defective units determined in the selected sampling plan. There is confidence if the acceptance procedure is followed and the sample is random that one is accepting a good program. A defective rate is determined using an iterative process where the number of defective units in the sample is less than the acceptable number of defective units. The caution to be taken with this statistical method is that while random sampling is good for large-quantity manufactured items, care must be exercised in applying this method to software units, which are newly developed, individual items.

The following, taken from Cho's book,[12] is an example of a procedure for testing the uniform random number generator:

```
SUBROUTINE RANDU (N,R)
N = N*65539
IF(N.LT.0) N = N + 2147483647 + 1
R = N
R = R/2147483647
RETURN
END
```

The testing of this generator is accomplished by the following step-by-step procedure:

(1) Define Product Unit. The product unit of the generator is defined for an application as follows: A sequence of 1,000 digits is produced by the generator by using an initial seed and calling the generator 1,000 times. Each digit is obtained by multiplying 10 by a number returned via the variable R in the generator, $0 < R < 1$, and by truncating the result to an integer digit.

(2) Define Product Unit Defectiveness. The product unit, a sequence of 1,000 digits, is defined as defective if the digits are not random, as determined by failure to pass at least one of the frequency tests, serial tests, poker tests, and gap tests, as discussed in Cho's book. It is nondefective if it passes all four tests. (Note: There are many other tests that could be used to determine the randomness of the digits. The four tests cited here are given for discussion purposes only.)

(3) Understand Sampling Plan. An appropriate sampling plan for testing the generator would be the simple sampling plan for estimating the defective rate of the product unit population produced by the generator.

(4) Implement the Test Design. Once the product unit and product unit defectiveness have been defined and a sampling plan selected, the test design can be implemented as follows: First, 300 random "seed" numbers are generated independently of the generator to be tested. Each of these seeds will be used by the generator to pro-

duce a sequence of 1,000 digits. There will be, therefore, 300 product units to be tested for randomness. Implementation of the test
design requires development of a Chi-square test program to automate the frequency, serial, poker, and gap tests. The complete
implementation of the test program and the random number generator is shown in Cho's book.

(5) Generate Test Results. The generator is used to produce 300
sequences of 1,000 digits, that is, 300 product units. It is impossible at this point to determine whether the results are those expected, that is, sequences of random numbers. Thus, the results must
be analyzed further to determine whether the product units are
defective or nondefective.

(6) Estimate the Defective Rate of the Product Unit Population of the
Generator. The estimation of the product unit population defective
rate requires two steps: analyzing the test results and performing
statistical inference.

    a.   Analyzing Test Results. Figure 6.2 shows a step-by-step result
of sampling and determination of the sample size required.
Initially, 20 product units (i.e., 20 sequences of 1,000 digits)
are sampled, using the first 20 seeds described in step 4. The
product units are analyzed by the Chi-square test program.
The sample defective rate is:

$$1 - 14/20 = 0.30.$$

The sample size is found to be 57 with:

$$\hat{\sigma} = 0.30,$$
$$a = 0.40,$$
and
$$z = 1.96.$$

Since 20 is less than 57, 37 additional product units must be
sampled. After 30 additional product units are generated, the
sample defective rate remains 0.30. To reach the required sample size of 57, another seven product units must be generated.
After another 30 additional product units are sampled, the
defective rate is found to be 0.25 with a total of 80 sequences.
(Theoretically, 57 sequences would have been sufficient.
Because more sampling results in greater accuracy, 80
sequences are sampled.) The sample size is found to be 73,
which is less than 80; therefore, the sampling process is completed.

    b.   Performing Statistical Inference. The sampling process dis-
cussed above represents taking outputs at random from a
binomial distribution.

The sample defective rate is found to be:

$$\overline{O}^\circ = 0.25.$$

The next step is to estimate the mean μ and the variance σ of the product unit population. This can be done by testing the hypotheses as follows:

Let the hypotheses be formulated as:

$$H_1: \mu = \mu_1 = 19.2$$

$$H_2: \mu = \mu_2 = 19.2$$

on the basis of the mean $\overline{X}$ and variance s^2 of the sample of 80 sequences at the five percent level of significance. The sample mean $\overline{X}$ and variance s^2 can be computed by:

$$\overline{X} = n\overline{O}^\circ = 80 \times 0.25 = 20$$

$$s^2 = n\overline{O}^\circ(1 - \overline{O}^\circ) = 80 \times 0.25 \times 0.75 = 15$$

The procedure for testing the mean of a binomial distribution having an unknown variance can be used for testing the hypotheses. The student t value is:

$$\text{value of } t_{n-1,/2} = t_{80-1, 0.005/2} = 1.96.$$

The value:

$$(\overline{X} - \mu_1)\sqrt{n}/s = \frac{(20 - 19.2)\sqrt{80}}{3.87} = 1.85$$

Since $-1.96 < 1.85 < 1.96$, the hypotheses H_1 is accepted. In other words, the sample mean 20 is not different from 19.2 at the five-percent level of significance.

This conclusion can be verified by the μ confidence interval of the population mean as follows. The $(1 - 0.05)$ percent confidence interval of the mean of the population is:

$$[\overline{X} \pm t_{n-1,\alpha/2} \frac{s}{\sqrt{n}}] = [20 \pm 1.96 \frac{3.87}{\sqrt{80}}] = [19.152, 20.848]$$

(7) **Determine Whether or Not to Use the Generator.** The 95 percent confidence interval of the mean of the product unit population produced by the generator is found to be [19.152, 20.848]. The defective rate of the population is found to be from 18.152/80 to

20.848/80, or from 0.2394 to 0.2606. If an application requires that
the rate must be less than 0.05, this generator is not usable.

It is important to note that generalizations about the usability
of the generator, as determined previously, should be avoided. The
determination that the generator is usable or not usable is valid
only for a given test design. If a different test design is used, then
the defective rate of the product unit population may also be different, even though the generator is the same. Thus, although a piece
of software may not be usable under one set of conditions, it may
be 100 percent usable under another set.

It is also important to note that the usability of the generator is
determined by four characteristics: efficiency, reproducibility, long
period, and statistical acceptability. None of these characteristics
is related to the number of errors in the generator.

In fact, there is no error in the generator. This generator serves
as a counterexample to almost all of the software reliability models currently existent in literature.[13]

A sample result chart from a uniform random number generator
program on a 32-bit computer is given in Table 6.2 using:

$$n_{i+1} = \frac{Z^2(1 - \sigma_i^0)}{a^2 \sigma_i^0}$$

So, the product unit defective rate is about 25 percent, that is, the
probability of getting a defective product unit from the population is
0.25. So the "mean time to failure" is one in every four units *independent of time*. If different definitions are given for product unit and
product unit defectiveness, then the defective rate may not be 0.25.
The fact that the generator contains no defects, but with a defective
rate of 0.25 on this computer, should alert the reader that zero defect
software may not always be usable.

The software reliability models (reference items 14 and 15) below
would measure the reliability of the random number generator as follows:

(1) MTTF Model. Since $E_T = O$ and $E_C(m) = O$ the MTTF is infinite
by the equation:

$$\text{MTTF} = \frac{1}{K(E_T/I_T - E_C(m))} = \frac{1}{K(0/I_T - 0)} \rightarrow \infty$$

This says the generator will never fail, but as seen from Cho, the generator will fail 25 percent of the time.

TABLE 6.2.   Estimating the Defective Rate[13]

i	n_{i+1}	n_i	$n_{i+1}-n_i$	$\overset{0}{\theta}_i$
1	57	20	37	0.30
2	57	50	7	0.30
3	73	80	−7	0.25

Copyright © 1987, John Wiley & Sons, Inc. Reprinted by permission.

(2) Jelinski-Moranda Model. The hazard function is:

$$Z(t) = M[0 - (0 - 1)] = M$$

where N = 0 and k = 0. Plugging Z(t) in, the MTTF is:

$$MTTF = \frac{1}{M}$$

Thus, the mean time to failure of the generator can be arbitrarily selected from 0 to infinity, as the value of M is an arbitrary constant, which is not the case.

(3) Schick-Wolverton Model. N and k are both 0, thus:

$$Z(t) = M[N - (K - 1)]t = M[0° - (0° - 1)]t = Mt$$

Plugging Z(t) in, the MTTF is:

$$MTTF = \frac{1}{Mt}$$

Again, the mean time to failure would range from 0 to infinity, depending on the operation time t. Since the random number generator contains no error, there is no need to use operation time for error correction. Therefore t, would be equal to 0, and the mean time to failure would be infinite, which is not the case.

(4) Musa Model. Since $M_0 = 0$ the equation is:

$$T = T_0 e[t'C/0] \rightarrow \infty$$

Again, the mean time to failure is predicted to be infinite, which is not the case.

(5) Nelson Model. As there are no errors remaining in the software,

the size of the error:

$$S(E_r) = 0,$$

therefore

$$n_f = 0,$$

which is not the case.[16]

According to Richard Hamlet, "The failure-rate model is not widely accepted. Its assumptions do not seem appropriate for programs, and the mathematics is tractable for only the simplest cases. Some results are intuitively wrong. For example, the number of tests required to force high confidence in a low failure rate does not depend on the size of the program or on the size of the input domain. Even if failure-rate models are wrong, probabilistic analysis seems appropriate for testing theory because it is capable of comparing methods and assessing confidence in successful tests."[17]

There are other problems with these failure-rate models. One is that their use requires careful and complete gathering of data during testing (not after), which implies integration of the technique into the overall management approach. Another problem is the cost to the project; it is significantly greater because of the discipline involved in data gathering when software reliability models are used.[18]

To conclude this section on software reliability, a summary of the ideas by Dr. C. K. Cho concerning software warranty is appropriate. Both the developer and the user must allocate time and resources to make a meaningful software warranty possible. The user has to tell the developer what is required of the software in order to demand a software warranty. The developer must develop the foundations that will make reliance on statistical evidence of product quality an integral part of the software industry in order to deliver a software warranty.[19]

STATISTICS AND INSPECTIONS

We now move away from the software reliability discussion to a discussion on the wider use of statistical methods. Statistical quality methods have been widely used for more than 30 years. In the 1950s, W. Edwards Deming, Ph.D., instructed the Japanese on statistical methods for improving quality in the factory. Later, J. M. Juran, Ph.D., discussed quality management techniques with the Japanese. The observations made by Shigeo Shingo concerning statistics are particularly applicable. The use of statistics and their effect on different inspection types are introduced here and further explored in detail in Chap. 7. Mr. Shingo observed the following concerning inductive statistics:

- Inductive statistics remains an excellent technique for manufacturing process control.

- Statistics is extremely effective in the planning phase of management.

- Statistics is not always effective in control and execution phases.

- Information inspections are a major feature of Statistical Quality Control Systems and must be pursued to the limit.

- Inductive statistics is an excellent technique for making methods more rational.

In 1951, Shigeo Shingo understood quality control to mean efforts to inspect products, make high quality goods, and eliminate defects. A representative from Nippon Electric Co. said, "It's not quality control unless you use statistics." He described experimental planning methods, determination of significant differences, factor charts, histograms, and control charts for informative inspections. He continued with such other things as standard limits and control limits, control charts and three standard deviation limits, $\overline{X}.R$ control charts, P control charts, and sampling inspections based on statistical science.

Informative inspections that could reduce defects in the future impressed Shigeo Shingo. With this approach, control charts would be drawn up, and whenever values were outside the control limits and improvement feedback made, work methods would be improved. Especially impressive was determining whether a situation was normal or not through three standard deviation control limits. The theory-based techniques of experimental planning methods and determining significant differences were extremely effective.

"The characteristics of so-called Statistical Quality Control (SQC) Systems include, first of all, the notion of informative inspections, which use statistically based control charts as inputs to reduce future defects by feeding back information about defects to the offending processes; work methods are then corrected accordingly. Also, characteristic of SQC systems is the use of statistics to set control limits that distinguish between normal and abnormal situations. The number of samples taken to detect abnormal values is similarly determined according to statistical principles. Thus, the use of statistical principles may be considered to be the essential condition identifying a method of inspection as an SQC method."[20] This statistical approach to quality control was invented in the United States in the 1920s, but its integration as a system is new to the United States.[21]

Hewlett-Packard cites a specific example of SQC applied to software development. First, defects actually encountered in the past from an application program are listed in Fig. 6.2. These definitions and cate-

		Pareto Analysis
A.	User Interface/Interaction	
	1. User needs additional data fields	15
	2. Existing data needs to be organized/presented differently	16
	3. Edits on data values are too restrictive	9
	4. Edits on data values are too loose	9
	5. Inadequate system controls or audit trails	4
	6. Unclear instructions or responses	12
	7. New function or different processing required	18
B.	Programming Defects	
	1. Data incorrectly or inconsistently defined	11
	2. Initialization problems	10
	3. Database processing incorrect	3
	4. Screen processing incorrect	
	5. Incorrect language instruction	2
	6. Incorrect parameter passing	2
	7. Unanticipated error condition	8
	8. Operating system file handling incorrect	
	9. Incorrect program control flow	5
	10. Incorrect processing logic or algorithm	7
	11. Processing requirement overlooked or not defined	1
	12. Changes required to conform to standards	
C.	Operating Environment	
	1. Terminal differences	
	2. Printer differences	1
	3. Different versions of systems software	
	4. Incorrect JCL	
	5. Incorrect account structure or capabilities	
	6. Unforeseen local system requirements	1
	7. Prototyping language problem	1

Figure 6.2   Categories of software defects.[23]

gories are relatively unique to the particular application and development environment.

Then, a Pareto analysis (Fig. 6.2) identifies the most frequently occurring defects. Over one-third of the defects correspond to categories A7, A2, and A1 from Fig. 6.2. The probable causes of these defects are then determined by using SQC, and changes are instituted into the development process.[22]

Mr. Shingo points out some of the pluses and minuses associated with SQC systems. Informative inspections have shown the possibility of defect rate reductions, and this has yielded phenomenal developments. Also statistical science methods are of considerable value. In management planning, analytical techniques, such as experimental planning method and the determination of significant differences, have led to improvements in the establishment of standard work processes and operating procedures. Statistics also provided a highly reliable way to determine appropriate sample sizes for establishing control limits and for finding abnormalities.

On the minus side, the initial effectiveness of SQC systems as statistical techniques led many people to say, "If it doesn't use statistics, it's not quality control."

"The beliefs that you cannot carry out quality control," said Mr. Shingo, "without drawing up control charts, or that sampling inspections are rational because they are backed up by statistical science, led people to forget that these are no more than streamlined inspection methods and that they do not make quality assurance any more rational." The confidence such people had in the powers of statistical science was a bit excessive.

Major conceptual advances of informative inspections were obscured by inductive statistics. Consequently, qualitative improvements in informative inspections, i.e., the performance of 100 percent checks of the development process or increases in the speed of corrective action, were neglected.

Mathematical techniques, such as inductive statistics, dominated discussions among scholars and theory-oriented technicians who excelled in "desktop" mathematical processing. It frequently alienated those responsible for quality control, to the point of giving them a headache. Probably the reason for the tardy pursuit of real quality control systems aimed at *zero defects* was that the quality control efforts in Japan were led by certain highbrow theorists with no real connection to the workplace.[24]

STATISTICS FOR ZERO DEFECTS

This section is modified from a paper entitled "Quality Control Techniques for 'Zero Defects' " by Thomas W. Calvin of IBM Corporation.* Exposure to the "zero defects philosophy as a goal for manufacturing is increasing. Much attention has been given to implementing a program to get to zero defects. Little consideration has been given to statistical techniques necessary to assure that the product or process stays at zero defects. Does an attribute control chart at zero defects convey much useful information when only zeros are plotted?

---

*Adapted courtesy of the author from the *Proceedings of Qual Test–2*, Copyright © 1983, American Society for Nondestructive Testing, American Society for Quality Control and the Society of Manufacturing Engineers.

For conventional acceptance sampling inspection near zero defects, sample sizes approach lot sizes or 100 percent inspection. The challenge is to couple control chart and sampling inspection philosophies more closely with defect prevention. Two statistical techniques, a control chart and a sampling procedure, help to accomplish the goal of making it right the first time for zero defects.

Zero defects is used as a descriptor of a process with blemishes and nonconformities approaching zero which produces no defects or failure. In labor-intensive processes, people may have bad days, and the result can be that the processes capable of zero defects may only approach zero. With testing and inspection procedures combined with process shutdowns encouraging "make it right the first time," process improvements will result in a process more and more resistant to those bad days.

Some techniques are inadequate at zero defects and require modification or new approaches. How useful is the information provided by a percent defective chart that displays mainly zeros? Assurance via an attributes acceptance sampling procedure requiring a sample approaching the size of the lot is no longer a sample plan. Of particular concern are those statistical techniques associated with attributes data. Variables data requires an increased awareness of the relationship between the specifications and the process capability.

Typically, variables data considers one characteristic at a time, while attributes data can lump together many characteristics into one measure. Thus, variables control charts and sampling plans typically involve an individual characteristic of a critical nature. Attributes control charts and sampling plans consider multiple characteristics relative to their specifications and combine them into one measurement, such as a fraction defective or defects-per-unit. Thus, only the count of incidents not satisfying the specification is recorded, and the numerical magnitude of the characteristic is lost. This loss of information is compensated for by taking larger sample sizes. The sample sizes for variables data are smaller, reflecting the greater amount of information retained. The variables data percent defective, which may not be measurable, can often be estimated.

The choice between using variables or attributes data depends upon the situation. Destructive testing or very difficult, time-consuming inspection would necessitate a small variables sample. However, easy inspection of many characteristics may make a larger attributes sample economical. But at zero defects, attributes samples become prohibitively large. Sometimes only an attributes measure is possible.

Variables techniques for control charts and sampling plans are adaptable for zero defects. The more standard deviations that the specification limits are from the process average, the closer the process comes to zero defects. Under a normal assumption, 4.75 standard deviations, S, from the average, $\overline{X}$, represents a fraction defective of 1 ppm (part per million), which is approaching zero defects.

$$\frac{USL - \overline{X}}{S} \quad \text{or} \quad \frac{\overline{X} - LSL}{S} = 4.75$$

Both $\overline{X}$ and R charts and variables acceptance sampling procedures, adequately described in A. J. Duncan, *Quality Control and Industrial Statistics,* depend upon the relationship between specification limits, standard deviations, and averages. It is important to recognize that one route to zero defects is the proper synergism between performance and reliability specifications and manufacturing process capability. Be aware early in a program of any incompatibility between product specifications and the process producing the product. Challenge the specifications to see if they can be relaxed and still maintain performance and reliability, at the same time pursuing ways to improve process capability. This will greatly enhance the ability to reach zero defects by providing the capability of making it right the first time.

Assessing the properties of an item by counting the number of undesirable characteristics or the number of characteristics exceeding specifications becomes a measurement problem as zero defects are approached. Suppose lot sizes of 1,000 at 10 ppm are monitored on a control chart. How useful is a chart plotting only zeros? What sort of limits would indicate statistical control? For example, 99 zero-defect lots are expected with 100 percent inspection. But if, say, a sample of 100 is inspected, now 999 zero-defect samples are expected. Additionally, many subproducts, such as cards and boards, have average lot sizes much less than 100 items. Plotting the number of defective items does not provide any meaningful information on a timely basis. Also, for attribute acceptance sampling, low ppm targets yield large sample sizes or 100 percent inspection. Since it is unlikely that the latter is 100 percent efficient, traditional approaches to attributes inspection are inadequate to assure product quality. Certainly some new approaches need to be considered. Rather than dwelling on the number of bad items or lots, we should concentrate on the number of good items or lots between the bad ones.

For example, how about a cumulative count control chart which cumulates the number of good items between bad? This could be plotted on semi-logarithmic paper with a logarithmic vertical scale for cumulative count and a linear horizontal scale for the time periods as measured by lots, days, weeks, etc. The number of good items prior to a bad one would follow a geometric distribution. The expected number of good items is:

$\overline{n} = 10^{+6}/\text{ppm}$ $\overline{n} = 1/p$ or $10^6/p$ for p in ppm

$\text{median} = 0.693\,\overline{n}$

$\text{LCL} = \alpha\,\overline{n}$ and $\text{UCL} = -\overline{n}\,\ln\alpha$

where α is the probability of a count less than the Lower Control Limit, LCL, or a count greater than the Upper Control Limit, UCL. Thus, given the ppm, the center line and upper and lower limits are easily obtained.

Any count between defects below the lower limit is indicative of an out-of-control process, as is five or more defects below the median. Any line exceeding the upper limit or five or more defects above the median indicates a significant improvement in the process. This is now a very positive chart, highlighting the number of good items produced in a sequence. Out-of-control situations are immediately visible. Thus, the control chart provides more meaningful, timely information, and the variation in the number of units produced in each period is unimportant as only the total cumulation is considered. This type of control chart can replace either percent defective or defects per unit charts to monitor statistical quality control of a process, as at low ppm, these charts are equivalent.

A second procedure involves acceptance sampling where low ppm also creates problems. Statistically determined samples become larger and larger and result in 100 percent inspection. Thus traditional attributes acceptance sampling is not satisfactory at zero defects. Rather than attribute acceptance sampling plans that strictly accept or reject lots, how about plans that also accept or reject a process? The latter rejection is implemented by process shutdown or stop shipment, either of which prevents potential substandard products from exiting to the customer or next operation. Of course, this is not a new concept, since the MIL-STD-105D, *Sampling Procedures and Tables for Inspection by Attributes,* scheme allows for termination of sampling inspection, which applies pressure on the producer to maintain the AQL (Acceptable Quality Level).

The procedure described requires the same sample sizes as dictated by the lot sizes. The downward arrows in Table 6.3 will be replaced by the minimum number of accepted lots between rejected lots for process acceptance. If a second rejection occurs at or prior to that number being attained, the process is rejected and either the process is shut down or shipment is stopped. Table 6.4 shows these numbers, which are obtained from the following relationship:

$$PR = npk = 0.08$$

where

PR = the probability of rejection given a rejected lot

n = the sample size

p = the AQL

k = the minimum number of accepted lots between rejected lots

With PR fixed at 0.08, the k can be obtained for any combination of n and p. Since np is constant along the diagonals, calculation of the first column using $p = 0.0001$ yielded

$$k = \frac{0.08}{0.0001n} = \frac{800}{n}$$

with rounding to an integer. Then the diagonals were completed. Using these numbers provides a constant conditional probability of process rejection given a lot rejection. The absolute probability of rejection is the probability of a lot rejection:

$$Pr = np,$$

multiplied by the above conditional probability:

$$PR = npk = 0.08,$$

yielding:

$$knp = 0.08 \, np.$$

Thus the smaller:

$$Pr = np,$$

the less likely is process rejection but, given a lot rejection, the longer the decision period, k, for process acceptance.

Much attention has been given to implementing and managing a program to get to zero defects. Little consideration has been directed toward the statistical techniques necessary to assure that a product or process stays at zero defects. New approaches to acceptance sampling and control charting are required at zero defects. Two procedures based upon cumulative counts have been suggested. The suggestion was made that they could be implemented with a stop shipment or process shutdown procedure. This is a feasible approach, since at the

TABLE 6.3 Single Sampling Plans for Normal Inspection (Master Table)[25]

Acceptable Quality Levels (normal inspection) — Percent

Arrows: ↓ = Use first sampling plan below arrow. ↑ = Use first sampling plan above arrow. (Values shown as "Ac Re".)

Sample size code letter	Sample size	0.010	0.015	0.025	0.040	0.065	0.10	0.15	0.25	0.40	0.65	1.0	1.5	2.5	4.0	6.5	10.0
A	2	↓	↓	↓	↓	↓	↓	↓	↓	↓	↓	↓	↓	↓	↓	0 1	1 2
B	3	↓	↓	↓	↓	↓	↓	↓	↓	↓	↓	↓	↓	↓	0 1	1 2	2 3
C	5	↓	↓	↓	↓	↓	↓	↓	↓	↓	↓	↓	↓	0 1	1 2	2 3	3 4
D	8	↓	↓	↓	↓	↓	↓	↓	↓	↓	↓	↓	0 1	1 2	2 3	3 4	5 6
E	13	↓	↓	↓	↓	↓	↓	↓	↓	↓	↓	0 1	1 2	2 3	3 4	5 6	7 8
F	20	↓	↓	↓	↓	↓	↓	↓	↓	↓	0 1	1 2	2 3	3 4	5 6	7 8	10 11
G	32	↓	↓	↓	↓	↓	↓	↓	↓	0 1	1 2	2 3	3 4	5 6	7 8	10 11	14 15
H	50	↓	↓	↓	↓	↓	↓	↓	0 1	1 2	2 3	3 4	5 6	7 8	10 11	14 15	21 22
J	80	↓	↓	↓	↓	↓	↓	0 1	1 2	2 3	3 4	5 6	7 8	10 11	14 15	21 22	↑
K	125	↓	↓	↓	↓	↓	0 1	1 2	2 3	3 4	5 6	7 8	10 11	14 15	21 22	↑	↑
L	200	↓	↓	↓	↓	0 1	1 2	2 3	3 4	5 6	7 8	10 11	14 15	21 22	↑	↑	↑
M	315	↓	↓	↓	0 1	1 2	2 3	3 4	5 6	7 8	10 11	14 15	21 22	↑	↑	↑	↑
N	500	↓	↓	0 1	1 2	2 3	3 4	5 6	7 8	10 11	14 15	21 22	↑	↑	↑	↑	↑
P	800	↓	0 1	1 2	2 3	3 4	5 6	7 8	10 11	14 15	21 22	↑	↑	↑	↑	↑	↑
Q	1250	0 1	1 2	2 3	3 4	5 6	7 8	10 11	14 15	21 22	↑	↑	↑	↑	↑	↑	↑
R	2000	1 2	2 3	3 4	5 6	7 8	10 11	14 15	21 22	↑	↑	↑	↑	↑	↑	↑	↑

↓ = Use first sampling plan below arrow. If sample size equals, or exceeds, lot or batch size, do 100 percent inspection.
↑ = Use first sampling plan above arrow.
Ac = Acceptance number.
Re = Rejection number.

TABLE 6.4   Single Sampling Plans for Normal Inspection (Master Table), extended for zero defects [26]

Acceptable Quality Levels (normal inspection) — Percent. For each AQL column the heading is **K / Ac Re**. Cells show the K value (single number), the Ac Re pair, or an arrow (↑ = use first sampling plan above arrow).

Sample size code letter	Sample size	0.010	0.015	0.025	0.040	0.065	0.10	0.15	0.25	0.40	0.65	1.0	1.5	2.5	4.0	6.5	10.0
A	2	400	250	160	100	64	40	25	16	10	6	4	3	2	1	0 1	1 2
B	3	250	160	100	64	40	25	16	10	6	4	3	2	1	0 1	1 2	2 3
C	5	160	100	64	40	25	16	10	6	4	3	2	1	0 1	1 2	2 3	3 4
D	8	100	64	40	25	16	10	6	4	3	2	1	0 1	1 2	2 3	3 4	5 6
E	13	64	40	25	16	10	6	4	3	2	1	0 1	1 2	2 3	3 4	5 6	7 8
F	20	40	25	16	10	6	4	3	2	1	0 1	1 2	2 3	3 4	5 6	7 8	10 11
G	32	25	16	10	6	4	3	2	1	0 1	1 2	2 3	3 4	5 6	7 8	10 11	14 15
H	50	16	10	6	4	3	2	1	0 1	1 2	2 3	3 4	5 6	7 8	10 11	14 15	21 22
J	80	10	6	4	3	2	1	0 1	1 2	2 3	3 4	5 6	7 8	10 11	14 15	21 22	↑
K	125	6	4	3	2	1	0 1	1 2	2 3	3 4	5 6	7 8	10 11	14 15	21 22	↑	↑
L	200	4	3	2	1	0 1	1 2	2 3	3 4	5 6	7 8	10 11	14 15	21 22	↑	↑	↑
M	315	3	2	1	0 1	1 2	2 3	3 4	5 6	7 8	10 11	14 15	21 22	↑	↑	↑	↑
N	500	2	1	0 1	1 2	2 3	3 4	5 6	7 8	10 11	14 15	21 22	↑	↑	↑	↑	↑
P	800	1	0 1	1 2	2 3	3 4	5 6	7 8	10 11	14 15	21 22	↑	↑	↑	↑	↑	↑
Q	1250	0 1	1 2	2 3	3 4	5 6	7 8	10 11	14 15	21 22	↑	↑	↑	↑	↑	↑	↑
R	2000	1 2	2 3	3 4	5 6	7 8	10 11	14 15	21 22	↑	↑	↑	↑	↑	↑	↑	↑

K = Minimum number of accepted lots between rejected lots for process acceptance when nAQL ≤ 0.08.

⇩ = Use first sampling plan below arrow. I² sample size equals, or exceeds, lot or batch size, do 100 percent inspection.

⇧ = Use first sampling plan above arrow.

Ac = Acceptance number.

Re = Rejection number.

99

low target levels, very few shutdowns would result. As more and more problems are resolved and the process approaches zero defects, process shutdowns become a rarity and "making it right the first time" becomes a reality.[27]

AQL AND SPC

Three other statistically based programs are in use and are briefly discussed below. Shipped-product quality level (SPQL), acceptable quality level (AQL), and in a different vein, Statistical Process Control are these methods.

Companies help their people not meet the requirements in some of the following ways:

- Shipped-product quality level (SPQL) means that a certain number of defects are recognized as inevitable. Refrigerators and television sets have perhaps three or more, and computers eight or more. SPQL lets managers know how many field service people will be needed.

- Acceptable quality level (AQL), established usually for suppliers, is supposed to establish an acceptance plan for inspection (about 2.5%). It really represents the number of nonconforming items that can come in an acceptable lot. AQL is discussed in more detail in Chap. 10.

There are other variations that convince people that the determination to get things done right just is not there. People continually explain that zero defects is impossible. Yet, in companies, there are routine examples of no known defects.[28]

SPC (Statistical Process Control) is the application of statistical measures along the process key points in the development of the product. By sampling product while it is being built, instead of just when it is completed, the developers can fix errors/discrepancies early. In that manner, the component aspects of the process are kept under control at the earliest possible stage. This concept is quite similar to the methods applied to the software development process leading to zero defect software.

"No longer will we accept quality by inspection. Our contractors need to understand that their manufacturing process controls the quality of the products they are producing. We want them to maintain quality by inspecting the process," said Maj. Gen. Monroe Smith, deputy chief of the Air Force Systems Command for product assurance and acquisition logistics, in 1987.

The prospective policy requires contractors to control the quality of their products by continually examining critical assembly processes throughout the production line. This is called SPC because each process is analyzed statistically to ensure that every part is being produced correctly. SPC allows workers to uncover poor workmanship when the problem occurs, instead of after products are assembled.[29]

Fixing the manufacturing system, not the products, then appears to be the correct way to improved quality. In this manner, the causes of product deficiency are detected at the source rather than after the completion of assembly. SPC measures a manufacturing process by monitoring progress in production. SPC helps locate potential difficulties before they result in defective product.[30]*

SPC gauges the performance of the manufacturing process by carefully monitoring changes in whatever is being produced. It is the goal to detect potential problems before they result in defective products, then pinpoint the reason for the deviation and make the process more stable. The problem is the extensive amount of variables and large number of processing steps that need to be controlled to achieve zero defects. Sophisticated statistical analyses make sense out of the relationships among all the variables within all the processes.[31]

SPC is a valuable technique because it helps to make continual improvements to processes. If the control limits are too wide, SPC provides a method for experimentation, enabling one to see the effects on the process of any improvements made to it. There is a way in which control charts can be used to good effect even in small batch manufacturing. With this method, instead of trying to control the accuracy of each individual batch, the aim is to monitor and improve the machine or process which is being used to manufacture the work—even when batch quantities are down to one. Since SPC monitors the capability of the process, this method can be used for manufacturing one unit and is the only way in which monitoring can be performed in a flexible manufacturing system. When used as a long-term monitoring device, it can show if a machine is starting to deteriorate. SPC also provides useful information which can be sent to the design department, so that designers know what tolerances can realistically be applied to work going into the factory.[32]

Similar to SPC for software development is the cleanroom software development method. It has three main attributes: a set of attitudes, a series of carefully prescribed processes, and a rigorous mathematical basis. Cleanroom strives for zero defects, which means that errors become rare events in the statistical sense. Every cleanroom team

---

*Excerpted from *Mini-Micro Systems,* Dec. 1985, copyright © 1985 by Cahners Publishing Company.

member must have successes and know that the zero defects goal is not only possible, but is expected.[33]

Dr. C. K. Cho in his book, *Quality Programming: Developing and Testing Software with Statistical Quality Control,* also addresses similar issues but from a different perspective. He says that the manufacturing system is equivalent to the software system. The process of making the manufacturing system is equivalent to the process of developing software.

In any manufacturing system, in general, there is no way to fix the products, he goes on to say. The only way to produce better products is to make sure the manufacturing system works right. In software development, if the product is software and the manufacturing system is the development process, then fixing the process does not necessarily work.

REFERENCES

1. West, Andrew H., *No Major Defects Program Overview* presentation at Westinghouse Electric Corp., Jan. 1987, p. 3.
2. Schneidewind, Norman F., "The Applicability of Hardware Reliability Principles to Computer Software," in *Software Quality Management,* Matthew J. Fisher and John D. Cooper, eds., Petrocelli Books, Princeton, NJ, 1979, p. 171.
3. *Ibid.,* p. 180.
4. Schulmeyer, G. Gordon and C. K. Cho Ph.D., "Software Reliability—A Statistical Approach," *Proceedings of E & AT Statistics Symposium III,* Westinghouse, Oct. 19–20, Pittsburgh, 1987, p. 2.
5. Preface in *Software Quality Management,* Matthew J. Fisher and John D. Cooper, eds., Petrocelli Books, Princeton, NJ, 1979, p. viii.
6. Hecht, Herbert and Myron Hecht, "Fault-Tolerant Software", in *Fault-Tolerant Computing: Theory and Techniques,* vol. II, D. K. Pradham, ed., Prentice Hall, Inc., Englewood Cliffs, NJ, Copyright © 1986, p. 659. Reprinted by permission.
7. *Ibid.,* p. 659.
8. *Ibid.,* p. 659.
9. Software Engineering Technical Committee of the IEEE Computer Society, *IEEE Standard Glossary of Software Engineering Terminology,* IEEE-STD-729-1983, IEEE, New York, 1983, p. 32.
10. *Draft Glossary of Software Quality Terms* prepared by ITT Research Institute, Rome, New York; prepared for Rome Air Development Center (RADC), Griffiss AFB, New York, November 8, 1985, p. 5.
11. Mills, Harlan D., Michael Dyer, and Richard C. Linger, "Cleanroom Software Engineering," *IEEE Software,* September 1987, Copyright © 1987, IEEE, New York, p. 23, Reprinted by permission.
12. Cho, Chin-Kuei, *Quality Programming: Developing and Testing Software with Statistical Quality Control,* John Wiley & Sons, Inc., New York, Copyright © 1987, pp. 302–311, 357, Reprinted by permission.
13. *Ibid.,* p. 391.
14. Farr, William H. Ph.D., "A Survey of Software Reliability Modeling and Estimation", NSWC TR 82-171, prepared for Naval Surface Weapons Center, Dahlgren, VA, September 1983.
15. "Quantitative Software Models", SRR-1, prepared by Computer Sciences Corporation, under contract to ITT Research Institute, prepared for Rome Air Development Center (RADC), Griffiss AFB, New York, March 1979.

16. Cho, Chin-Kuei, *op. cit.*, pp. 390–393.
17. Hamlet, Richard, "Special Section on Software Testing", *Communications of the ACM,* vol. 31, no. 6, June 1988, Copyright © 1988 by ACM, pp. 665, 666, Reprinted by permission.
18. Schulmeyer, G. Gordon and Halsey B. Chenoweth, Ph.D., "The Trouble with Software Reliability," *IEEE COMPSAC Proceedings,* IEEE Press, Oct. 8–10, 1986, Copyright © 1986 IEEE, New York, p. 258.
19. Cho, Chin-Kuei, *op. cit.*, p. 25.
20. Shingo, Shigeo, *Zero Quality Control: Source Inspection and the Poka-yoke System,* Andrew P. Dillon (trans.), Productivity Press, Cambridge, MA, 1986, pp. 41, 42, 54, 56, 59, Published with permission.
21. Stuelpnagel, Thomas R., "Improved U.S. Defense, Total Quality Control," *National Defense,* vol. LXXII, no. 438, May/June 1988, Copyright © 1988, American Defense Preparedness Association, Arlington, VA, p. 47, Reprinted by permission.
22. Grady, Robert B. and Deborah L. Caswell, *Software Metrics: Establishing a Company-wide Program,* Prentice Hall, Inc., Englewood Cliffs, NJ, Copyright © 1987, p. 123. Reprinted by permission.
23. *Ibid.,* p. 124.
24. Shingo, Shigeo, *op. cit.*, pp. 66, 67.
25. Calvin, Thomas W., "Quality Control Techniques for 'Zero Defects' ", *Proceedings of Qual Test-2,* American Society for Nondestructive Testing, American Society for Quality Control, and Society of Manufacturing Engineers, Oct. 25–27, 1983, Dallas, pp. 14-10.
26. *Ibid.,* p. 14-10.
27. *Ibid.,* p. 14-2 to 14-7.
28. Crosby, Philip B., *Quality Without Tears,* McGraw-Hill Book Company, New York, 1984, p. 75.
29. Beyers, Dan, "AF Eyes Tough Directive To Contractors on Quality," *Defense News,* vol. 2, no. 21, May 25, 1987, Reprinted courtesy of *Defense News,* Copyright © 1987 by Times Journal Publishing Company, Springfield, VA, p. 1.
30. Kotelly, George V., "Competitiveness = Quality", *Mini-Micro Systems,* vol. XX, no. 12, December 1985, Copyright © 1985, Cahners Publishing Co., Div. of Reed Publishing, Denver, CO., p. 9.
31. "The Push for Quality", *Business Week,* no. 3002, June 8, 1987, McGraw-Hill Publications Company, New York, p. 132.
32. Cullen, Joe and Jack Hollingum, *Implementing Total Quality,* IFS (Publications) Ltd., Bedford, U.K., 1987, pp. 149–151.
33. Mills, Harlan D. and J. H. Poore, "Bringing Software Under Statistical Quality Control," *Quality Progress,* vol. XXI, no. 11, November 1988, Copyright © 1988 American Society for Quality Control, Inc., Milwaukee, WI, p. 53.

Manual Error Detection

"When workmen strive to do better than well
They do confound their skill in covetousness;
And oftentimes excusing of a fault
Doth make the fault the worse by the excuse:
As patches set upon a little breach
Discredit more in hiding of the fault
Than did the fault before it was so patch'd."
SHAKESPEARE
King John, Act IV, Scene 2

This chapter and the next are directed at error detection. In this chapter, consideration is given to the manual methods of error detection with prime emphasis on Mr. Shigeo Shingo's inspection discussion. The following chapter discusses automated error detection emphasizing the poka-yoke concepts of Mr. Shingo.

Inspections flow throughout the software development process chart (App. A), and so a detailed explanation of the types and applicability is provided. Inspections are used in the software development process, and it is through source and successive inspections that it is possible to achieve zero defect software. Inspections of the proper type as a manual error-detection method are clearly of great benefit for software development. That proper type is defined in this chapter.

The other major portion of this chapter relates various manual error-detection methods to be used with software development. Items such as human verification methods, user-intent errors, code reading, and static analysis are covered. Highlighted within this section are the evaluations required by the *Defense System Software Development* (DOD-STD-2167A) standard. This chapter concludes with a table from the American Society for Quality Control showing the techniques and tools for software quality in use throughout the United States of America.

INSPECTIONS

"In a closed system, the number of mistakes made expands to fill the inspection capacity available" is posited as a corollary to Parkinson's law.[1] If this corollary is correct, most companies have a system in place for development in which it is guaranteed that more mistakes than ever will be made! It even seems that the recommended increase in inspections at many points in software development would increase the number of mistakes. This is not likely.

Mr. Shigeo Shingo provides an overview of inspections as related to the production process. Production is a network of processes and operations. Process can be further broken down into work, inspection, transportation, and delay. Inspections consist of comparisons with standards which are merely descriptions of the act of inspection. Within a process, inspections reveal and prevent defects in the course of work, transportation from one process to the next, and in the course of delays.

So inspections supplement work, transportation, and delays. Strictly speaking, inspections can be thought of as secondary to production, with inspections playing only a passive role.

From an operation's point of view, maximally efficient inspections must be conducted. The fact that inspections are of little value on the process side means that even efficient inspections are nothing more than efficiently wasteful. It is necessary, therefore, to examine why we conduct inspections at all. There also needs to be ways of work, transportation, and delays that obviate the need for inspections. The following focus is on inspections with respect to work, or processing, excluding transportation and delays.

Sensory inspections are inspections performed by means of the human senses, which makes it subjective. Physical inspections involve the use of measuring devices, such as calipers. Subjective inspections are made by the same person who performed the work—it is dangerous. Objective inspections are made by someone other than the individual who performed the work.

Inspections carried out at the same place where the work was performed are process-internal inspections, and inspections carried out at a different place are process-external inspections. Because of rapid transmission of information, or feedback, process-internal inspections are superior.

The number of samples chosen to be inspected may be chosen either in accordance with statistical theory or not. It is more rational to use statistical inspections for products manufactured in large quantities. Sampling inspections inspect an appropriate number of samples constituted statistically, whereas 100 percent inspections inspect every processed item. One hundred percent inspections are "inspections in which specified characteristics of each unit of product are examined or tested to determine conformance with requirements."[2] It is sometimes claimed that 100 percent inspections generally take a great deal of trouble and increase the risk of oversights.

Information sent back to the work process that an error occurred is known as inspection feedback. Action is the devising of countermeasures to alter the work process where the error occurred.

Measurement refers to the determination of numerical values through the use of measuring devices such as calipers. A decision to accept or reject is made on the basis of these numerical values.

Judgment inspections distinguish acceptable from unacceptable goods sometime without numerical measurements. Quantity inspections determine if the correct amount is available. Quality inspections ensure items are within permissible limits.[3]

Two important quotes seemingly contradict the value of inspections: John Guaspari, an author and lecturer on quality, says, "Once we changed our way of thinking from an inspection to a prevention mindset, things began to fall into place."[4] And Robert Costello, the Secretary of Defense for acquisition, says, "The key to quality control is for companies to learn to build things right the first time rather than rely on inspections to catch defects."[5]

But the inspections they both speak of are judgmental inspections and not the source inspections which help build the product right, and this is what is illuminated in detail next.

INSPECTION METHODS

There are three major inspection methods: (1) judgment inspections that discover defects, (2) informative inspections that reduce defects, and (3) source inspections that eliminate defects.[6]

Judgment inspection

Since defects are generated during the process, you are only discovering those defects by inspecting goods at the end of the process. Adding inspection workers is pointless because you will not reduce defects without using processing methods that prevent defects from occurring in the first place. A defective process will produce a defective product.

It is an unalterable fact that processing produces defects and all that inspections can do is find those defects. So approaching the problem only at the final inspection stage does nothing to prevent defects from entering the process. Defects will not be reduced merely by making improvements at the final inspection stage, although such improvements may eliminate defects in delivered goods.

One of W. Edwards Deming's fourteen steps to industrial survival is, "cease dependence on inspection to achieve quality. Eliminate the need for inspection on a mass basis by building quality into the product in the first place."[7] Remember he is speaking of judgment inspections that discover defects.

Richard Zultner has taken Deming's fourteen points for quality and applied them to software development/management. He highlights to cease dependence on mass inspection (especially testing) to achieve quality. [Judgment] inspection is not the answer; it is too late and unreliable. It does not produce quality. Quality must be built into the system, or it doesn't exist. Quality comes from improving the development process, thereby preventing errors.[8]

The most fundamental concept is to recognize that defects are generated by work and all that final inspections—judgmental inspections—do is discover those defects. This point was made clear earlier by the quotes from John Guaspari and Robert Costello. Zero defects can never be achieved if this concept is forgotten.[9]

Informative inspection

An informative inspection is an inspection in which information of a defect occurring is fed back to the specific work process, which then corrects the process. Consequently, adopting informative inspections regularly should gradually reduce production defect rates. There are three categories of informative inspections: **Statistical Quality Control Systems (SQCS)**, **Successive Check Systems (SuCS)**, and **Self-Check Systems (SeCS)**.

Statistical Quality Control Systems (SQCS) include the notion of informative inspections and use statistically based control charts. SQC Systems use statistics to set control limits that distinguish between normal and abnormal situations. The essential condition identifying a method of inspection as an SQC method is the use of statistical principles.

SQC Systems suffer from the shortcomings of using sampling and of being too slow giving feedback. The question should be asked that if sampling is used, would not it be better to use 100 percent inspections to find *all* abnormalities. One hundred percent inspections, however, are expensive and time consuming. If low-cost 100 percent inspections could be devised, would not they be preferable? This led to poka-yoke devices. SQC methods are too slow to be fully effective concerning feedback and corrective action.

The best way to speed up feedback and corrective action would be to have the worker who finds any abnormality carry out 100 percent inspections and immediately take corrective action. But objectivity is essential to the performance of inspections, and that is why inspections have been carried out by independent inspectors. An inspection can be carried out by any worker other than the one who did the processing. If this task is given to the nearest person, then one could have a successive check system of the following sort:

1. When A completes processing, she passes it on to B for the next step.

2. B first inspects the item processed by A and then carries out the processing assigned to him. Then B passes the item to C.

3. C first inspects the item processed by B and then carries out the processing assigned to her. Then C passes the item to D.

4. Similarly, each successive worker inspects items from the previous process.

5. If a defect is discovered in an item from the previous process, the defective item is immediately passed back to the earlier process. There, the item is verified and the defect corrected. Action is taken to prevent the occurrence of subsequent defects.

Successive check systems represent an advance over control chart systems because a successive check system makes it possible to conduct 100 percent inspections, perform immediate feedback and action, and have inspections performed by people other than the workers involved in the processing. This does not imply a look at the entire output data population for software, but a look at the computer programs and associated documentation.

Mr. Shingo in *Zero Quality Control: Source Inspection and the Poka-yoke System* reports that a successive check system was put into place at Matsushita Electric's Moriguchi Television Division with the following results. In a month, the defect rate went from 6.5 percent to 1.5 percent. Three months later, the rate went to 0.65 percent, and the defect rate at the last process had gone as low as 0.016 percent.

The nature of informative inspections remains such that rapid feedback and swift action are desirable, and it would be ideal to have the actual worker involved conduct 100 percent inspections to check for defects. However, there are two flaws to be reckoned with: workers are liable to make compromises when inspecting items that they themselves have worked on, and they occasionally forget to perform checks on their own.

If these flaws could be overcome, then a self-check system would be superior to a successive check system. In cases where physical, rather than sensory, inspections are possible, poka-yoke devices can be installed within the process boundaries, so that when abnormalities occur, the information is immediately fed back to the worker involved. Because abnormalities are discovered within the processes where they occur, rather than at subsequent processes, instant corrective action is possible. So to cut defects even further, a self-check system is a higher order approach than the successive check system.

The incidence of defects can be strikingly reduced through the use of successive checks, self-checks, and other techniques. We were giving feedback and taking action only after defects had been detected. Was there not some inspection system that would prevent defects from occurring in the first place? Since defects result from errors, perhaps there is a way to use control mechanisms to prevent errors at an earlier stage. This led to source inspections.[10]

SOURCE INSPECTIONS

Source inspections are inspection methods that are based on discovering errors in conditions that *give rise to defects* and performing feedback and action at the error stage so as to keep those errors from turning into defects, rather than stimulating feedback and action in response to defects.

Many people maintain that it is impossible to eliminate defects from tasks performed by humans. This stems from the failure to make a clear separation between errors and defects. Defects arise because errors are made; the two have a cause-and-effect relationship.

It is impossible to eliminate all errors from any task performed by humans. Inadvertent errors are possible and inevitable. If feedback and corrective action occur, errors will not turn into defects. The principal feature of source inspections eliminates defects by distinguishing between errors and defects, i.e., between causes and effects.

Mr. Shingo reports the following success when source inspections were combined with the poka-yoke system. It produced zero monthly defects in a 30,000-units-per-month washing machine assembly process in 1977. Poka-yoke can be effective alone and can be even more effective when combined with successive checks and self-checks. Zero QC system, however, *requires* poka-yoke techniques be combined with source inspections. The poka-yoke system must not obscure the functions of source inspections.

Management systems in the past have carried out control in large cycles (Fig. 6.8); an error takes place (cause), a defect occurs as a result, information is fed back, and corrective action is taken accordingly.

In source inspections, control or management is carried out in small cycles; an error takes place (cause), feedback is carried out at the error stage before the error turns into a defect, and corrective action is taken accordingly. This has been pictorially represented in Fig. 1.9. Zero defects are achieved because errors are not allowed to turn into defects, and management cycles are very rapid.

Imagine five situations in which defects occur:

1. Cases in which either inappropriate standard work processes or inappropriate standard operating procedures are established at the planning stage.

2. Cases in which actual operations show excessive variation even though standard methods are appropriate.

3. Cases where sections of raw material are damaged or material thicknesses fluctuate excessively.

4. Cases where friction in machine bearings results in excessive play or worn tools throw off measurements.

5. Cases where some defects clearly occur due to inadvertent errors by workers or machines. Since it is difficult for sampling inspections to capture these defects because they occur unpredictably and randomly, 100 percent inspections are indispensable here.[11]

This fifth case is of specific interest because it raises the question of 100 percent inspections. Do not confuse these 100 percent inspections with 100 percent inputs to test all possible cases of the software—that is impossible for all but the most trivial cases. These inspections are the source inspections that *all* software developers are required to perform in the zero defect software program. These inspections are the successive inspections that software developers and software quality personnel must conduct for every product as it moves through the process of software development.

A summary of the various characteristics of the three inspection types is given in Fig. 7.1. To conclude this section on inspections, an example software case study is provided. IBM established a major quality program for the on-board software for NASA's shuttle missions, which has been applied over the last fifteen years. The project had approximately 300 software professionals responsible for delivering 500,000 lines of on-board software and 1.7 million lines of ground-support software. The quality program involved:

performing a process assessment

defining the software process

adopting advanced software engineering methods

conducting rigorous process inspections

performing defect cause analysis

utilizing specialized testing tools and methods

This resulted in a product error rate of 2.0/KLOC in 1982 to 0.11/KLOC in 1985.[12] This author believes a significant contributor to the success was the "rigorous in-process inspections".

HUMAN VERIFICATION

An examination of manual error detection methods employed other than inspections is made. Their relationship to the zero defect software program is drawn where applicable.

The Software Cost Reduction (SCR) project run by Dr. David Parnas since 1977 applied software engineering principles to a Navy real-time program. In 1985, David Parnas wrote, "The project made two things clear: (1) much of what the academics proposed can be done; (2) good software engineering is far from easy. The methods reduce, but do not eliminate errors ..."[13] In remembering the distinction between errors and defects, there is easy agreement with his observation.

Human verification of software, even though fallible, could replace automated error removal in software development—even informal human verification can produce software sufficiently robust to go to system testing without automated error removal.

A positive development effect was the combining of formal design methods and mathematics-based verification. Normally 60 percent of product defects is found before first execution, but this combination method found more than 90 percent. This seems to relate to the added care and attention given to design instead of rushing into code and relying on test to achieve product quality.

With a cleanroom focus on error prevention rather than error detection, the defect count was practically cut in half. Since industry averages appear to be around fifty to sixty defects per 1,000 lines of code, halving these numbers is significant.[15]

William Perry, the director of the Institute for Quality Assurance in Florida, has authored many books on quality data processing. His books are filled with checklists (a human verification method) to pre-

Characteristics of inspection types

Object of checks	Number of samples	Inspection agent	Inspection technique	Speed of action	Judgment inspections	Control charts	Successive checks	Self-checks	Source inspections (zero QC)
Results	(Statistical or other) sampling	Others	Sensory	Long-term	☆				
Results	(Statistical or other) sampling	Others	Sensory	Momentary		☆			
Results	(Statistical or other) sampling	Others	Sensory	Immediate					
Results	(Statistical or other) sampling	Others	Material	Long-term	☆				
Results	(Statistical or other) sampling	Others	Material	Momentary		☆			
Results	(Statistical or other) sampling	Others	Material	Immediate					
Results	(Statistical or other) sampling	Self	Sensory	Long-term					
Results	(Statistical or other) sampling	Self	Sensory	Momentary					
Results	(Statistical or other) sampling	Self	Sensory	Immediate					
Results	(Statistical or other) sampling	Self	Material	Long-term					
Results	(Statistical or other) sampling	Self	Material	Momentary					
Results	(Statistical or other) sampling	Self	Material	Immediate					
Results	All items	Others	Sensory	Long-term	☆				
Results	All items	Others	Sensory	Momentary					
Results	All items	Others	Sensory	Immediate			⊙		
Results	All items	Others	Material	Long-term	☆				
Results	All items	Others	Material	Momentary					
Results	All items	Others	Material	Immediate			⊙		
Results	All items	Self	Sensory	Long-term					
Results	All items	Self	Sensory	Momentary					
Results	All items	Self	Sensory	Immediate				⊙	
Results	All items	Self	Material	Long-term					
Results	All items	Self	Material	Momentary					
Results	All items	Self	Material	Immediate				⊙	
Causes	(Statistical) sampling	Others	Sensory	Long-term					
Causes	(Statistical) sampling	Others	Sensory	Momentary					
Causes	(Statistical) sampling	Others	Sensory	Immediate					
Causes	(Statistical) sampling	Others	Material	Long-term					
Causes	(Statistical) sampling	Others	Material	Momentary					
Causes	(Statistical) sampling	Others	Material	Immediate					
Causes	(Statistical) sampling	Self	Sensory	Long-term					
Causes	(Statistical) sampling	Self	Sensory	Momentary					
Causes	(Statistical) sampling	Self	Sensory	Immediate					
Causes	(Statistical) sampling	Self	Material	Long-term					
Causes	(Statistical) sampling	Self	Material	Momentary					
Causes	(Statistical) sampling	Self	Material	Immediate					
Causes	All items	Others	Sensory	Long-term					
Causes	All items	Others	Sensory	Momentary					
Causes	All items	Others	Sensory	Immediate					
Causes	All items	Others	Material	Long-term					
Causes	All items	Others	Material	Momentary					
Causes	All items	Others	Material	Immediate					
Causes	All items	Self	Sensory	Long-term					
Causes	All items	Self	Sensory	Momentary					
Causes	All items	Self	Sensory	Immediate					
Causes	All items	Self	Material	Long-term					
Causes	All items	Self	Material	Momentary					
Causes	All items	Self	Material	Immediate				⊙	⊙

Inspection method: Judgment inspections; Control charts, Successive checks, Self-checks (Informative inspections); Source inspections (zero QC).

Figure 7.1 Characteristics of inspection types.[14]

vent software developers from forgetting a major point. An item in the data error checklist of relevance here is, "Are controls in place covering the process of identifying, correcting, and reprocessing data rejected by the computer programs?"[16]

The question goes right to the heart of the steps in the software development process chart and the related software activities checklist. These techniques provide the framework for keeping the development process under control.

USER-INTENT ERROR

A user-intent error is an error that occurs because the user did not properly think through a problem before committing the problem to software. Errors in user intent are difficult to catch because a program containing them can be consistent and complete but yet give undesired, although correct, results. Some errors of intent arise from oversights—the equivalent of typographical errors in code—while others come from a genuine confusion on the user's part as to what the program should actually do.

Problems of incorrect user intent are only a small proportion of the total software errors in most projects. More common and more subtle are interface errors—those resulting from interactions between two software modules coded with different premises about each other's function and syntax, or between software modules and the rest of the system. Formal specification techniques and software tools for checking those specifications can eliminate inconsistencies in all phases of software development, except the inconsistency between requirements the user puts on paper and those in the user's head.[17]

These two error types—user intent and interface—are addressed by the source inspections method suggested with the zero defect software process.

CODE READING

On the software development process chart is a box called "personally inspect code", and it seems "desk-checking" (or code reading) can mean any of the following:

(1) Looking over the code for obvious errors

(2) Checking for correct procedure interfaces

(3) Looking for a subset of the following errors:

- Logic and control

    unreachable code

    improper nesting of loops and branches

inverted predicater

incomplete predicater

improper sequencing of processes

infinite loops

instruction modification

failure to save or restore registers

unauthorized recursion

missing labels or code

unreferenced labels

- Data operations and computations

  missing validity tests

  incorrect access of array components

  mismatched parameter lists

  initialization faults

  anachronistic data

  undefined variable

  misuse of variables, both locally and globally

  data fields unconstrained by natural or defined data boundaries

  inefficient data transport

- All others

  calls to subprograms that do not exist

  improper program linkages

  input-output faults

  prodigal programming

  failure to implement the design

(4) Reading comments to sense what code does and then comparing that to the external specifications

(5) Comparing comments to design documentation

(6) Stepping through with input conditions contrived to "exercise" all paths, including those that are not directly related to the external specifications

(7) Checking for compliance with programming standards

(8) Any combination of the above, but rarely more than two or three of the items

The problem with desk-checking of another's computer program is that it takes an unusual degree of discipline for a software developer, lacking team play reinforcement, to grind through someone else's code. There are people able to do this, but they are rare. It is certainly important to distinguish between code reviews, independent desk-checking and desk-checking performed by the author of the code.[18] Once these units have achieved a known reliability, they should go into a reusable library.

Two major aspects for improving software reliability are reusing existing units and avoiding errors in the first place. The best way to build reliable software systems is to use units that have proved reliable and link them together with reliable constructs.

This implies that a system for creating reliable programs could be built by limiting software developers to design methods that are provably correct. The user of such a system would construct hierarchies of units, using only such methods together with reliable preexisting units, to develop a reliable system regardless of its size or complexity. Methods to develop zero defect software should leave as few errors as possible for the dynamic testing phase of a system. All errors except those of user intent should be found earlier through static methods.[19]

STATIC ANALYSIS

A summary of existing static methods is given in "Static Analysis and Dynamic Analysis Applied to Software Quality Assurance"[20] by Bradley J. Brown. The key methods are highlighted in Table 7.1. The purpose of static analysis and dynamic analysis is to improve software quality by detecting and correcting errors while the software development is in its lowest level of complexity.

Static analysis is used during all phases of the software development cycle. There are methods which examine, test, and exercise system requirements and design, but more commonly, there are methods which are used to analyze source code.

EVALUATION CRITERIA

In DOD-STD-2167A[21], there are charts provided (Figs. 7.2 to 7.8) which give product evaluation criteria for the development phases: system requirements analysis/design, software requirements analysis, preliminary design, detailed design, coding and CSU (computer software unit) testing, CSC (computer software component) integration and testing, and CSCI (computer software configuration item) testing.

The evaluation criteria listed in these figures are not that obvious, so the DOD-STD-2167A provides an elaboration of them. Since the criteria define those elements that make a quality software product, they are given here for the convenience of the reader. The definitions use the word "document" for the item being evaluated, even though, in some instances, the item being evaluated may be other than a document.

Internal consistency. Internal consistency, as used in this standard, means that: (1) no two statements in a document contradict one another, (2) a given term, acronym, or abbreviation means the same thing throughout the document, and (3) a given item or concept is referred to by the same name or description throughout the document.

Understandability. Understandability, as used in this standard, means that (1) the document uses rules of capitalization, punctuation, symbols, and notation consistent with those specified in the *U.S. Government Printing Office Style Manual,* (2) all terms not contained in the *U.S. Government Printing Office Style Manual* or *Merriam-Webster's New International* dictionary (latest revision) are defined, (3) standard abbreviations listed in MIL-STD-12 are used, (4) all acronyms and abbreviations not listed in MIL-STD-12 are defined, (5) all acronyms and abbreviations are preceded by the word or term spelled out in full the first time they are used in the document, unless the first use occurs in a table, figure, or equation, in which case, they are explained in the text or in a footnote, and (6) all tables, figures, and illustrations are called out in the text before they appear, in the order in which they appear in the document.

Traceability to indicated documents. Traceability, as used in this standard, means that the document in question is in agreement with a predecessor document to which it has a hierarchical relationship. Traceability has five elements: (1) the document in question contains or implements all applicable stipulations of the predecessor document, (2) a given term, acronym, or abbreviation means the same thing in the documents, (3) a given item or concept is referred to by the same name or description in the documents, (4) all material in the successor document has its basis in the predecessor document, that is, no untraceable material has been introduced, and (5) the two documents do not contradict one another.

Consistency with indicated documents. Consistency between documents, as used in this standard, means that two or more documents that are not hierarchically related are free from contradictions with one another. Elements of consistency are: (1) no two statements contradict one another, (2) a given term, acronym, or abbreviation means the same thing in the documents, and (3) a given item or concept is referred to by the same name or description in the documents.

Appropriate analysis, design, and coding techniques used. The contract may include provisions regarding the requirements analysis, design, and coding techniques to be used. The contractor's Software Development Plan (SDP) describes the contractor's proposed implementation of these techniques. This criterion consists of compliance with the techniques specified in the contract and SDP.

Appropriate allocation of sizing and timing resources. This criterion, as used in this standard, means that: (1) the amount of memory or time allocated to a given element does not exceed documented constraints applicable to that element, and (2) the sum of the allocated amounts for all subordinate elements is within the overall allocation for an item.

Adequate test coverage of requirements. This criterion, as used in this standard, means that: (1) every specified requirement is addressed by at least one test, (2) test cases have been selected for both "average" situation and "boundary" situations, such as minimum and maximum values, (3) "stress" cases have been selected, such as out-of-bounds values, and (4) test cases that exercise combinations of different functions are included.

TABLE 7.1   Static Analysis

Information Analysis
   Cross-Reference Reports
   Interface Descriptions
   Design Charts
   Metrics
   Statistical Reports
   Directed Graphs
   Configuration Identification (Comparator vs. Checksum)

Static Error Analysis
   Syntax Errors Analysis
   Variable Declaration Analysis
   Variable Content Analysis
   Data Flow Analysis
   Expression Analysis
   Interface Analysis
   Standards Analysis
   Executability Analysis

Symbolic Evaluation

Figure 7.2 Evaluation criteria of system requirements analysis/design.

Item to be Evaluated	Internal Consistency	Understandability	Traceability to the indicated documents	Consistency with the indicated documents	Appropriate analysis, design or coding techniques used	Appropriate allocation of sizing and timing resources	Adequate test coverage of requirements	Notes: Clarification or Additional Criteria
System/Segment Design Document (SSDD)	●	●	See Notes					Traceability to System Specification and SOW
Software Development Plan (SDP)	●	●	SOW CDRL					
Preliminary Software Requirements Specification(s) (SRSs)	●	●	See Notes	See Notes	●	●	●	Traceability to System Specification and SOW Consistency with IRS and other specifications for interfacing items Testability of requirements Adequacy of quality factor requirements
Preliminary Interface Requirements Specification (IRS)	●	●	See Notes	See Notes	●	●		Traceability to System Specification and SOW Consistency with other specifications for interfacing items Testability of requirements

119

Item to be Evaluated	Internal Consistency	Understandability	Traceability to the indicated documents	Consistency with the indicated documents	Appropriate analysis, design or coding techniques used	Appropriate allocation of sizing and timing resources	Adequate test coverage of requirements	Notes: Clarification or Additional Criteria
Software Requirements Specification(s) (SRSs)	●	●	See Notes	See Notes	●	●	●	Traceability to System Specification and SOW Consistency with IRS and other specifications for interfacing items Testability of requirements Adequacy of quality factor requirements
Interface Requirements Specification (IRS)	●	●	See Notes	See Notes	●			Traceability to System Specification and SOW Consistency with other specifications for interfacing items Testability of requirements

Figure 7.3 Evaluation criteria of software requirements analysis.

Item to be Evaluated	Internal Consistency	Understandability	Traceability to the indicated documents	Consistency with the indicated documents	Appropriate analysis, design or coding techniques used	Appropriate allocation of sizing and timing resources	Adequate test coverage of requirements	Notes: Clarification or Additional Criteria
Software Design Document(s) (SDDs) —Preliminary Design	●	●	IRS SRSs	IDD	●	●		Adequacy of requirements allocation for CSCI to CSCs
Preliminary Interface Design Document (IDD)	●	●	IRS SRSs	SDDs				
Software Test Plan (STP)	●	●	SSDD IRS SRSs	SDP				Adequacy of data recording, reduction, and analysis methods
CSC test requirements	●	●						

Evaluation Criteria

Figure 7.4 Evaluation criteria of preliminary design.

Item to be Evaluated	Internal Consistency	Understandability	Traceability to the indicated documents	Consistency with the indicated documents	Appropriate analysis, design or coding techniques used	Appropriate allocation of sizing and timing resources	Adequate test coverage of requirements	Notes: Clarification or Additional Criteria
Software Design Document(s) (SDDs) Detailed Design	●	●	IRS SRSs	IDD	●	●		Consistency between data definition and data use. Accuracy and required precision of constants
Interface Design Document (IDD)	●	●	IRS SRSs	SDDs				
CSU test requirements and test cases	●	●		SDDs IDD			●	Adequate detail in specifying test inputs, expected results, and evaluation criteria
CSC test cases	●	●	IRS SRSs	SDDs IDD			●	Adequate detail in specifying test inputs, expected results, and evaluation criteria
Contents of CSU and CSC SDFs	●	●	See Notes	See Notes				Traceability of CSU SDFs to CSC SDFs
Software Test Descriptions (STDs) Test cases	●	●	IRS SRSs				●	Adequate detail in specifying test inputs, expected results, and evaluation criteria

Figure 7.5 Evaluation criteria of detailed design.

Item to be Evaluated	Internal Consistency	Understandability	Traceability to the indicated documents	Consistency with the indicated documents	Appropriate analysis, design or coding techniques used	Appropriate allocation of sizing and timing resources	Adequate test coverage of requirements	Notes: Clarification or Additional Criteria
Source code	●	●	SDDs IDD	SDDs	●	●		Compliance with design and coding standards; Compliance with maintainability requirements; Compliance with CSU requirements
CSU test procedures	●	●	CSU test cases	SDDs IDD		●		Adequate detail in specifying test procedures
CSU test results	●	●	See Notes		●	●		Conformance to expected results; Completeness of testing; Adequacy of CSU to enter the Developmental Configuration
CSC test procedures	●	●	CSC test cases	SDDs IDD		●		Adequate detail in specifying test procedures
Contents of CSU and CSC SDFs	●	●	See Notes	See Notes				Traceability of CSU SDFs to CSC SDFs

Evaluation Criteria

Figure 7.6 Evaluation criteria of coding and CSU testing.

Item to be Evaluated	Internal Consistency	Understandability	Traceability to the indicated documents	Consistency with the indicated documents	Appropriate analysis, design or coding techniques used	Appropriate allocation of sizing and timing resources	Adequate test coverage of requirements	Notes: Clarification or Additional Criteria
CSC integration test results	●	●	See Notes			●	●	Conformance to expected results Completeness of testing Completeness of retesting Adequacy of integrated CSCI for FOT testing
Software Test Descriptions (STDs) Formal test procedures	●	●	IRS SRSs See Notes				●	Adequate detail in specifying test procedures Traceability to formal test cases
Updated source code	●	●	SDDs IDD	SDDs	●	●		Compliance with design and coding standards Compliance with maintainability requirements
Contents of updated SDFs	●	●		See Notes				Consistency with updated code and SDD Adequacy of updated test results

Figure 7.7 Evaluation criteria of CSC integration and testing.

Item to be Evaluated / Evaluation Criteria	Internal Consistency	Understandability	Traceability to the indicated documents	Consistency with the indicated documents	Appropriate analysis, design or coding techniques used	Appropriate allocation of sizing and timing resources	Adequate test coverage of requirements	Notes: Clarification or Additional Criteria
Software Test Report (STR)	●	●	STDs	See Notes		●		Conformance to expected results Completeness of testing Completeness of retesting Adequacy of the tested CSCI
Updated Source Code	●	●	SDDs IDD	SDDs	●	●		Compliance with design and coding standards Compliance with maintainability requirements

Figure 7.8 Evaluation criteria of CSCI testing.

125

TABLE 7.2   Quality Techniques and Tools[24]

Techniques and tools	% Usage
Complexity Analyzer—an automated tool used to determine the complexity of a software design or of code using some metric like fan-in/fan-out, degree of nesting or other characteristic.	6
Database Analyzer—an automated tool used to investigate the structure of and flow within a database to determine whether performance goals can be realized.	6
Error Lists—a list of common errors typically distributed at a walkthrough or an inspection to help reviewers understand what to look for as they go through a design or code.	24
Histograms—frequency distributions in which heights of rectangles placed upon on the horizontal axis are used to indicate frequency information.	10
Logic Analyzer—an automated tool used to inspect the use of control logic within a program and determine if it is proper and mechanizes the specified design.	6
Reliability Models—automated packages used to assess the probability with which the software will perform its required functions during a stated period of time.	4
Simulators—automated tools (both hardware and software) used to represent certain features or functions of the behavior of a physical or abstract system.	10
Standards Analyzer—an automated tool used to determine whether prescribed development standards have been followed.	7
Test Drivers—an automated tool that invokes an item under test and often provides test inputs and reports test results.	20
Cause and Effect Graphs—a diagrammatic tool used to show cause and effect relationships for analysis purposes.	5
Comparator—an automated tool used to compare two software programs, files or data sets to identify commonalities and/or differences.	14
Consistency Analyzer—an automated tool employed to identify inconsistencies in conventions used in requirements, designs, or programs.	4
Data Flow Analyzer—an automated tool used to determine if a data-flow diagram is complete, consistent, and adheres to those rules established that govern flow.	13
Fishbone Diagrams—a diagrammatic tool used to illustrate multiple relationships all at the same time.	5
Interface Analyzer—an automated tool used to determine if range of variables is correct as they cross interface boundaries.	1
Metrics Analyzer—an automated tool used to collect, analyze, and report the results of metrics quantification and analysis activities.	4
Requirements Tracer—an automated tool used to trace how the requirements were realized in the design and code.	16

TABLE 7.2   Quality Techniques and Tools[24] *(Continued)*

Techniques and tools	% Usage
Test Analyzers—automated tools used to determine test case coverage (whether a segment of code had been tested by tests).	7
Test Generators—automated tools used to generate test cases directly from some specification.	12
Standards—formalized basis for comparative evaluations.	69
Brainstorming Sessions—groups of people tossing out ideas without initial regard to usefulness.	44
Checklists—used as structuring guides for ensuring that everything that should be done is completed.	79

Additional criteria. The following definitions apply to criteria that are not self-explanatory and that appear in the NOTES column of Figs. 7.2 through 7.8. These criteria are not included in each figure, but appear only as appropriate.

Adequacy of quality factors. This criterion applies to the quality factor requirements in the Software Requirements Specification (SRS). Aspects to be considered are: (1) trade-offs between quality factors have been considered and documented, and (2) each quality factor is accompanied by a feasible method to evaluate compliance, as required by the SRS DID (Data Item Description).

Testability of requirements. A requirement is considered to be testable if an objective and feasible test can be designed to determine whether the requirement is met by the software.

Consistency between data definition and data use. This criterion applies primarily to design documents. It means that each data element is defined in a way that is consistent with its usage in the software logic.

Adequacy of test cases, test procedures (test inputs, expected results, evaluation criteria). Test cases and test procedures should specify exactly what inputs to provide, what steps to follow, what outputs to expect, and what criteria to use in evaluating the outputs. If any of these elements are not specified, the test case or test procedure is inadequate.

Completeness of testing. Testing is complete if all test procedures have been performed, all results have been recorded, and all acceptance criteria have been met.

Completeness of retesting. Retesting consists of repeating a subset of

5.1 Evaluation of software
    a. complies with contract
    b. adheres to software plans
5.2 Evaluation of software documentation
    5.2.1 Evaluation of software plans
        a. software plans required by contract have been documented
        b. software plans comply with contract
        c. plans consistent with each other
    5.2.2 Evaluation of other software documentation
        a. adheres to format
        b. complies with contract
5.3 Evaluation of processes used in software development
    5.3.1 Evaluation of software management
    5.3.2 Evaluation of software engineering
    5.3.3 Evaluation of software qualification
        a. cover all requirements
        b. conducted as specified in software plans and as required by contract
        c. document version number
        d. record and analyze results
        e. all required for qualification are available
    5.3.4 Evaluation of software configuration management
        a. complies with contract
        b. adheres to software plans
    5.3.5 Evaluation of software corrective action process
        a. report all problems
        b. classify problems and identify trends
        c. achieve resolution, track status, and maintain records
        d. evaluate corrective action so that
            1. problems resolved
            2. reverse adverse trends
            3. correctly implemented changed
            4. any new problems introduced
        e. adheres to software plans
    5.3.6 Evaluation of documentation and media distribution
        a. complies with contract
        b. adheres to software plans
    5.3.7 Evaluation of storage, handling, and delivery
        a. complies with contract
        b. adheres to software plans

Figure 7.9 Evaluation of software (DOD-STD-2168).

        5.3.8   Evaluation of other software development processes
             a.   complies with contract
             b.   adheres to software plans

5.4 Evaluation of software development library
    a.   complies with contract
    b.   adheres to software plans
    c.   most recent authorized version of materials identified and available
    d.   previous versions identified and available for an audit trail

5.5 Evaluation of nondevelopmental software
    a.   objective evidence that it performs required functions
    b.   under internal configuration control
    c.   data rights provisions consistent with contract

5.6 Evaluation of nondeliverable software
    a.   objective evidence that it performs required functions
    b.   under internal configuration control

5.7 Evaluation of deliverable elements of software engineering and test environments
    a.   complies with contract
    b.   objective evidence that it performs required functions
    c.   under internal configuration control
    d.   documented in software plans

5.8 Evaluation of subcontractor management
    a.   subcontract satisfies prime contract
    b.   baseline requirements established and maintained
    c.   software quality program requirements levied
    d.   access for contractor reviews
    e.   access for contracting agency reviews

5.9 Evaluations associated with acceptance inspections and preparation for delivery
    a.   software products ready for contracting agency inspection
    b.   required procedures performed and satisfactory completion evidence available for contracting agency inspection
    c.   all software and documentation to be delivered updated

5.10 Participation in formal reviews and audits
    a.   prior to
       1.   products ready for contracting agency review
       2.   preparations completed
    b.   during
       1.   present evaluation and status of products
    c.   after
       1.   assure action items accomplished

Figure 7.9 Evaluation of software (DOD-STD-2168). *(Continued)*

the test cases and test procedures after software corrections have been made to correct problems found in previous testing. Retesting is considered complete if: (1) all test cases and test procedures that revealed problems in the previous testing have been repeated, their results have been recorded, and the results have met acceptance criteria, and (2) all test cases and test procedures that revealed no problems during the previous testing, but that test functions that are affected by the corrections, have been repeated, their results have been recorded, and the results have met acceptance criteria.

These evaluations are key elements to be tied with the software development process chart. They provide elements of what manual error detections should look for along the way.

Another software evaluation method of value to mention here is the summary of evaluation of software development from DOD-STD-2168, *Defense System—Software Quality Program.*[22] They are shown in Fig. 7.9.

QUALITY TECHNIQUES AND TOOLS

The American Society for Quality Control (ASQC) conducted a survey concerning software quality in the United States industry.[23] Table 7.2 highlights the quality techniques and tools in use throughout industry and provides a brief description of each of these. An average usage percent is provided with each entry listed in the table, which gives the reader a sense of what is popular; i.e., successful in industry.

Since the survey contains manual error detection (techniques) and automated error detection (tools) together, it is provided as a bridge to the next chapter.

REFERENCES

1. Guaspari, John, *I Know It When I See It,* AMACOM, New York, Copyright © 1985 American Management Association, Reprinted by permission, p. 42.
2. U.S. Dept. of Defense, MIL-STD-109B, *Military Standard—Quality Assurance Terms and Definitions,* NAVMAT 09Y, Washington, DC, April 4, 1969, p. 4.
3. Shingo, Shigeo, *Zero Quality Control: Source Inspection and the Poka-yoke System,* Andrew P. Dillon, trans., Productivity Press, Cambridge, MA, 1986, pp. 18–21. Published with permission.
4. Guaspari, John, *op. cit.,* p. 49.
5. Van Voorst, Bruce, "Mission: Just About Impossible," *Time,* vol. 131, no. 5, February 1, 1988, Time Inc., New York, p. 44.
6. Shingo, Shigeo, *op, cit.,* pp. 58, 59.
7. Pellerin, Cheryl, "Father of Industrial Revolution's Third Wave Takes On the Defense Department," *Defense News,* vol. 3, no. 23, June 6, 1988, Reprinted courtesy of *Defense News,* Copyrighted © 1988 by Time Journal Publishing Company, Springfield, VA, p. 16.
8. Zultner, Richard, "The Deming Approach to Software Quality Engineering," *Quality*

Progress, vol. XXI, no. 11, November 1988, Copyright © 1988, American Society for Quality Control, Inc., Milwaukee, WI, p. 60, Reprinted by permission.

9. Shingo, Shigeo, *op. cit.,* pp. 35–39.
10. *Ibid.,* pp. x–xiv, 48, 58, 59, 67–69, 77.
11. *Ibid.,* pp. x–xiv, 83–85.
12. Humphrey, Watts S., "Statistically Managing the Software Process," *Chance: New Directions for Statistics and Computing,* vol. 2, no. 2, 1989, Copyright © 1989, Springer-Verlag, Berlin, p. 38.
13. Parnas, David L., "Software Aspects of Strategic Defense Systems," *Communications of the ACM,* vol. 28, no. 12, December 1985, Copyright © 1985, Association of Computing Machinery, Inc., New York, p. 1331, Reprinted by permission.
14. Shingo, Shigeo, *op. cit.,* p. 55.
15. Mills, Harlan D., Michael Dyer, and Richard C. Linger, "Cleanroom Software Engineering," *IEEE Software,* September 1987, Copyright © 1987, IEEE, New York, pp. 19, 20.
16. Perry, William E., *Effective Methods of EDP Quality Assurance,* Q.E.D. Information Science, Inc., Wellesley, MA, 1988, pp. 204, 205.
17. Brown, Bradley J., "Static Analysis and Dynamic Analysis Applied to Software Quality Assurance," *IEEE Spectrum,* vol. 23, no. 3, March 1986, Copyright © 1986, IEEE, p. 48, 49.
18. Dunn, Robert, *Software Defect Removal,* McGraw-Hill Book Company, New York, 1984, pp. 108–111.
19. Brown, Bradley J., *op. cit.,* p. 50.
20. Brown, Bradley J., "Static Analysis and Dynamic Analysis Applied to Software Quality Assurance," in *Handbook of Software Quality Assurance,* G. Gordon Schulmeyer, James I. McManus, eds, Van Nostrand Reinhold Co. Inc., New York, 1987, pp. 268–284.
21. U.S. Dept. of Defense, DOD-STD-2167A, *Military Standard—Defense System Software Development,* NAVMAT 09Y, Feb. 29, 1988, Washington, DC, pp. 20–32, 45, 46.
22. U.S. Dept. of Defense, DOD-STD-2168, *Military Standard—Defense System Software Quality Program,* NAVMAT 09Y, April 29, 1988, Washington, DC.
23. Reifer, Donald, J., Richard W. Knudson, and Jerry Smith, *Final Report: Software Quality Survey,* prepared for American Society for Quality Control, ASQC, Milwaukee, WI, 1987.
24. *Ibid.,* pp. 17–20.

Automated Error Detection

"O hateful error melancholy's child!
Why dost thou show to the apt thoughts of
men
The things that are not? O error! soon
conceiv'd
Thou never com'st unto a happy birth
But kill'st the mother that engender'd thee."
                                        SHAKESPEARE
              Julius Caesar, Act V, Scene 3

In this chapter, there is a shift from the manual error detection method—inspections in the zero defect software process. For automated error detection, source inspections with poka-yoke is the special method derived from Shigeo Shingo. Poka-yoke leads to dynamic analysis, just as manual error detection leads to static analysis. It should be understood that poka-yoke in the zero defect software process is interpreted as the use of software tools.

Some special automated tools are then covered with discussion of their benefits. The tools explosion embedded in the development process through computer-aided software engineering (CASE) environments is given some exposure.

How Artificial Intelligence (AI) fits into the automated error detection arena is also covered. Briefly, some automated correction programs are surveyed, and an expert system for specifying software quality is introduced.

The chapter concludes with a discussion of the use of software tools to aid the testing process.

POKA-YOKE

Baka-yoke is Japanese for "foolproofing". A foolproofing device to prevent seat parts from being spot-welded backwards was installed in Arakawa Auto Body plant around 1963. A worker asked hysterically if she were a "fool" who could mix up left-and-right hand parts. She was told she was not a "fool", but the device was inserted because anyone could make an inadvertent mistake.

When Shigeo Shingo was told that story he sought a suitable term. He gave the name *poka-yoke* (mistake-proofing) to the devices because they serve to prevent or "proof" (*yoke* in Japanese) the sort of inadvertent mistakes (*poka* in Japanese) that anyone could make. Since the word poka-yoke has been used untranslated into English, French, Swedish, and Italian books, it is now current throughout the industrialized world.

A poka-yoke system is a means and not an end. Poka-yoke systems can be combined with successive checks or self-checks and can fulfill the needs of those techniques by providing 100 percent inspections and prompt feedback and action. Successive checks and self-checks function only as informative inspections, in which feedback and action take place after a defect has occurred. In cases where repairs can be made, it looks as though no defects occurred, but these methods are inherently unable to attain zero defects.

Because the adoption of appropriate poka-yoke devices results in the total elimination of defects, Mr. Shingo began to doubt the conventional view of exclusive reliance on statistical quality control methods. The source of the doubt lay in the fact that the poka-yoke approach uses 100 percent inspections to guard against inadvertent mistakes. If we admit the existence of inadvertent mistakes, then 100 percent inspections are superior to sampling inspections based on statistical theory. It seems the total elimination of defects has been an effect of 100 percent inspections. But if the significance of checking actual working conditions was noted, the concept of "source inspections" would have come sooner.

The old-fashioned belief that 100 percent inspections take too much trouble and cost too much is solved by poka-yoke systems involving 100 percent inspections and requiring immediate feedback and action when errors occur.

Because of the considerable effect achieved by poka-yoke devices, people have the false impression that simply putting in such devices eliminates defects. Poka-yoke devices are only an aid in preventing human errors.

A poka-yoke system possesses two functions: it can carry out 100 percent inspections, and, if abnormalities occur, it can carry out immediate feedback and corrective action.

Two regulatory functions are performed by poka-yoke systems: control and warning.

Control mechanisms are, when abnormalities occur, methods that shut down machines or lock clamps to halt operations, thereby preventing the occurrence of compounded serial defects. Maximum efficacy in achieving zero defects is obtained by using control-type systems.

Warning methods call abnormalities to workers' attention by activating a buzzer or a light. Since defects will continue to occur if workers do not notice these signals, this approach is less powerful than the control methods. The use of warning methods may be considered either where the impact of abnormalities is slight or where technical or economic factors make the adoption of control methods extremely difficult.

The setting functions of poka-yoke systems can be divided into three categories: contact methods, fixed-value methods, and motion-step methods.

Methods in which mechanized sensing devices detect abnormalities in product shape or dimension by whether or not contact is made between the products and the sensing devices are called contact methods.

With fixed-value methods, abnormalities are detected by checking for the specified number of motions in cases where operations must be repeated a predetermined number of times.

Motion-step methods are methods in which abnormalities are detected by checking for errors in standard motions in cases where operations must be carried out with predetermined motions.

Source inspections and poka-yoke measures must be combined to eliminate defects. The combination of source inspections and poka-yoke devices make quality control systems for zero defects possible. This same combination applies to the software development process as outlined in the chart in App. A. One must never forget that the poka-yoke system refers to a means, not an end.[1]

Whenever possible a poka-yoke method should be inserted to ensure the success of the self-check or source inspection. Some standard poka-yoke methods already exist in the process, such as, a compiler syntax checker, an automated standards checker, and code path tests. More work needs to be done in every step of the process to have poka-yoke methods available everywhere, such as, the direction computer-aided software engineering (CASE) environments is taking.

DYNAMIC ANALYSIS

Dynamic analysis is the execution of a unit or collection of units using simulated or actual input data to induce behavior which can be observed as a means of inferring correctness. Dynamic analysis (see Table 8.1) is most efficient when used after all the errors that can be detected by less expensive means (code inspection, for example) have been corrected, and before the software is examined by more expensive methods.[2]

Gelperin and Hetzel in "The Growth of Software Testing" say, "As computer applications increased in number, cost, and complexity, testing came to assume more significance because of greater economic risk." To enforce this proposition, they provide the stages of growth of testing:

–1956	The Debugging-Oriented Period
1957–1978	The Demonstration-Oriented Period
1979–1982	The Destruction-Oriented Period
1983–1987	The Evaluation-Oriented Period
1988–	The Prevention-Oriented Period

For this prevention testing methodology, Gelperin and Hetzel subsumed the IEEE unit testing process to all levels of testing. They call it STEP (Systematic Test and Evaluation Process), which defines a system of testing tasks, products, and roles for the consistent and cost-effective achievement of test objectives.[3] This dynamic analysis method holds good promise for post-1988 because, like the zero defect software process, it is prevention-oriented.

SOFTWARE TOOLS

Emphasis is now focused on software tools which are the poka-yoke method as applied to software development. These automated tools are a key part of the development of zero defect software. It must not be forgotten to apply them in conjunction with source and successive inspections.

TABLE 8.1   Dynamic Analysis

DYNAMIC ANALYSIS

Test case preparation
Test coverage assessment
  Source code test coverage
  Error test coverage
Test result examination

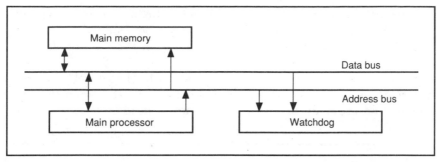

Figure 8.1   Error detection using a watchdog.[6] (*Copyright ©1988, IEEE.*)

"Encapsulation" technique

At the beginning of the software development process, there are recent tools to check program specifications for inconsistencies, ambiguities, and incompleteness similar to the way compilers check the syntax of program code.[4]

An error in a multiprocessing environment is sometimes difficult to repeat because the application programs do not usually run in an identical fashion, so there is no way to know exactly what led up to it. That is, there is no easy way to repeat the fault and no easy way to capture the state of the software during the fault.

To handle this problem, an "encapsulation" technique has been used. It simulates those operations whose results could be affected by activity external to the code, while the other operations are left intact.

Random tests are then generated and repeated as needed by rerunning a random-number generator. Some 700 lines of microcode were tested using this method for a month, and 38 errors were fixed. For two more weeks, the code was run under combined test and live execution, and five more errors were found. The code then ran for a year without defects in a multiprocessing environment.[5]

Watchdog processor

A watchdog processor is a small and simple coprocessor used to perform concurrent system-level error detection by monitoring the behavior of a main processor. Figure 8.1 shows the organization of a system using a watchdog processor.

Error detection by a watchdog processor is a two-phase process; the setup phase provides the watchdog with information about the processor or process to be checked, and during the checking phase, it monitors the processor and collects the relevant information concurrently. Error detection is accomplished by comparison of information collected concurrently with the information provided during setup. Information provided to the watchdog to detect errors can be about memory access behavior, the control flow, the control signals, or the reasonableness of results.

Semantic or data manipulation errors can be detected by having a watchdog execute assertions concurrently about the program being executed on the main processor. It is a problem to be able to transfer

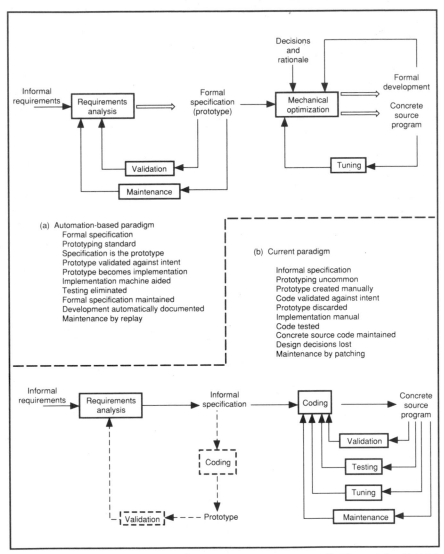

Figure 8.2 Software development paradigm comparison.[10] (*Copyright ©1983, IEEE.*)

TABLE 8.2   CASE Productivity Advantages[11]

Program size	Projected savings (%) with CASE* Compared with current methods		
	COST	TIME	STAFFING
SMALL	95	97	0
MEDIUM	94	92	50
LARGE	92	83	88
VERY LARGE	87	80	37

*Computer Aided Software Engineering

data from the main processor to the watchdog without excessive time overhead. A great advantage of the watchdog processor is that it provides an independent circuitry for error detection, at a reasonable cost. Also, the use of a watchdog processor is more in the spirit of distributed computing, where dedicated processors are used to perform specialized tasks.[7]

Automation-based paradigm

A software initiative toward incremental improvement in each phase of the existing software cycle is a conservative, evolutionary approach with short-term payoff. This incremental initiative is based on the existing software development paradigm, which was conceived in the era prior to computer support of software development. Thus, there is a clear need to investigate a software paradigm based on automation to achieve orders-of-magnitude improvement. Such a paradigm is shown pictorially in Fig. 8.2.

The formal manipulation needed to realize optimizations are automated as part of the new software development paradigm. This yields some benefits: (1) no clerical errors, (2) increased optimization, (3) better documentation, and (4) reasonable software.[8]

CASE

When software tools are the drivers in a computer-aided software engineering (CASE) environment for development, the user first develops a system definition, then software analysis tools check the definition for logical correctness, and finally a resource allocation tool produces source code. This is a tool-based proposed way of developing zero defect software.[9] This CASE methodology also has some productivity advantages as shown in Table 8.2.

Rather than supporting a single development methodology, Software Life-Cycle Support Environment (SLCSE) uses a modifiable tool-based

TABLE 8.3   Software Tool Types and Categories[13]

General support:
- text editor
- document formatter
- command-language editor
- electronic mail

Requirements analysis:
- requirements generator
- requirements documenter
- consistency analyzer

Design:
- design generator
- design documenter
- consistency checker

Coding:
- language-sensitive editor
- assembler
- compiler
- linker
- debugger
- assertion translator

Testing:
- instrumenter
- postexecution analyzer
- test-summary reporter
- test manager
- simulator

Prototyping:
- window prototyper

Verification:
- data tracer
- code auditor
- static analyzer
- dataflow analyzer
- interface checker
- quality analyzer

Configuration management:
- software manager
- documentation manager
- test-data/results manager
- change-effect manager

Project management:
- project planner
- project tracker/reporter
- problems-report processor
- change-request

Environment management:
- method script editor
- menu editor
- keypad editor
- command-procedure editor
- global-command setup
- tool installer/deleter

approach where tools can be integrated to support various methodologies limited only by system resources. Off-the-shelf or custom tools may be used so that changes in the modes or the development paradigm may be supported. Table 8.3 shows initial tool categories and representative generic tool types for each category that will be supported by SLCSE. The tool categories reflect life-cycle phases or activities that span the entire cycle.[12] These tools are the equivalent of poka-yoke techniques for the software development process.

The automation of the entire software development process is a helpful idea that introduces poka-yoke methods throughout and so is very valuable to lead toward zero defect software.

ARTIFICIAL INTELLIGENCE

Even the use of Artificial Intelligence (AI) helps in the goal for zero defect software. The usefulness of an automatic programming assistant depends on what it offers to counter errors. If an error arises, the user can:

- correct the program in midexecution
- automatically exit the part of the program where the error was, but not in midexecution
- ask the automatic correction subsystem to prepare alternate corrected versions
- enter into an inspection loop to change variables, back up the history of computation, exit, ask for documentation, etc., and then continue computation[14]

Pragmatic rules formalize the knowledge and make it explicit for the detection and correction of errors. From a certain point of view, pragmatic rules implementation lies totally within D. Lenat's analysis of Artificial Intelligence: "One very significant reason for doing Artificial Intelligence research is that it starts the metamorphosis of the nature of scientific fields from incomprehensible guilds into well-understood technical crafts. It leads to a science of science, AI programs make explicit, in a very usable form, the knowledge necessary to perform some complicated activity, thereby demystifying it."[15] The implementation of pragmatic rules makes the reading and correcting of programs accessible; the pragmatic rules make explicit implicitly utilized knowledge and techniques. This knowledge and these techniques can either be very general or very precise. The pragmatic rules of thumb of an AI tool correspond to the rules of thumb of experienced programmers.[16]

Automatic detection programs

Below is a survey of the group of systems for automatic detection and correction of programming errors currently in existence:

DRAWL detects, not corrects, strictly syntactic errors.

DWIM interactively detects unbound variables, undefined functions, and certain bracketing errors, and corrects errors due to evaluation of atom T in functional position in LISP and spelling errors.

RUTH'S ANALYZER detects and corrects underlying errors in programs which implement sort algorithms. It is specific in that it only detects errors corresponding to structures of anticipated errors.

MYCROFT detects and corrects errors in simple programs. To understand and correct a program, a description of the programmer's intention is needed.

THE PROGRAMMER'S APPRENTICE is a system for understanding LISP programs based entirely on interactive use. The apprentice writes a plan for the program which is checked against the developed program automatically.

LAURA detects and corrects FORTRAN programs. It compares the correct, teacher's version with the incorrect, student's version.

MENO-II and PROUST are programming tutors possessing stereotyped knowledge about programming. Along with the stereotyped knowledge, they need a programmer's plan.

THE ALGORITHMIC CORRECTOR is an interactive corrector of Prolog programs. Three types of errors can be detected: (1) termination of a program with an erroneous result, (2) termination of a program with a missing result, and (3) nontermination of a program.

Φ is a debugging aid system that combines searching for errors, both syntactic and semantic, with their stereotyped correction: for the same class of errors, Φ produces the same correction, independent of the particular program where that error occurs. It is the only semantic-error correction system not to use any specific knowledge about the program to be improved. It is fully implemented and given further exposure in the following chapter.[16]

Assistant for specifying the quality of software

Finally, the Assistant for Specifying the Quality of Software (ASQS) is an expert system for specifying quality. The knowledge base contains expertise about the RADC (Rome Air Development Center) quality framework and various functional areas. To assist the user in describing the system, the ASQS can explain why it is asking any question as well as how it arrived at any conclusions. These may be done repetitively to receive increasingly detailed information.

The ASQS asks the user questions about system quality factors, the structure of the software, the need for individual functions, and other properties of the system whose quality is being specified. The user can answer "unknown", thus incomplete and uncertain information capabilities are provided for tracking. ASQS then divides the thirteen quality factors for each software component into four categories: excellent, good, average, and not important. ASQS can identify the effects of complementary and contradictory quality goals. ASQS also tailors the metrics framework for each phase. It also records version information, thus allowing the user to experiment with different quality goals and to reconstruct the history of a system's quality goals.[17]

1. Creating too few tests:	Letting too many defects get to the customer
2. Creating the wrong tests:	Letting the wrong defects get to the customer
3. Creating too many tests:	Doing redundant work

Figure 8.3 Most probable errors in testing.[19] (*Copyright ©1988, IEEE.*)

SOFTWARE TESTING

The final attention of this chapter on automated error detection is on that tool set which is relevant to testing software. The process of testing software invites errors. Tests must be selected from infinite inputs and paths for a finite list of requirements in a limited time period. There is greater probability for error by making judgments and trade-offs about what to test and when to test it further. So, one should apply a most probable errors list (Fig. 8.3) to the software testing process. Dr. C. K. Cho purports to allow the tester to *know* the correct amount of tests to run, as mentioned previously.

To find an error in the testing process, the inputs, outputs, and acceptance criteria for the outputs must be defined. Capture the outputs and evaluate them to reveal errors in the process. That is, test the testing process.[18]

In terms of its effect on defect density, testing borders on the irrelevant. In the United States, the range of defects per thousand lines of executable code is from 0.016 to 60, a factor of nearly 4,000. Dr. C. K. Cho says that (when the software is usable for the customer) this kind of measure is irrelevant. The way to make a drastic improvement in the quality of code that comes out of the testing process is to make a drastic improvement in the quality of code that goes into the testing process. However, it is still important to remember that testing is a weapon that prevents poor quality software from getting to the customer.

Figure 8.4 shows the predictive model of a particular project from Hewlett-Packard and the actual rate of error discovery and resolution during testing. A "calculated stop point" was used to estimate when testing was complete. Testing actually stopped based on a predefined number of hours without any errors, plus spending two weeks beyond the calculated stop point.

The calculated stop point is the error rate below which the project is willing to stop testing. The rate is determined by considering the cost to find and fix an error prerelease versus postrelease. The stop point determines the most cost effective amount of testing; it does not aim at

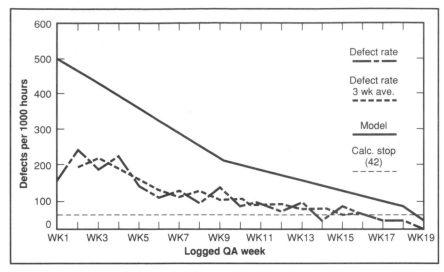

Figure 8.4 Actual defect rate.[21]

zero defects in all cases. In Fig. 8.4, the calculated stop point of 42 is the reciprocal of the number of hours of error-free testing that has been spent after the "last" error has been found.[20]

There are different incentives directed toward optimizing quality prior to testing in low-error environments. These incentives begin by separating the testing function from the rest of development.

Most often the justification for a separate test group is that it improves the effectiveness of testing. When the people responsible for writing and inspecting code are not allowed to test that code, then their last chance to prove the excellence of their work is past when they submit it for testing. In this environment, they get the attitude to improve quality, which is to tie all their self-esteem to producing error-free code directly from the coding/inspection process.

Total separation of testing creates strong new incentives to maximize the quality of untested code. The developer wants to hand over a superior product to the tester. It affords a good mechanism for error data collection during the project. People should not test their own code (except unit testing) and ought not to be allowed to try.[22]

Testing and automated error removal tools are emerging as allies in the battle for fast and cost-effective program development. There are a variety of tools (Fig. 8.5) to assist developers in testing and automated error removal. They fall into two basic categories: interactive tools or "debuggers"; and batch mode tools or testers. "Debuggers" are great for identifying the source of an error, but they do not identify new coding errors. Testing tools that work in batch mode help with this. As is seen in Fig. 8.4, the foundation of these strategies is the use of incremental testing at each step of software development, rather than at the end of the process, as is traditional.[23]

Programming Environments' **T** automatic test-generation tool is not designed to do exhaustive testing of every program combination and permutation, nor can it guarantee that the tested software will work

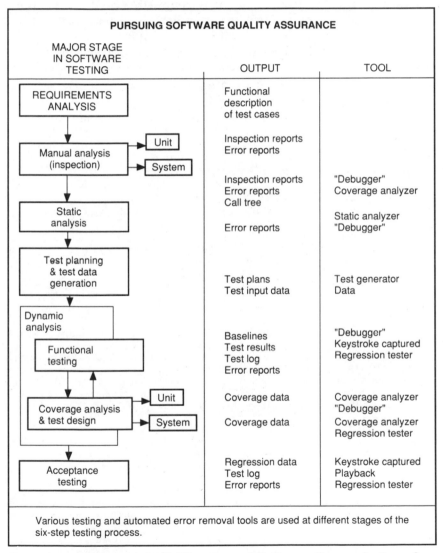

PURSUING SOFTWARE QUALITY ASSURANCE		
MAJOR STAGE IN SOFTWARE TESTING	OUTPUT	TOOL
REQUIREMENTS ANALYSIS	Functional description of test cases	
Manual analysis (inspection) → Unit, System	Inspection reports Error reports	
Static analysis	Inspection reports Error reports Call tree Error reports	"Debugger" Coverage analyzer Static analyzer "Debugger"
Test planning & test data generation	Test plans Test input data	Test generator Data
Dynamic analysis — Functional testing	Baselines Test results Test log Error reports	"Debugger" Keystroke captured Regression tester
Coverage analysis & test design → Unit, System	Coverage data Coverage data	Coverage analyzer "Debugger" Coverage analyzer Regression tester
Acceptance testing	Regression data Test log Error reports	Keystroke captured Playback Regression tester

Various testing and automated error removal tools are used at different stages of the six-step testing process.

Figure 8.5 Testing tools.[24] (*Courtesy of Software Research, Inc., San Francisco. Reprinted with permission of "Software Magazine," October 1987, Sentry Publishing, Inc., Westborough, MA 01550.*)

under all conditions. But **T** generates at least one test case for each testable specification and for every piece of entered data, so that all of the most probable errors are checked at least once.

Software Research's Smarts provides for automatic test reruns (regression), and up to 1,500 tests can be included. A database maintains information on output evaluation, activity and history recording, execution timing, and regression-test management.[25]

Westinghouse Electronic Systems Group's RAVE (Regression and Verification Engineering) test tool handles 8,000 test cases. It has automatic rerun, a pass/fail indicator, and global database validation.

There have been a collection of publications of software tool directories and taxonomies[26, 27, 28, 29, 30] which contain pertinent references to testing tools. A more recent list contained in *Software Magazine*[31] lists seventy-one test and automated error removal tools. So, test automation is available for the enterprising software development organizations to use.

REFERENCES

1. Shingo, Shigeo, *Zero Quality Control: Source Inspection and the Poka-yoke System,* Andrew P. Dillon, trans., Productivity Press, Cambridge, MA, 1986, pp. 45, 46, 92, 93, 99–106. Published with permission.
2. Brown, Bradley J., "Static Analysis and Dynamic Analysis Applied to Software Quality Assurance," in *Handbook of Software Quality Assurance,* G. Gordon Schulmeyer, and James I. McManus, eds, Van Nostrand Reinhold Co. Inc., New York, 1987, pp. 268–284.
3. Gelperin, David and Bill Hetzel, "The Growth of Software Testing," *Communications of the ACM,* vol. 31, no. 6, June 1988, Copyright © 1988 by Association for Computing Machinery, New York, NY, pp. 689–691, Reprinted by permission.
4. Hamilton, Margaret H. "Zero-defect software: the elusive goal," *IEEE Spectrum,* vol. 23, no. 3, March 1986, Copyright © 1986, IEEE, New York, p. 48.
5. Falk, Howard, "New Tools Help Exterminate Software Bugs," *Computer Design,* vol. 26, no. 18, October 1, 1987, Westford, MA, pp. 52, 55.
6. Mahmood, Aamer and McCluskey, E. J., "Concurrent Error Detection Using Watchdog Processors—A Survey," *IEEE Transactions on Computers,* vol. 37, no. 2, February 1988, Copyright © 1988, IEEE, New York, p. 160, Reprinted by permission.
7. *Ibid.,* p. 160, 172.
8. Balzer, Robert, Thomas E. Cheatham, Jr., and Cordell Green, "Software Technology in the 1990's: Using a New Paradigm," *IEEE Computer,* vol. 16, no. 11, November 1983, Copyright © 1983, IEEE, New York, pp. 39–42, Reprinted by permission.
9. Hamilton, Margaret H., *op. cit.,* p. 50.
10. Balzer, Robert, Thomas E. Cheatham, Jr., and Cordell Green, *op. cit.,* p. 40.
11. "The Software Trap: Automate—or Else," *Business Week,* No. 3051, May 9, 1988, Data provided by Software Productivity Research Inc., McGraw Hill, Inc., NY, p. 150.
12. Cavano, Joseph P. and Frank S. LaMonica, "Quality Assurance in Future Development Environments," *IEEE Software,* September 1987, Copyright © 1987, IEEE, New York, p. 29, Reprinted by permission.
13. *Ibid.,* p. 30.
14. Wertz, H., *Automatic Correction and Improvement of Programs,* John Wiley & Sons, New York, 1987, pp. 165, 166.

15. Lenat, D. B., "The Ambiguity of Discovery," *Artificial Intelligence* 9(3), p. 283, 1978, Computers and Thought Lecture, 1977.
16. Wertz, H., *op. cit.,* p. 46, 135–151.
17. "Assistant for Specifying the Quality of Software (ASQS)," DACS Bulletin, vol. VII, no. 8, November 1987, Griffiss AFB, New York, RADC/COEE, p. 2.
18. Poston, Robert, "Preventing Most-probable Errors in Testing," *IEEE Software,* March 1988, Copyright © 1988, IEEE, New York, p. 86, Reprinted by permission.
19. *Ibid.,* p. 86.
20. Grady, Robert B., and Deborah L. Caswell, *Software Metrics: Establishing a Company-Wide Program,* Prentice Hall Inc., Englewood Cliffs, NJ, Copyright © 1987, pp. 128, 129, Adapted with permission.
21. *Ibid.,* p. 129.
22. DeMarco, Tom, *Controlling Software Projects,* Yourdon, Inc., New York, Copyright © 1982, pp. 216–218, Adapted with permission from Prentice Hall Inc., Englewood Cliffs, NJ.
23. Rubin, Charles, "To Get Quality Code, Admit Bugs are a Reality," *Software Magazine,* vol. 7, no. 11, October 1987, Copyright © 1987, Sentry Publishing Company, Inc., Westborough, MA, Source of chart is Software Research Inc., San Francisco, pp. 61–72, Reprinted by permission.
24. *Ibid.,* p. 62.
25. Falk, Howard, *op. cit.,* pp. 52, 53.
26. Reifer, Donald J. and Harold A. Montgomery, *Final Report: Software Tool Taxonomy,* SMC-TR-004 prepared for National Bureau of Standards, Contract NB79SBCA0273, NBS, Washington DC, 1980.
27. Houghton, Jr., R. C., *The NBS/ICST Taxonomy of Software Tool Features* prepared for National Bureau of Standards Institute for Computer Sciences and Technology (NBS/ICST), NBS, Washington DC, January 1982.
28. Houghton, Jr., R. C., *A Taxonomy of Tool Features for the Ada Programming Support Environment (APSE),* Technical Report NBSIR 82-2625 prepared for National Bureau of Standards Institute for Computer Sciences and Technology (NBS/ICST), NBS, Washington DC, December 1982.
29. Brement, G., *Software Life Cycle Tools Directory,* Technical Report STI185 prepared for Rome Air Development Center by IIT Research Institute/Data & Analysis Center for Software RADC/DACS, Rome, NY, March, 1985.
30. Kean, E. S. and F. S. LaMonica, *A Taxonomy of Tool Features for a Life Cycle Software Engineering Environment,* Technical Report RADC-TR-85-112 prepared for Rome Air Development Center, In-House Report, RADC, Rome, NY, June 1985.
31. Philips, Roger A. "No-Test Software is 'Unobtainware' ", *Software Magazine,* vol. 8, no. 15, December 1988, Copyright © 1988 by Sentry Publishing Company, Inc., Westborough, MA, pp. 36–43.

Writing Correct Software

"to be a well-favoured man is the gift of fortune, but to write and read comes by nature."

SHAKESPEARE
Much Ado About Nothing, Act III, Scene 3

The theme of this chapter picks up from the prior discussion on how software is developed today. This chapter emphasizes some of the available methods and tools for writing correct software. A major drawback is that these methods and tools have been used only on small projects on single programs. But, for completeness, and for future consideration to tie into the zero defect software process, these points must be covered.

An introduction to program proving theories is given with particular comment on proofs of correctness. The flow of an automated verification system is covered. The section concludes with the benefits that may accrue from program provers.

Next, a distinction is given between small and large system development. The hypothetical formal development of a software method for large software systems is enumerated. The section concludes with a functional classification for a sample tool set for a software evaluation system in large system development.

The automated test generation section covers two main categories. The interplay between automated testing and proof of program correctness is discussed. An automated program corrector called $\bar{\Phi}$, which is an Artificial Intelligence implementation, is discussed.

When the software developer has available a computer-aided software engineering (CASE) environment, he/she will be more able to experiment with the various tools in large scale development projects. Specific tools of proof of correctness and automated test generation may be brought into the CASE environment and tried out. It is with that type of proaction that software developers will move more rapidly toward development of zero defect software.

PROGRAM PROVING THEORIES

We can all remember from mathematics classes that the problem was not simply to get the right answer, but it was to find the right process for getting the answer. Often we received only part credit for a correct answer because we did not show how we got it. There was a reason. If we do simple mathematical problems by guessing the answers, then when we move on to harder problems, we will not be able to guess the answers. That is exactly the role of the new math in computer programming—to go from programming as an instinctive, intuitive process to a more systematic, constructive process that can be shared as a professional activity.[1]

To try the integer multiplication of two 27-bit integers, there are 2^{54} multiplications that are required. If each case on a computer took a few microseconds, this finite set of multiplications would exceed 10,000 years. As long as the multiplier is considered as a black box, one can only test by sampling. Whole classes of, in some sense, "critical" multiplications may remain untested. The conclusion is that a convincing demonstration of correctness is impossible as long as the mechanism is regarded as a black box. Hope, therefore, lies only in *not* regarding the mechanism as a black box. One must take the structure of the mechanism into account.[2] When one considers the structure of the mechanism in software development, it leads one to the concept of structured programming. The term structured programming is the case where mathematics models the mental processes of programming—of inventing algorithms suitable for a given computer to meet prescribed logical specifications.[3]

By taking the structure into account, one is led to a use of mathematics to prove that the structure is correct. "Correctness" is being used here as a technical term which is a relative, not absolute, notion. A program is considered correct if it is correct relative to some given specification. Generally, the specification of a programming problem consists of a precondition describing the properties of the supplied data and a postcondition describing the desired effect of the computation. The precondition and postcondition that make up a program specification are predicates (relative truths) that depend on the values of the program variables.[4]

A proof of correctness, then, is a mathematical demonstration of the consistency between a program and its specifications, relative to sets of statements about the environment and the semantic behavior of the program.

The basic steps in a proof are: 1) establishing the assertions, 2) constructing the proof, and 3) checking the result.[5]

The assertion is the basis of most formal verification systems. An assertion is a statement that is considered to be always true. It is this statement that is used as a check against the code to demonstrate program consistency.

A verification condition is a theorem in logic. If the theorem is shown to be valid, then the program is said to be consistent with its assertions. A verification condition is formed by stating, as the premise of the theorem, the initial assertion that is true on entry to the program. The theorem may be stated as:

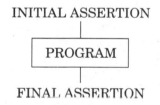

INITIAL ASSERTION

PROGRAM

FINAL ASSERTION

If the initial assertion is true and the program is executed, then the final assertion is true.

Using symbolic execution, programs are executed with the *names* of the data instead of their *values*. There is forward symbolic execution, backward symbolic execution, symbolic execution over all variables, and symbolic execution over one variable or selected variables. Whereas, interactive systems often choose forward symbolic execution over a single path for selected variables, batch systems use backward symbolic execution for all variables and all paths.[6]

An example system that has been automated is based on the conventional inductive assertion method of proving properties of programs and consists of five major components: a standard text editor, a program and assertion parser for Pascal programs, a verification condition generator, a simplification and substitution package, and an interactive theorem prover.

The verification condition generator is an implementation of the axioms and rules of inference which constitute the axiomatic definition of the Pascal language. By invoking these semantic rules, the consistency question between program and specifications is reduced to proving a set of mathematical lemmas sufficient to show that the initial assertion of the program always implies the final assertion.

The use of an axiomatic definition of a programming language as the basis of a verification condition generator is to implement the axioms and rules of inference in such a way that, for each type of program statement, exactly one axiom or rule of inference is applicable to the type. It is then possible to generate recursive subgoals deterministically, i.e., to compute without search sufficient lemmas to imply the desired properties about the program.

The first step in proving the verification conditions is the application of a simplification and substitution package. Each verification condition is assigned a unique name and is processed individually under interactive control. The package consists of 1) a symbolic evaluator that applies reduction rules to expressions within the verification condition and 2) an interactively controlled substitution routine that is triggered by equalities in the main hypotheses of the verification condition. Working together, the evaluator and substitution routine achieve many of the simple proofs and reductions that typically arise in proving programs.

Those verification conditions that do not simplify to TRUE are passed on to the interactive theorem prover. Briefly speaking, the prover is a natural deduction system that proves theorems by subgoaling (splitting), matching, and rewriting. The theorems (and subsequent subgoals) are shown on the user terminal in a natural, easy-to-read form, and the user is provided with several interactive commands for communicating with the prover.[7]

Benefits of program provers

This practice of proving programs would seem to lead to solution of three pressing problems in software development, namely, reliability, documentation, and compatibility.

When the correctness of a program, its compiler, and the hardware of the computer have all been established with mathematical certainty, it will be possible to place great reliance on the results of the program and predict their properties with a confidence limited only by the reliability of the electronics.

Documentation informs a potential user of how to use the program and what it accomplishes; and also assists in further development when it is necessary to update a program to meet changing circumstances or to improve it in light of increased knowledge. The most rigorous method of formulating the purpose of a program, as well as the conditions of its proper use, is to make assertions about the values of variables before and after the program's execution. Furthermore, when it becomes necessary to modify a program, it will always be valid to replace any program by another which satisfies the same criterion of correctness.

Now, the advantages to compatibility of using program proving theories is explored. Even when written in a so-called machine-independent programming language, many programs inadvertently take advantage of some machine-dependent property of a particular implementation, and unpleasant surprises can result when attempting to transfer it to another machine. However, the presence of a machine-dependent feature will always be revealed in advance by the failure of an attempt to prove the program from machine-independent axioms. The programmer will then have the choice of formulating his or her algorithm in a machine-independent fashion, possibly with the help of environment enquires; or, if this involves too much effort or inefficiency, the programmer can deliberately construct a machine-dependent program and rely for proof on some machine-dependent axiom. In the latter case, the axiom must be explicitly quoted as one of the preconditions of successful use of the program. The program can still be transferred to any other machine which happens to satisfy the same machine-dependent axiom; but if it becomes necessary to transfer it to an implementation which does not, then all the places where changes are required will be clearly annotated by the fact that the proof at that point appeals to the truth of the offending machine-dependent axiom.[8]

LARGE SYSTEM DEVELOPMENT

Laszlo Belady sums up large system development as opposed to small development; 'The world of intermodule communication is the "Programming in the Large", in contrast to the implementation of individual modules—the "Programming in the Small".[9]

Another way to view the distinction is to review the subtitles for "Programming in the Small" versus "Programming in the Large" posited by Harlan Mills and others. The subtitles in the section for "Programming in the Small" are:

- How to write correct programs and know it
- What is a correct program?
- Proofs of program correctness
- An intuitive approach to program correctness

whereas the subtitles in the section for "Programming in the Large" are:

- Conceptual integrity
- The difference between heuristics and rigor
- Structured programs and good design
- The difference between detailing and design
- Design validation by top-down development
- The basis for software reliability is design, not testing[10]

Notice the emphasis on good modern programming practices in the subheadings for "Programming in the Large", whereas "Programming in the Small" focuses on proof of correctness for a program or code unit.

The development of reliable large-scale software systems presents a number of problems and challenges not generally encountered in small projects. Here, a small project is one in which a single individual can encompass and resolve any and all of the significant macro and micro issues involved in developing the system.

On large projects, problems such as interface definition, ambiguity resolution, management visibility, and consistency of assumptions are dominant ones. Error distributions on large projects differ considerably from the most familiar data on software error sources.

On a sample large-scale project, there is a striking contrast with respect to the relative difficulty of eliminating design and coding errors. Not only did the number of types of design error outweigh the coding error types, 64 percent to 36 percent, but also the design errors took the longest by far to detect and correct. Of the 54 percent of the error types typically not caught until acceptance, integration, or delivery testing, only 9 percent were coding errors; the other 45 percent were design errors.

Based on analysis of observational data for this sample large-scale project, a hypothesis was derived regarding the potential cost-effectiveness of an automated aid in detecting inconsistencies between assertions about the nature of inputs and outputs of various elements (functions, modules, data bases, data sources, etc.) of the software design. This hypothesis was tested by developing a prototype of such an aid, the Design Assertion Consistency Checker (DACC), and using it on a large-scale software project with 186 elements and 967 assertions about their input and output. Of the 121,000 possible mismatches between input and output assertions, DACC found 818, at a cost in computer time of $30.[11] This experiment showed the value of a tool in helping to track down design differences on a large-scale development project, and should induce others to try to provide similar tools on their large-scale development project.

Previous experience with actual proofs of a variety of programs and with various experimental program verification systems seems to support three preliminary conclusions. First, proofs of significant programs are possible. Second, automatic program verifiers can be of considerable help in proving real programs. Third, proof methods can best be applied to a sizable program if the program is structured so that it can be broken into many parts that can be proved independently.

If we are to prove large programs, such programs and their specifications must be expressed in sufficiently abstract terms so that their proofs can be carried out in terms of intellectually manageable segments. Second, proofs of large programs will require information about the domain of the problem being solved, and this information will be stated explicitly either in the program or its specifications.[12]

Bringing together the first section on program proving theories and this section, hypothetical formal development of software method for large software systems (Fig. 9.1) is outlined:

1. The system is initially described by a formal specification.

2. The formal specification is shown to be well formed by being passed through automated checks for syntactic correctness and semantic consistency.

3. Once confidence is gained that the specification is well formed, it is validated, or shown to describe a system that satisfies the goals of the developers. Validation is primarily performed by inspection. It may be aided by "symbolic execution" (interpretation of specifications) or by automated interpreters for specification. These tools permit input values to be submitted to functions in a specification and then return the output values that the specification defines for these inputs. Validation may also include formal proofs of properties such as security and fault tolerance.

4. After confidence is gained that the formal specification is well formed and describes the intended system, it is used to guide the implementation (programming) of the system.

5. The programs are verified by proofs of correctness which show that they correspond to the validated specification. Proofs are heavily supported by automated tools.

6. Testing is used selectively to double-check the proofs. Test strategies are automatically developed from the specifications using tools.[13]

However, formal proof of program correctness is currently infeasible for large systems. Automated tools can be defined that check the pres-

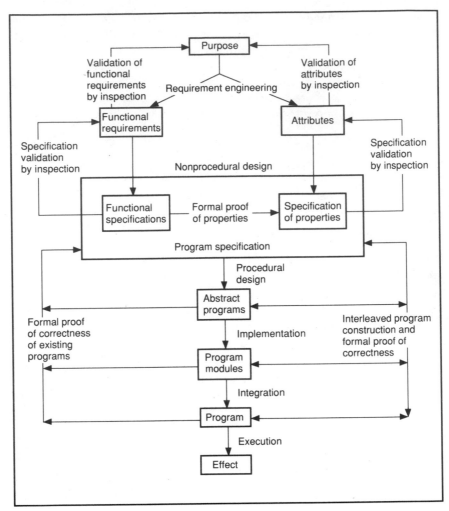

Figure 9.1   Verification method.[14]

ence of certain software attributes which can be program syntax correctness, proper program control statements, proper module interface, testing completeness, and so forth. By ascertaining the construction of the program, it is assured to contain no major flaws. Such a software evaluation system is a composite system consisting of a set of automated tools for the purposes of system design analysis, automated error removal, testing, and partial validation. Partial validation is the process of demonstrating the validity of a program to an acceptable degree of reliability and performance. Current software evaluation systems only partially fulfill this definition.

A sample tool set for a software evaluation system would be based upon the following functional classifications:

System Design Analysis

   A. Automated Design Tools

   B. Automated Simulation Tools

Source Program Static Analysis

   C. Tools for Code Analysis

   D. Tools for Program Structure Checks

   E. Tools for Proper Module Interface Checks

   F. Tools for Event Sequence Checks

Source Program Dynamic Analysis

   G. Tools for Monitoring Real Time Behavior

   H. Tools for Automated Test Case Generation

   I. Tools for Checking Assertions

   J. Tools for Inserting Software Defenses

Maintenance

   K. Tools for Documentation Generation

   L. Tools for Validating Modifications

Performance Enhancement

   M. Tools for Program Restructuring

   N. Tools for Extract and Validate Parallel Operations

Software Quality Evaluation

   O. Tools for Software Quality Evaluation[15]

AUTOMATED TEST GENERATION

Software quality enhancement can be achieved in the near term through the use of a systematic program testing methodology. The methodology attempts to relate functional software test cases with formal software specifications as a means to achieve correspondence between the software and its specifications. To do this requires generation of appropriate test-case data. Such automatic test-case generation is based on *a priori* knowledge of two forms of internal structure information: a representation of the tree of subschema automatically identified from within each program text, and a representation of the iteration structure of each subschema. This partition of a large program allows for efficient and effective automatic test-case generation using backtracking techniques.

During backtracking, a number of simplifying, consolidating, and consistency analyses are applied. The result is either early recognition of the impossibility of a particular program flow, or efficient generation of input variable specifications which cause the test case to traverse each portion of the required program flow.

Generating test-case data which meets specific testing objectives for medium and large computer programs is a difficult problem, however. In typical, large computer programs, the total number of possible program patterns (not counting the number of loop traversals within each pattern) is in the range of 10^5 to 10^7. A systematic automatable methodology for identifying test-case forms, finding appropriate test-case data, and verifying the effectiveness of the test-case data is a desirable tool to have available when imposing a uniform testedness measure on a large-scale software system.[16]

A few known automated tools in the area of automation test generation follow. The Automated Unit Test system developed by IBM operates on object modules and is independent of the language in which the target program was coded. The FORTRAN Test Procedure Language testing system developed by General Electric operates on source code and, therefore, can specify software tests based on the internal structure of the target program. The Test Procedure Language 2.0 developed by General Electric Research and Development Center features automatic assistance in the production and revision of test procedures.[17] Software Research, Inc., offers the Test Coverage Analysis Tool, which measures structural test completeness at the module level; the System Test Coverage Analysis Tool, which measures system level test coverage at the system interface level; the Software Maintenance and Regression Test System, which automates the work of creating, controlling, and analyzing the behavior of complex sets of tests; and the Test Data Generator, which is a test file generator with built-in random and sequential generation options.[18] General Research Corporation has developed the Research Software Validation Package (RSVP) to perform the backtracking and test-case generation discussed above.

Testing and program correctness

A previously published program example was noted to contain seven problems. A history of the errors found by others is provided: a reviewer of the original publication of the program found error 3, and a later published article corrected errors 1, 3, 4, and 7, but not errors 2, 5, and 6, even though it "proves" the updated version of the program correct. If the program were coded and run with test data, errors 1, 2, 3, and 7 would have been detected, but errors 4, 5, and 6 would not have been revealed.

To detect errors reliably, it is generally necessary to execute a *statement* under more than one combination of conditions to verify that its effect is appropriate under all circumstances. It is usually inadequate to exercise any statement just once.

Also, the same *path* through a loop will usually have to be exercised more than once before the right combination of conditions is found to reveal a missing path or inappropriate path selection error.

A reliable test is designed not so much to exercise program paths as to exercise paths under circumstances such that an error is detectable if one exists. Tests based solely on the internal structure of a program are likely to be unreliable.

Exhaustive testing, defined either in terms of program paths or a program's input domain (although these definitions are not equivalent), is usually cited as the impractical means of achieving a reliable and valid test.

Just because testing is not a completely reliable means of demonstrating program correctness does not mean it is sensible to rely solely on proofs. Proofs are not completely reliable either. Proofs can only provide assurance of correctness if all the following are true:

1. There is a complete axiomatization of the entire running environment of the program—all language, operating system, and hardware processors.

2. The processors are proved consistent with the axiomatization.

3. The program is completely and formally implemented in such a way that a proof can be performed or checked mechanically.

4. The specifications are correct in that if every program in the system is correct with respect to its specifications, then the entire system performs as desired.

These requirements are far beyond the state of the art of program specification and mechanical theorem proving, and so one must settle for less: informal specifications, axiomatizations, and proofs.

The goal is to define how to select test data for a particular program such that if the program processes all test data correctly, we can be reasonably confident the program will process *all* data correctly. For this to be possible, the test data must cover all errors in the program being tested, i.e., test-data selection must ensure that data revealing any errors will be selected.

Test data, the actual value from a program's input domain that collectively satisfy some test-data selection criterion.

Test predicates, a description of conditions and combinations of conditions relevant to the program's correct operation.

In short, test predicates describe what aspects of a program are to be tested; test data cause aspects to be tested.

There are two main features of the method of test-data selection—the use of test predicates and the use of a condition table.

Test predicates are the motivating force for data selection. A test predicate is found by identifying conditions and combinations of conditions relevant to the correct operation of a program. Conditions arise first and primarily from the program specifications. As implementations are considered, further conditions and predicates may be added. Conditions can arise from many sources, and as they come to mind, they are written down in the condition stub of a table. The columns of the table are then generated and checked. The checking process may suggest further conditions to be added.

The emphasis is on a systematic approach, and the condition table fulfills this purpose by recording conditions and their combinations in an orderly and mechanically checkable fashion. It forces attention toward specifications and what the program should do rather than an actual program structure and what a program seems to do. It avoids the flaws of testing methods that focus solely on the internal structure of a program, but it is not necessarily divorced from a program's internal structure, since all program predicates must ultimately be represented in the condition table if the table is to define a reliable set of test predicates.

The type of reasoning used in selecting test predicates is much like that used in creating assertions and, hence, the approach focuses attention on the abstract properties of the program and its specifications. A test predicate analysis of a program may be a practical first step toward program proving with the advantage that both testing and proving could be performed sequentially or in parallel.[19]

Automated Program Correction

A discussion follows of an Artificial Intelligence program called Φ that functions in a classroom environment to aid students in producing correct LISP programs. Although, not an automated test generated, this program has the capability of proposing new statement structure to lead toward a correct program.

An outline of Φ is given in Fig. 9.2. Φ first analyzes a program to translate it into a *syntactically correct* form. For this analysis, Φ utilizes a collection of *specialist* modules which are automatically invoked by the appearance of their associated function values. In parallel with this analysis, Φ constructs an internal description of the program which expresses all the information Φ can directly deduce from the text of the program. This always results in a syntactically correct LISP program.

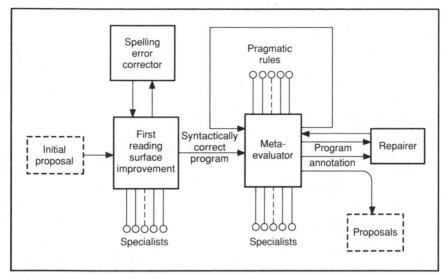

Figure 9.2 An outline of $\bar{\Phi}$.[20]

Next, the syntactically correct program is reanalyzed to detect *inconsistencies* (errors directly deducible from the explicit text of the program, not programmer's intentions) in it. $\bar{\Phi}$ then uses a process of *meta-evaluation* and a library of *pragmatic rules*—expressing knowledge about good program formation and error correction—as well as a second collection of specialist modules which possess knowledge about the semantics of LISP functions. This results in one or more *proposals* for improvement of the same program.

A large part of the body of knowledge is expressed in the form of a set of rules for rewriting expressions (the syntactic level) and rules for restrictions depending on the context and on their applicability (the semantic level). These first rules are accompanied by a collection of methods of simplification to make the resulting expressions clearer and more readable (the aesthetic level).

The pragmatic rules of $\bar{\Phi}$'s rules of thumb correspond to the rules of thumb of experienced programmers. They include notions about definition of procedures, calling procedures, local variables versus global variables, iteration, recursion, infinite loop, and termination condition.

By integrating $\bar{\Phi}$ in a programming environment, if an error arises, the user can

- Correct the program in midexecution—for spelling errors and variables or functions not defined.

- Automatically commence editing the part of the program where the error has been produced—for simple errors not able to be corrected in midexecution.

- Ask the automatic correction subsystem, Φ , to propose corrected versions of the erroneous program fragment.

- Enter into an inspection loop—allows the working of any change within the entire environment—and then continue execution in the modified environment.[21]

REFERENCES

1. Mills, Harlan D., "The New Math of Computer Programming," *Communications of the ACM*, vol. 18, no. 1, January 1975, Copyright © 1975, Association for Computing Machinery, New York, p. 44.
2. Dahl, Ole-Johan, Edsger W. Dijkstra, and C. A. R. Hoare, *Structured Programming*, Academic Press, New York, 1972, p. 4.
3. Mills, Harlan D., *op. cit.,* p. 44.
4. Backhouse, Roland C., *Program Construction and Verification*, Prentice Hall International, Englewood Cliffs, NJ, 1986, pp. 8, 9, 16.
5. Miller, Jr., Edward F., "Software Testing Technology: An Overview," *Handbook of Software Engineering*, Van Nostrand Reinhold Co., New York, 1984, C. R. Vick and C. V. Ramamoorthy, eds., p. 375.
6. Saib, S. H., "Formal Verification," *Handbook of Software Engineering*, Van Nostrand Reinhold Co., New York, 1984, C. R. Vick and C. V. Ramamoorthy, eds., pp. 381, 384, 386.
7. Good, Donald I., Ralph L. London and W. W. Bledsoe, "An Interactive Program Verification System," *Transactions on Software Engineering*, vol. SE-1, no. 1, March 1975, Copyright © 1975, IEEE, New York, p. 60–63, Reprinted by permission.
8. Hoare, C. A. R., "An Axiomatic Basis for Computer Programming," *Communications of the ACM*, vol. 12, no. 10, October 1969, Copyright © 1969, Association for Computing Machinery, New York, pp. 579, 580, Reprinted by permission.
9. Belady, Laszlo A., "Modifiability of Large Software Systems," collected in *Operating Systems Engineering*, M. Maecawa and L. A. Belady, eds., Springer-Verlag, Berlin, 1982, p. 167.
10. Linger, Richard C., Harlan D. Mills, and Bernard I. Witt, *Structured Programming: Theory and Practice*, Addison-Wesley Publishing Co., Reading, MA, 1979, pp. 1–13.
11. Boehm, Barry W., Robert K. McClean, and D. B. Urfrig, "Some Experience with Automated Software Evaluation Systems," collected in Edward Miller and William E. Howden, *Tutorial: Software Testing & Validation Techniques*, Copyright © 1978, IEEE, New York, pp. 134, 135, Reprinted by permission.
12. Good, Donald I., Ralph L. London, and W. W. Bledsoe, *op. cit.,* pp. 59, 66.
13. Berg, Helmut K. et al, *Formal Methods of Program Verification and Specification* Prentice Hall, Inc., Englewood Cliffs, NJ, Copyright © 1982, p. 180. Reprinted by permission.
14. *Ibid*, p. 7.
15. Ramamoorthy, C. V. and Siu-Bun F. Ho, "Testing Large Software with Automated Software Evaluation Systems," collected in Edward Miller and William E. Howden, *Tutorial: Software Testing & Validation Techniques*, Copyright © 1978, IEEE, New York, pp. 151, 160, 161, Reprinted by permission.
16. Miller, Jr., E. F. and R. A. Melton, "Automated Generation of Testcase Datasets," collected in Edward Miller and William E. Howden, *Tutorial: Software Testing & Validation Techniques*, Copyright © 1978, IEEE, New York, p. 238, Reprinted by permission.
17. Panzl, David J., "Automatic Software Test Drivers," collected in Edward Miller and William E. Howden, *Tutorial: Software Testing & Validation Techniques* Copyright © 1978, IEEE, New York, p. 267, Reprinted by permission.
18. Software Research, Inc., *Product Summary,* 625 Third Street, San Francisco, CA 94107-1997.

19. Goodenough, John B. and Susan L. Gerhart, "Toward a Theory of Test Data Selection," collected in Edward Miller and William E. Howden, *Tutorial: Software Testing & Validation Techniques,* Copyright © 1978, IEEE, New York, pp. 22, 23, 26, 27, 29, 31, 33, 34, Reprinted by permission.

20. Wertz, H., *Automatic Correction and Improvement of Programs,* John Wiley & Sons, New York, 1987, p. 17.

21. *Ibid,* pp. 16, 46, 115, 165, 166.

10

Problems with Current Methods

"every one fault seeming monstrous till his
fellow fault came to match it"
Shakespeare
As You Like It, Act III, Scene 2

In this chapter, the initial thrust is on generic quality concepts and then focuses those concepts toward software. Zero defects is first discussed in terms of performance expectations and performance standards. Then, Shigeo Shingo's zero quality control building blocks are covered and the importance he gives to distinguishing between an error and a defect.

Categories of software errors from requirements, design, and code phases are covered. These categories are followed up with a set of error profile indicators to point a way for capturing how the development is going. Error clustering is discussed with the major point being to get rid of defect-prone code.

The quality costs for software are examined with particular attention paid to the portions allocated to prevention, appraisal, and failure. Current methods estimate that failure costs account for 25 percent of the cost of software development.

Various methods in use today that strive toward zero defect software are discussed: specification checking, software fault tolerance, real-time, process-monitoring programs, inspection and desk checking.

Finally, some current methods to aid corrective action include a one-page form, inclusion of severity levels on problem reports, and a method of documenting systemic defects discovered.

PERFORMANCE EXPECTATIONS

A wide spectrum of opinion exists regarding the utility of zero defects programs. Some say having a quality standard of less than 100 percent creates openings for unwanted errors[1]. Others say focusing on zero defects unnaturally constrains the work and creativity of people[2]. This section discusses the merits of setting zero defect goals.

Consider the three basic areas of performance in any organization: cost, schedule, and quality—all vital for success. Each requires an unambiguous performance standard. Everyone knows not to exceed cost, be it $160,000 or whatever. For schedules, we meet the deadline or we don't. What about quality? Most talk about AQL (acceptable quality level)—a commitment to produce imperfection. The only acceptable quality performance standard is zero defects.

People are conditioned to believe that error is inevitable. We not only accept error, we anticipate it. We figure on making errors in typing letters or in programming a computer, and management plans for errors to occur. We feel that human beings have a "built-in" error factor. However, as individuals we do not have the same standard of error acceptance. We do not go home to the wrong house periodically or drink salt water for lemon juice. We have a double standard—one for ourselves, one for the company. The family creates a higher performance standard for us than the company. The company allows 20 percent of sales for scrap, rework, warranty, service, test, and inspection. Errors by people cause this waste. We must concentrate on preventing the defects and errors that plague us to eliminate waste.

The defect that is prevented does not need repair, examination, or explanation. All personnel must adopt an attitude of zero defects in the company.[3] This zero defects attitude is a performance standard for companies that approximates the performance standard created by the family.[4]

In some areas, people are willing to accept imperfections; in others, the amount of defects must be zero. Mistakes are caused by lack of knowledge and/or lack of attention. Knowledge can be measured and deficiencies corrected. Lack of attention must be corrected by the person. Lack of attention is an attitude problem that may be corrected if there is a personal commitment to watch each detail and carefully avoid error. This leads to zero defects in all things.

When this was explained to management and employees, in an example, everyone agreed to make it happen. A strong communication program began, and everyone submitted ideas for an error-cause removal system. The error rates in manufacturing, engineering, purchasing, and other places where measurements were made, dropped 40 percent almost immediately.

Zero defects is a management performance standard, not a "motivation" program. In 1980, in Tokyo, there was a party for Philip Crosby to celebrate sixteen years of zero defects programs in Japan. The United States, particularly in the defense industry, went zero defects-happy for two years. Then the "motivation" wore off because the American quality professional never took time to understand zero defects.

The quality control people are cynical. "Zero defects is Eastern mechanical thinking." "We have to satisfy the customer's perception of quality." "It just isn't possible for people to do things right the first time." "The economics of quality require errors; you have to consider the trade-offs." All these are part of the cynical wisdom that has kept nonconformance an acceptable concept. The swing in the quality control profession is toward the absolute of zero defects.

Setting requirements is a process that is readily understood, but the need for meeting those requirements every time is not so readily understood. Every action must be done just as planned in order to make everything come out right. The performance standard is the device for making the company happy by having everyone understand the importance of every action. When a company allows people not to do everything right, they cause some actions not to happen, so no one knows *exactly* what will occur.

People make the results in a company. Each service or product is created by thousands of tasks that go on in the company and in its dealing with its suppliers. Every task must be done properly, and people must know that they can depend on each other. This is the reason for a performance standard that cannot be misunderstood. The performance standard must be zero defects, not "that's close enough." [5]

ZERO QUALITY CONTROL

Shigeo Shingo has portrayed the road to total quality control (Fig. 10.1) with zero defects as a major step along the way. His methodology of zero quality control—quality control for zero defects—is built on the following ideas:

1. Use source inspections (see Chap. 7), i.e., inspections to eliminate defects entirely. It means applying control functions at the stage where defects originate.

2. Always use 100 percent inspections rather than sampling inspec-

tions. When applied to software, this relates to the development process, not the software product.

3. Carry out corrective action as close as possible to when abnormalities occur.

4. Human workers are not infallible. Set up poka-yoke devices recognizing that people are human. Poka-yoke devices fulfill control functions that must be effective in influencing execution functions (see Chap. 8).

The notion of clearly distinguishing between errors and defects and of running through control cycles at the stage of defect discovery is the most basic idea behind Shingo's Zero QC system. It is imperative that this point be clearly understood.

"Rather than detecting resulting defects and then carrying out feedback and action, zero defects will only be achieved if you detect the causal error behind the defect at the error creation stage and then perform feedback and action so that the error doesn't turn into a defect. What we absolutely cannot prevent are errors, but we can keep those errors from generating defects."[7]

Software developers are seldom given to contemplating their errors. Faults, once found and corrected, are forgotten as attention is quickly redirected to achieve forward progress. Failures are regarded as unscheduled impediments to the completion of testing, not to be dwelt upon. Yet, analysis of failures, the faults that cause them, and the errors that underlie faults are an important part of modern software development.[8]

Five basic questions would help the software developers to think twice about errors uncovered:

1. When in the life cycle do errors occur?

2. What causes, and what could have prevented, the errors that do occur?

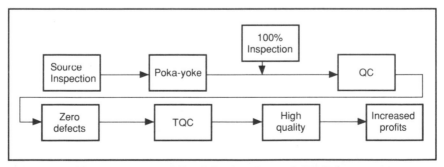

Figure 10.1   Movement toward Total Quality Control (TQC).[6]

3. When and how are the errors detected?
4. What could have been done to detect the errors earlier?
5. When are the errors corrected and at what cost?

These questions would help all of us achieve the major improvements we seek in error prevention, earlier error detection, and decreased error correction costs.[9]

SOFTWARE ERRORS

Even though in Chap. 3 there is a rather detailed discussion of error categories and creation times, a refresher of that idea is appropriate here with a slightly different slant. Emphasized here are requirements, design, and code phase errors:

Errors created during the definition of requirements include:

- Incorrect reflection of operational environment
- Incomplete requirements
- Infeasible requirements
- Conflicting requirements
- Ambiguous requirements
- Software requirement specification inconsistent with other specifications
- Improper description of the initial state of the system
- Insufficient requirements
- Incorrect allocation of error

Errors created during the design phase include:

- Range limitations
- Infinite loops
- Unauthorized or incorrect use of system resources
- Computational error improperly analyzed
- Logic errors
- Conflicting data representations
- Software interface anomalies
- Defenseless design
- Inadequate exception handling
- Nonconformance to specified requirements

Errors created during the coding phase include:

- Misuse of variables
- Mismatched parameter lists
- Improper nesting of loops and branches
- Undefined variables and initialization errors
- Infinite loops
- Missing code
- Unreachable code
- Inverted predicates
- Incomplete predicates
- Failure to save or restore registers
- Missing validity tests
- Incorrect access of array components
- Failure to implement the design as documented[10]
- Language semantics errors

A major concern in software development is the detection of errors. The manager needs to know if the tests being run are exercising the software to a degree that gives confidence that all errors will be uncovered.

Testing shows the presence of errors, it cannot prove their absence. This lack of positive evidence of correctness makes it difficult for managers to assess test completeness and sufficiency. Numbers of errors uncovered may be due to poor quality code or efficient testing, or both.

Two indicators address management concerns about completeness and efficiency of the error detection practices. The test coverage indicator measures the completeness of software testing activities as shown in Fig. 10.2. High test coverage provides intuitive, not statistical, confidence that as many errors as possible are being discovered. The error detection efficiency indicator shows the degree to which the error detection process in each phase discovered all errors that could or should have been detected in that phase. An example for basis paths execution is given in Fig. 10.3.[11]

The most quantitative measure of a technical product's quality is the number of errors discovered by all error detection processes. We access quality by studying errors discovered and removed because, currently, we cannot prove correctness, that is, the absence of errors, for systems having normal size and complexity. Even if we can prove, how does one make sure there is no error in the proof? To prove the proof? In soft-

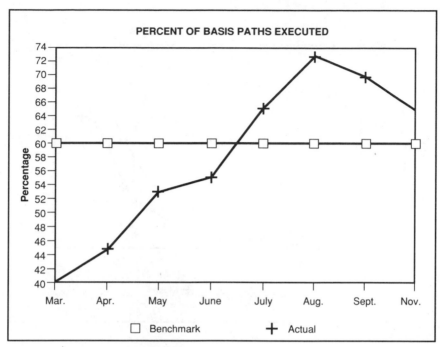

Figure 10.2 Test coverage indicator.[12]

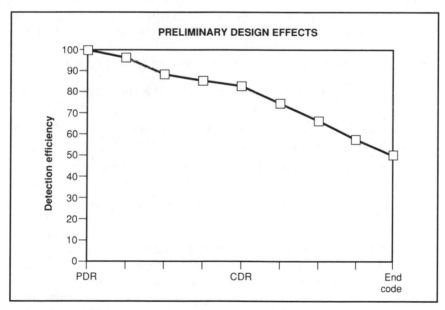

Figure 10.3 Error detection efficiency indicator.[13]

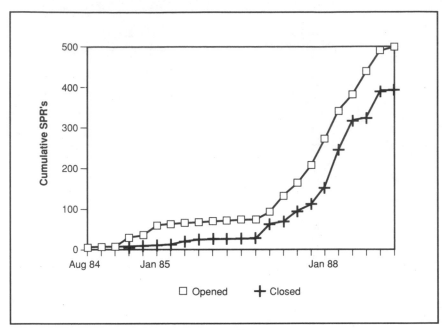

Figure 10.4   Error removal rate indicator.[15]

ware correctness proof, a proof ranges from five to ten times longer than the original program. If human beings cannot be sure there is no error in the program, how can one be sure that there is no error in the proof which is five to ten times longer?[14]

There are other quality indicators addressing error removal:

Error removal rate indicator (Fig. 10.4)—the rate at which errors are being found and resolved.

Another method of looking at error removal rate is contained in Fig. 10.5 that compares projected rates with actual rates.

Error density indicator (Fig. 10.6)—identifies error-prone system components.

Error age profile (Fig. 10.7)—promptness of error removal.[18]

Figures 10.2 through 10.7 are various error indicators and should be compared to the more general software quality indicators given in Chap. 4. Error indicators are specific to error control and tracking, whereas the software quality indicators look at more general indicators of the overall quality of the software product. This continual measurement must go on until zero defects is attained, but without the measurement, we will not know we attained it.

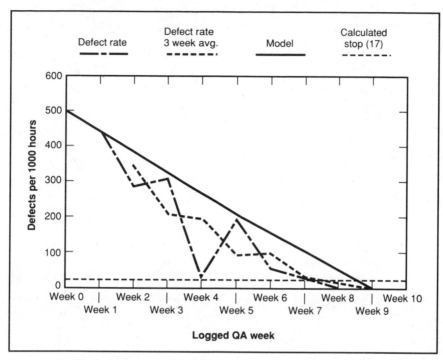

Figure 10.5   Projected versus actual error removal rates.[16]

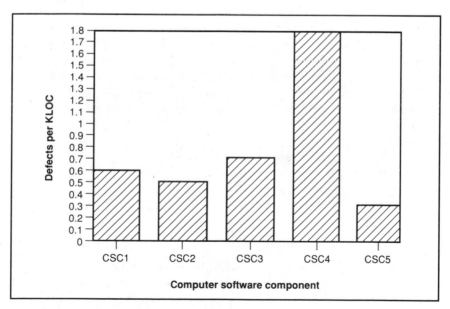

Figure 10.6   Error density indicator.[17]

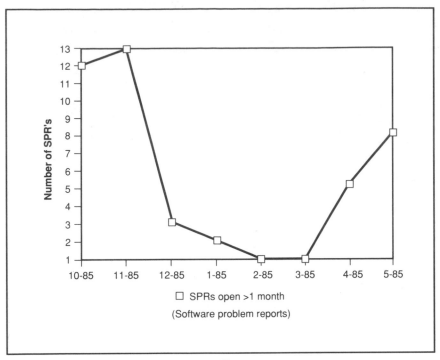

Figure 10.7 Error age profile indicator.[19]

Zero defects is not just a slogan that you pay lip service to in an attempt to achieve a surrogate goal of few defects. Zero defects is an attainable goal. You should not expect to deliver very large systems of software without defects. But the great majority of software units can be made to retire after a long productive life during which they never had need of defect repair. Most project workers can expect to deliver zero defect work.

IBM examples:

Information Management Systems (IMS):

300 of 425 modules defect-free

7.3% of modules had 57% of the defects

OS/360: 4% of modules had 47% of the defects

ERROR CLUSTERING

Early elimination of error clustered units is one of the main thrusts of zero defect development. "The probability of the existence of more errors in a section of a program is proportional to the number of errors already found in that section," said Glenford Myers in 1979. Myers' statement is a refutation of the mental model of error characteristics (all code starts with approximately the same degree of error; the more you test, the cleaner it gets). The next error found is more likely to be found in the module where twelve errors have already been found, rather than in the module where no errors have been found. A student of DeMarco said, "When you see a roach climbing up the wall of a restaurant you don't say, 'There goes *the* roach.' You say, 'The place is infested.' "

A basic strategy derived from the error clustering effect is: Do not spend money on defect-prone code, get rid of it. Coding cost is nearly irrelevant compared to the cost of repairing error-prone modules. If a software unit exceeds an error threshold, throw it out, and have a different developer do the recoding. Discard work in progress that shows a tendency toward errors because early errors predict late errors.

Is it possible for the number of compilation errors to be a predictor of the number of expected errors remaining? The average module is compiled thirty to fifty times during development, but those modules that are defect prone (more than 100 defects/KLOEC, where KLOEC is Thousand Lines of Executable Code) have to be compiled more than twice as often during development.

Collect your own error and defect data and build a family of curves:

- project-detected errors compared to defects detected after delivery
- unit test errors compared to system test errors
- first six months of spoilage compared to subsequent spoilage
- compilation errors compared to the rest of project-detected errors

or this similar, related family of curves:

- project detected errors—count of errors detected prior to delivery
- product defect density—defects per thousand lines of delivered executable code (KLOEC)
- delivered defects—defects discovered between product delivery and retirement[20]

ACCEPTABLE QUALITY LEVEL

There are conflicting schools of thought about quality. One says only zero defects is acceptable; the other says set an acceptable quality level (AQL) because the cost and effort to achieve zero defects is not worthwhile. Figure 10.8 gives an AQL chart where producing above AQL quality is out of control, but producing below AQL is too expensive to be practical.

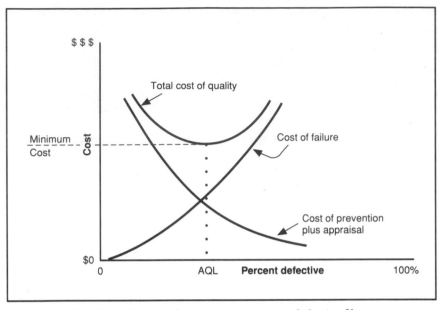

Figure 10.8   Traditional view of costs versus percent defective.[21]

Figure 10.8 does not adequately represent the cost of software systems (critical products) failure. Their malfunction can generate costs that are extremely large compared with the cost of system development. This means that the cost of failure rises steeply as the percent of defectives increase.

One view of the quality cost of software (Fig. 10.9) versus time provides the parts which comprise prevention, appraisal, and failure. Prevention focuses on building quality into software.

Primary prevention costs are:

- planning based on experience
- disciplined and lengthy analysis and design work
- acquisition of development support tools
- training developers in techniques and tools

Primary appraisal costs are:

- inspection of intermediate and final products
- auditing for compliance to procedures
- testing of the software
- error tracking and resolution[22]

Primary failure costs are:

- time expended to fix an error
- redesign to correct a misdesign
- time expended to respond to problems uncovered during audits
- legal liability for damage caused

It would be better to separate the prevention costs and the appraisal costs rather than what is shown in Fig. 10.8. Spending more on inspection and testing, the main ingredients of appraisal costs, will certainly reduce the amount of defective work getting through to the final product or to the end customer, but it is a method which gives diminishing returns, and beyond a certain point generates more expense in inspection person-hours than it saves in scrap, rework, and warranty.

Prevention work, on the other hand, can continue reducing failure costs almost indefinitely. Companies that have spent more and more on prevention have always found that their total quality cost has continued to fall. ITT's quality director proffers that the higher the prevention costs, on the whole, the better for the company.

A much better model for quality cost control, therefore, is that given by Burrill and Ellsworth and pictured in Fig. 10.10. Prevention costs, when effectively applied, reduce all other types of quality cost, includ-

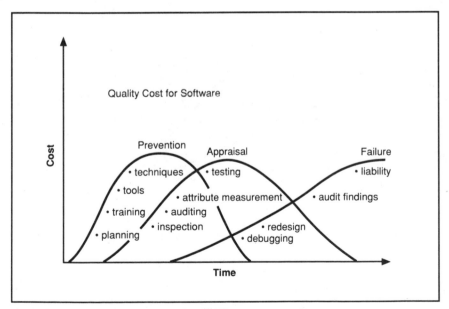

Figure 10.9   Quality cost for software.[23]

ing appraisal costs, and the result is a continuing reduction in overall quality costs. The key fact is that, for most companies, internal and external failure costs combined far exceed the cost of prevention.[24]

Consider the cost-of-prevention-plus-appraisal. The traditional view is that this cost must become almost infinite to achieve zero defects. But this is not true for software systems. Examples of no defect software in the first year of operation show that zero defects can be achieved at a cost-of-prevention-plus-appraisal that is finite and reasonable. Also, the increase in this cost is not excessive as the percent of defects trends to zero.

For failure costs and prevention-plus-appraisal-costs, as shown in Fig. 10.11, the total cost of failure decreases steadily as the percent

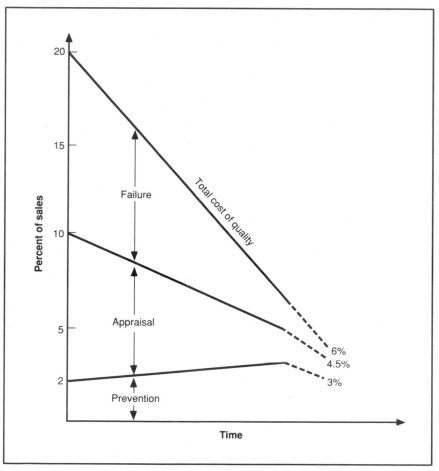

Figure 10.10   Prevention costs continuously drive down overall costs.[25]

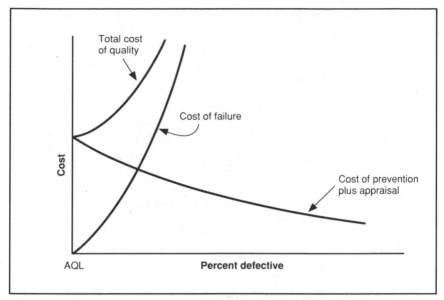

Figure 10.11   Cost versus percent defective for software systems.[27]

defective trends to zero. So the minimum total cost of failure is at the point of zero defects. For these curves, the AQL is zero defects.[26]

TOWARD ZERO DEFECT SOFTWARE

Defect-free software is an impossible goal in the opinion of most software developers. Some software developers believe complex software can be developed that approaches zero defects by using formal specification techniques and computer-based tools. These tools first check the consistency and logical completeness of a set of formal specifications and then generate program code that matches them. Checking the specifications for completeness and consistency with automated tools eliminates errors of logic that from the specifications might arise in implementing the specifications by hand.[28] This concept is detailed in Chap. 9.

Another method that strives to provide defect-free software is software fault tolerance. Software fault tolerance is a system's ability to provide uninterruptible operation in the presence of software faults through redundancy of a functional process. Notice "in the presence of software faults," so this method does not direct zero defect software, but software that will tolerate (or get around) the fault(s). Utilization of the concept of fault tolerance then, philosophically, denies the concept of zero defects in software.

A zero defect system will require "no" fault tolerance. The point is that systems have been designed with up to 30% (in software controlling nuclear power production) more software to make the systems fault tolerant in order to safeguard the software against defects.

Robert Poston and Mark Bruen, in a paper entitled "Counting Down to Zero Software Failures," give an example of a software system achieving significant progress toward reaching zero defect software. Leeds & Northrup Systems in North Wales, PA, achieved 0.072 failures per thousand lines for their Process Information Management Subsystem (PIMS) Trending project of 27,719 lines of source code. PIMS is a real-time, process-monitoring program embedded in a large process control system. The first full year of operation was 1986, where only two customer-reported failures occurred. Leeds & Northrup dropped from 1.3 failures per thousand lines to 0.072, for a 95 percent improvement in software quality.[29]

Tom DeMarco in *Controlling Software Projects* suggests that a workable zero defect software development program is predicated upon the following principles:

1. A stated goal of zero defects in the delivered product

2. Complete organizational separation of development, testing, and measurement

3. Pass *uncompiled code* from developers to testers

4. Failure to compile perfectly is treated as one defect

5. Use compilation defects to indicate degradation in the inspection process effectiveness

6. Repeated compilation failures are early indicators that code is defect prone, and should be recoded

Of these principles, passing uncompiled code from developers to testers is most controversial.

The formal inspection is the major tool in producing zero defect work. In order to keep the inspection process tuned and efficient, immediate feedback is required whenever the software fails. Whenever there are compiler-detected errors under a zero defects program, it is a sign of inspection failure because human inspectors let compile errors flow through.

Inspecting uncompiled code does away with the preconceived notion that it is not worth looking for errors because there probably are none.

Software developers should not feel free to produce error ridden code for the compiler to clean up. The attitude that it is okay to start with a product that is full of errors is unacceptable. The loss in syntax correction efficiency is a reasonable price to pay for a superior feedback mechanism to code and inspection quality.

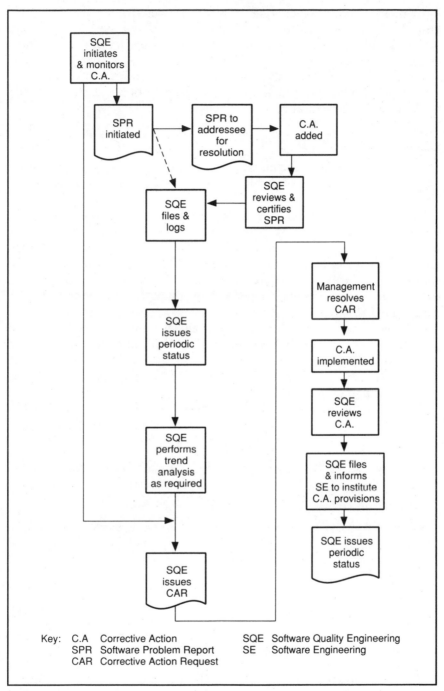

Key: C.A   Corrective Action   SQE   Software Quality Engineering
        SPR   Software Problem Report   SE   Software Engineering
        CAR   Corrective Action Request

Figure 10.12   Corrective action flow.[36]

In most cases, it is cheaper to build software right the first time than fixing it forever after. The first attempt to apply zero defect software should be toward a system with a long projected life and/or high reliability requirement.

For the doubters, identify just key units and target those units for zero defects in advance. This approach allows confidence in the reality of the concept to be built up little by little.[30]

CORRECTIVE ACTION

In the process of building up this confidence, it is necessary to have corrective action systems available to provide a method of closure on the errors made.

Corrective action provides a systematic method for resolving forever the problems that prevent meeting requirements or fail to meet customers' expectations. It is key that the problems are *resolved forever*. Corrective action deals too often with the symptom rather than the root cause of the problem. Often a quick fix is made that is only a bandage.[31] One way to protect against the quick-fix syndrome is to ask individuals to describe any problem that keeps them from performing error-free work on a simple, one-page form. Have them list only the problem. The appropriate functional group answers the problem described on the one-page form within twenty-four hours.[32] A method like this allows true corrective action to get at the root cause of the problem and to eliminate it forever.[33]

To aid in the corrective action process, the incorporation of the NASA-developed five levels of classification of severity of the error is recommended. These levels are:

Severity level 1—represents a factor that could lead to loss of crew and vehicle

Severity level 2—possible loss of mission objective

Severity level 3—loss of objective (with a possible workaround)

Severity level 4—insignificant violation of requirements

Severity level 5—no effect on operations[34]

There is an orderly process for handling problems, and one borrowed from Westinghouse is shown in Fig. 10.12. This figure contains the flow of activities for corrective action for a computer software release. The software quality engineer's involvement is highlighted.

Activity flows from the software configuration control board to the project configuration control board to the vault (formal release library) for the user. There are checks along the way that ensure the integrity of the product and provide safeguards against indiscriminate changes to a baseline.

Corrective action helps in the recognition of differences between a random defect (problem not repeatable as described) and a systemic defect (problem repeatable as described), with the result being that preventive action can be implemented accordingly. In this case, when a defect is discovered, it is treated as an opportunity to *improve* the process.[35]

REFERENCES

1. Peters, Thomas J. and Robert H. Waterman, Jr., *In Search of Excellence,* Harper & Row, Publishers, New York, Copyright © 1982 by Thomas Peters and Robert H. Waterman, Jr. p. 169, Reprinted by permission.
2. "60 Minutes," CBS Telecast, "Commandant Al Gray," March 27, 1988.
3. Crosby, Philip B., *Quality is Free,* New American Library, Inc., New York, 1979, pp. 145, 146.
4. DeMarco, Tom, *Controlling Software Projects,* Yourdon, Inc., New York, Copyright © 1982, p. 227, Adapted with permission from Prentice Hall Inc., Englewood Cliffs, NJ.
5. Crosby, Philip B., *Quality Without Tears,* McGraw-Hill Book Company, New York, 1984, pp. 54, 74, 83, 84.
6. Shingo, Shigeo, *Zero Quality Control: Source Inspection and the Poka-yoke System,* Andrew P. Dillon, trans., Productivity Press, Cambridge, MA, 1986, p. 272, 273. Published with permission.
7. *Ibid.,* p. 54, 278.
8. Dunn, Robert, *Software Defect Removal,* McGraw-Hill Book Company, New York, 1984, p. 253.
9. Kenett, Ron S. and Shage Koenig, "A Process Management Approach to SQA," *Quality Progress,* vol. XXI. no. 11 November 1988, Copyright © 1988, American Society for Quality Control, Inc., Milwaukee, WI, p. 69, Reprinted by permission.
10. Dunn, Robert H , "The Quest for Software Reliability", in *Handbook of Software Quality Assurance,* G. Gordon Schulmeyer, and James I. McManus, eds., Van Nostrand Reinhold Co. Inc., New York, 1987, pp. 343–348.
11. MacMillan, Jean and John R. Vosburgh, *Software Quality Indicators,* Scientific Systems, Inc., Cambridge, MA, 1986, contract number F33615-85-C-5108 AFBRMC/RDCB Wright Patterson Air Force Base, pp. 40, 41.
12. *Ibid.,* p. 43.
13. *Ibid.,* p. 46.
14. Cho, Chin K., *An Introduction to Software Quality Control,* Copyright © 1980, Wiley-Interscience, Reprinted by permission of John Wiley & Sons, Inc., New York.
15. MacMillian, Jean and John R. Vosburgh, *op. cit.,* p. 52.
16. Grady, Robert B., and Deborah L. Caswell, *Software Metrics: Establishing a Company-Wide Program,* Prentice Hall, Inc., Englewood Cliffs, NJ, Copyright © 1987, p. 27.
17. MacMillan, Jean and John R. Vosburgh, *op. cit.,* p. 59.
18. *Ibid.,* pp. 50, 51.
19. *Ibid.,* p. 56.
20. DeMarco, Tom, *op. cit.,* pp. 204–229.
21. Burrill, Claude W. and Leon W. Ellsworth, *Quality Data Processing,* Burrill-Ellsworth Associates, Inc., Tenafly, NJ, 1982, p. 50.
22. Daughtrey, Taz, "The Search for Software Quality," *Quality Progress,* vol. XXI, no. 11, November 1988, Copyright © 1988 American Society for Quality Control, Inc., Milwaukee, WI, p. 30, Reprinted by permission.

23. *Ibid.,* p. 29.
24. Cullen, Joe and Jack Hollingum, *Implementing Total Quality,* IFS (Publications) Ltd., Bedford, U. K., 1987, pp. 98–100.
25. *Ibid.,* p. 101.
26. Burrill, Claude W. and Leon W. Ellsworth, *op. cit.,* pp. 49–51.
27. *Ibid.,* p. 52.
28. Hamilton, Margaret H. "Zero-defect software: the elusive goal," *IEEE Spectrum,* vol. 23, no. 3, March 1986, Copyright © 1986, IEEE, New York, p. 48, Reprinted by permission.
29. Poston, Robert M. and Mark W. Bruen, "Counting Down to Zero Software Failures," *IEEE Software,* September 1987, Copyright © 1987, IEEE, New York, p. 54, Reprinted by permission.
30. DeMarco, Tom, *op. cit.,* pp. 229–231.
31. Cooper, Alan D., *The Journey Toward Managing Quality Improvement,* Westinghouse Electric Corp., Orlando, 1987, p. 28.
32. Crosby, Philip B., *op. cit.,* p. 117.
33. Cooper, Alan D., *op. cit.,* p. 28.
34. Doherty, Richard, "The Shuttle's Software—NASA goal: software with zero defects," *Electronics Engineering Times,* Issue #503, September 12, 1988, Copyright © 1988, CMP Publications, Inc., Manhasset, NY, p. 88, Reprinted by permission.
35. Schulmeyer, G. Gordon and Chenoweth, Halsey B., Ph.D., "The Trouble with Software Reliability," *IEEE COMPSAC Proceedings,* IEEE Press, Oct. 8–10, 1986, Copyright © 1986, IEEE, New York, pp. 257, 258, Reprinted by permission.
36. Westinghouse Quality System Implementation Procedure 5.1.1.9-C, *Software Corrective Action,* March 22, 1985, p. 16.

The Total Quality Concept

The Total Quality Concept

"...men's judgments are
A parcel of their future, and things outward
Do draw the inward quality after them, ..."
SHAKESPEARE
Anthony and Cleopatra, Act II,
Scene 10

An interlude at this point on the concept of Total Quality is provided because it is appropriate for a reflective aside. It covers concepts which are applicable to a zero defect software program. Elements, such as what is Total Quality and implementation elements including the internationally known quality circles and company sponsored quality programs, give the zero defect software program credibility as part of the company's Total Quality programs.

Westinghouse Electric Corporation defines Total Quality as "performance leadership in meeting customer requirements by doing the right things right the first time." Proper performance responds to "doing the right things", and "doing them right the first time" implies conformance to requirements in an error-free manner. It is important to understand that total quality improvement is an on-going, never-ending process.

The four Westinghouse imperatives of Total Quality are: customer orientation, human resources excellence, product/process leadership, and management leadership. Everything starts with the customer, and his or her perception of value is considered important to a zero defect software program. The most important resource for total quality is people who are motivated, trained, and educated. Product and process leadership is the focus for the total quality effort, and setting product and process requirements is a key strategic issue. Line and project management must exercise leadership in establishing total quality as a way of life with emphasis on training, objectives setting, communicating, incentives, measuring, and feedback. The conditions of excellence to fulfill total quality requirements are summarized in Figure IT.1.[1]

The Japanese have been perfecting Total Quality for the last forty years with results sufficiently noted in the Preface. This process is based on the principle that higher quality results in lower cost and shorter product lead time, all of which increase customer satisfaction and market share. There are seven steps to higher quality shown in Fig. IT.2, where United States industry is typically at step four.[3]

Although Fig. IT.2 shows many steps for Total Quality, there are underlying challenging principles behind the steps. The principles are training and management of people, the use of single-source suppliers, and the concept of continuous improvement in all processes. The most important principle, however, is to approach Total Quality as a system.[5]

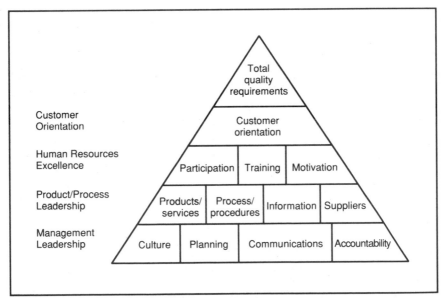

Figure IT.1   Conditions of excellence for Total Quality.[2]

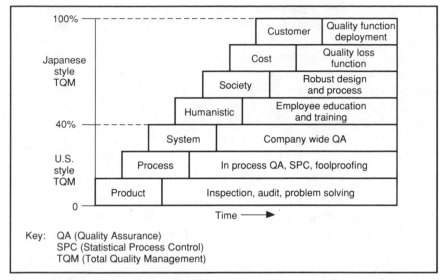

Figure IT.2   The build-up of quality in seven stages.[4]

Another view provided by the Delta Consulting Group lists eight actions similar to the seven steps shown above for Total Quality:

1. *Create tools and processes for quality improvement throughout the organization.*
2. *Invest in training to use those tools.*
3. *Provide technical support to follow the training.*
4. *Create measurement systems to track quality.*
5. *Focus on change in management behavior.*
6. *Create new management positions to implement the change.*
7. *Create new rewards and recognition.*
8. *Communicate need for quality.*[6]

The application of all these various actions for Total Quality as applied to software development is described throughout this book.

TOTAL QUALITY IMPLEMENTATION

David Kearns, CEO of Xerox Corporation, thought TQC meant quality control at the end of the manufacturing line. But he learned that it meant how to run a business in its entirety. It had nothing to do with checking quality as your products roll off the assembly line.

A quality vice-president was appointed around 1984 by Kearns, and the Xerox Corporation then put together a quality implementation team who worked out a basic plan emphasizing five broad areas. (1) Total commitment of senior management was the most important. (2) Standards and measurements of how work is done were worked out. (3) Training was provided for virtually *all of 100,000 employees*. (4) Recognition and rewards for quality improvements were instituted. (5) Communicating the quality culture was institutionalized.

After five years, the quality process has become part of the Xerox culture. There are 8,000 problem-solving teams (read *quality circles*) with approximately 75,000 employees. Employees must be trained in this process for results. All information must be shared with the quality improvement teams. If they do not get all the information they need, they cannot do the work. David Kearns recognized that it is most difficult for the top executives to give up a great deal of power, and information is one of the tools of power for management.

The experience of specific interest here is what occurred over the years at Xerox's Webster, New York, plant. In the early 1980s, about 92 percent of incoming parts were defect free. The situation today is 99.95 percent defect-free. "We believe that 100 percent defect-free is possible," said Kearns, "and that is our expectation now."

The Xerox quality statement says that quality is the basic business principle for Xerox. Quality means fully satisfying the requirements of internal and external customers with innovative products and services. Quality improvement is the job of every Xerox employee.[7]

This commitment to quality has paid off for David Kearns and Xerox Corporation because they received the 1989 Malcolm Baldridge National Quality Award.

QUALITY CIRCLES

Of special mention from item 1 in the Delta Consulting Group list for Total Quality is an application that has been successful in both United States and Japanese cultures—the Quality Circle. The Quality Control Circle, or Q-C Circle, share with management the responsibility for locating and solving problems of coordination and productivity. The success of Q-C Circles depends not only on technique, but on the human aspect. The circles notice all the little things that go wrong, then put up a flag. The fundamental purposes of the Q-C Circle are to:

- Contribute to the improvement and development of the enterprise
- Respect humanity and build a happy, bright workshop which is meaningful to work in

- Display human capabilities fully and eventually draw out infinite possibilities

As an example, the Q-C Circle group may begin a systematic study of a problem, collecting statistics about it, perhaps even counting the number of defects per part at each stage of the production process covered by circle members. When the study period ends, perhaps after six weeks, members analyze the data, drawing charts, and graphics to determine the source(s) of the problem. Once the problem is identified, circle members suggest steps to correct it.[8]

TRANSITION IMPROVEMENT PROGRAM

Total quality in software development is a very recent practice. Although total quality has not been widely used in the software area, it has been used in large software developments. Originally, quality-control activities were used on the production line, so there are lessons to be learned which are applicable to the software production process.

A part of the Total Quality activity at Westinghouse Electronic Systems Group (ESG) is the Transition Improvement Program (TIP). TIP is an implementation of items 1, 4, 5, and 8 in the Delta Consulting Group's list for Total Quality. The mission statement for TIP is to implement the corrective/preventative action necessary to improve the design/manufacturing transition process in order to reduce total product cost and cycle time, and to enhance total product quality. The key projects of TIP include design/layout reviews, part/process standardization, product transition facility, producibility guideline, zero defect software, and data feedback systems.[9] It is clear that software quality is a key part of the Total Quality activities at Westinghouse, and becoming so at most other major manufacturers using significant quantities of software in their products.

Total quality for software development is pursued at Westinghouse ESG for two reasons: To improve software quality in terms of decreasing defects, and to stimulate individual motivation and creativity in software development in the longer term. The more software development is industrialized, the more quality improvements such as Total Quality will be considered important.[10]

Total Quality means exactly what it says—zero defects in all products leaving the company. It means quality in every aspect of the company's operations. It also means more than it says. One might think that the achievement of near-perfection in quality would involve a cost penalty for the company. The reverse is true. The costs incurred in implementing Total Quality are far outweighed by the savings it produces, both directly, in terms of the elimination of wasted time, effort, and materials throughout the company, and in enhanced business resulting from greater competitiveness and better customer relations.[11]

REFERENCES

1. *Total Quality—A Westinghouse Imperative,* Management Overview, May 1986.
2. *Ibid.,* p. 4.
3. Stuelpnagel, Thomas R. "Total Quality Management," *National Defense,* vol. LXXI-II, no. 442, November 1988, Copyright © 1988, American Defense Preparedness Association, Arlington, VA, p. 57, Reprinted by permission.
4. *Ibid.,* chart from Ford Motor Co., "Company-Wide Quality Control," L. P. Sullivan, p. 57.
5. Stuelpnagel, Thomas R., "Improved U.S. Defense, Total Quality Control," *National Defense,* vol. LXXIII, no. 438, May/June 1988, Copyright © 1988, American Defense Preparedness Association, Arlington, VA, p. 46, Reprinted by permission.
6. Skrzycki, Cindy, "Making Quality a Priority," *The Washington Post,* October 11, 1987, p. k1.
7. Kearns, David, "Xerox: Satisfying Customer Needs with a New Culture," *Management Review,* February 1989, Copyright © 1989, American Management Association, New York, pp. 81–83, Reprinted by permission.
8. Ouchi, William, *Theory Z,* Addison-Wesley Publishing Co., Inc., Reading, MA, Copyright © 1981, pp. 261–265, Reprinted with permission.
9. Townshend, Rolph and Andrew H. West, *1987 Kickoff Meeting of No Major Defects* presentation at Westinghouse, Jan., 1987, pp. 2–23.
10. Kishida, Konichi, et al, "Quality Assurance Technology in Japan," *IEEE Software,* September 1987, Copyright © 1987, IEEE, New York, p. 17, Reprinted by permission.
11. Cullen, Joe and Jack Hollingum, *Implementing Total Quality,* IFS (Publications) Ltd., Bedford, U. K., 1987, p. 1.

Improvements

Taking Responsibility for Defects

"Condemn the fault, and not the actor of it"
SHAKESPEARE
Measure for Measure, Act II, Scene 2

Where does the responsibility lie for achieving zero defect software? Like any human activity, people must accomplish it. In this chapter, the spotlight is turned on people.

A Japanese model of cooperation versus the United States model of conflict is discussed first to set the stage for the cultural change required by the people to have the correct mindset. With the correct mindset then, how workers act as sensors in the inspection process which strides toward zero defect software is discussed.

The participation of the software developers is critical to the success of a zero defect software program. Ways to achieve effective participation are provided, and the role of how a company can provide the proper atmosphere for participation is discussed.

The fact that there are some poor performers doing software development and what to do about it is explored. Various sociological views of how to handle the poor performer are considered.

The question of discipline in software development is raised by addressing how software developers may believe discipline stifles their creativity. This is answered by the challenge to fly only on unregulated airlines, demonstrating a major point about the necessity of discipline.

The chapter concludes with strong statements to management about their role in any quality program, especially a zero defect software one.

HUMAN BEHAVIOR

Figure 11.1 shows a marked difference between European-American and Japanese systems of work. The Japanese push first for productivity which then creates profits, while Europeans and Americans use existing profits to pull up productivity. Human behavior is recognized as the cornerstone, and the work motivation stack tells much about our inherent differences on how we handle people. The result in the Euro-American system is conflict, and in the Japanese system, it is cooperation—a goal worth striving for. As a cogent reminder from the *One Minute Manager,* by Blanchard and Johnson, the aphorism provided is:

> "Take a minute:
> Look At Your Goals
>   Look At
>   Your Performance
> See If Your Behavior
>   Matches Your Goals"[1]

For software development, one would do well to review Dr. Barry Boehm's chart (see Fig. 1.13) on the importance of human relations in software engineering.

Corporate leadership that beats the quality drum has been found to be essential to implementing a quality revolution in a company, but the message has to be heeded by everyone. This is more an issue of people and motivation (work motivation) and less of capital and equipment (work methods) because it involves a cultural change.[3] How that cultural change is aided is touched upon in the Introduction and is discussed again in the following chapter.

There are some high-level concepts that quality experts agree with; which when understood, help bring about the necessary cultural change to achieve the goal of quality in software. First is the concept of: it is the responsibility of management to instill the quality message. The second concept is that for substantial, long-lasting quality improvements to be made, all employees must live the quality message.[4] So, the quality message of zero defect software must be accepted by *all employees.*

Regardless of the type of industry, manufacturing, retail, services, or whatever, there are four basic components of quality: (1) parts, (2) requirements, (3) processes, and (4) people. This is shown in Fig. 11.2 with the "people" box purposely on the top. The other three compo-

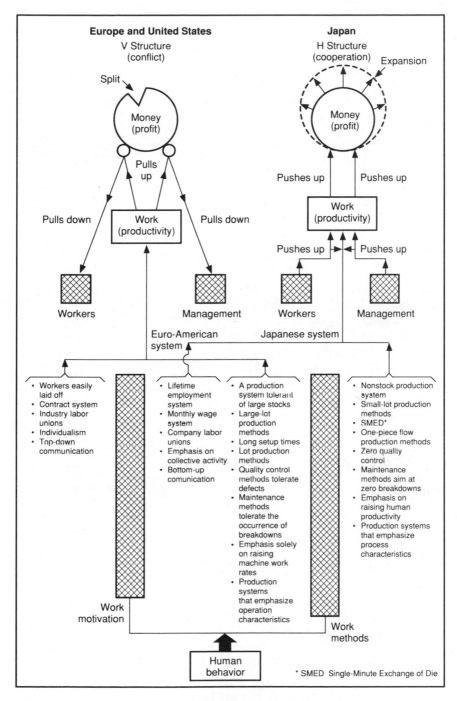

Figure 11.1   Euro-American system versus the Japanese system.[2]

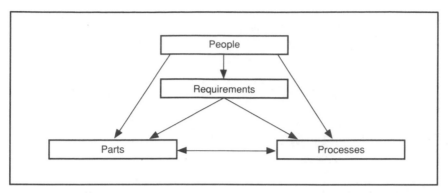

Figure 11.2 Four basic components of quality.[6] (*Copyright © 1987, Terry R. Sargent. Reprinted by permission.*)

nents are dependent entirely on the dictates of people's needs and desires.

The box labeled "People" represents each of us. We, as customers and employees, determine the level of quality that we wish to achieve. Do not confuse this with meeting or not meeting requirements; it is a recognition that there are different levels of acceptable quality as determined by the public. We determine the processes, as described in this book, we will perform and identify the parts we will use to meet that level of quality. This "People" box governs the contents of the other three, and changes made in this area will impact the other components, through a ripple effect.[5]

PEOPLE AS SENSORS

People play a major role as a sensing "device" and are classified in this sensing role as:

- where the basic job is to be a sensor (inspector, investigator, auditor, etc.)

- where the basic job is something else and the sensing duties are incidental

A person as a basic sensor compares the actual happenings against standard and records the difference.

In most situations of human sensing, the "real" job is something else; the sensing is only incidental. The "doers" tend to feel that record keeping (time-card logging, for example) is a nuisance, keeps them from their "regular" jobs, and is kind of low-grade, anyhow.

Securing acceptance of sensing responsibilities is not just a matter of convincing the sensor. It is no small job to convince those who are to be the subject of the checking that a constructive purpose is being served. Experience with getting "incidental" recording done has evolved some useful guides:

1. Explain the why of the records.
2. Minimize the amount of recording needed.
3. Automate recording where possible.
4. Be sure the data are actually used.
5. Assign the sensing to full-time sensors when dealing with variances or exceptions.[7]
6. Feed back the results of the recording to the sensors.

Certainly Japan, during the 1950s, made use of the human sensing idea, and the Japanese long ago instituted worker self-inspection.

However, many workers prefer that the next worker down the line perform checks on their work because it is more like having friends tell you to be careful than having complaints lodged by specialized inspectors. Workers prefer to be warned immediately than to wait until long after defective work is done. They support successive checks because their compliance in the identification of defects allows improvements to be made immediately and lowers defects.

When using successive checks, it is imperative to gain the thorough understanding and compliance of workers. Failure to do this will undermine interpersonal relations by creating an atmosphere in which each worker feels as though she or he is being criticized by the worker at the next process. Everyone must understand that inadvertent human errors are more easily sensed, i.e., detected by others and that workers help one another by checking each other's work.

As an example of this sensing activity, a management person narrowed down a defect caused by a particular worker when the successive check method was introduced. He realized that it was not the worker's skill or lack thereof, but technical leadership was lacking. With this realization, he was able to focus on similar phenomena and, with appropriate management, leadership was able to reduce defects by 90 percent.[8]

PARTICIPATION

What, then, are these self inspections and successive inspections but means of getting people committed to the quality goal. Commitment can be garnered from the people by fostering a participative climate.

Key objectives of individual participation are to have people at all levels involved in planning and implementing quality improvements, participating in problem-solving activities, working as a team, and exhibiting mutual dependence. The people performing tasks usually have the most knowledge about the quality and factors effecting quality of their output.

There are three conditions necessary for effective participation by the appropriate personnel. First, people must understand that they have the opportunity for participation. People must perceive that management wants them to participate. Second, people need training to be effective in the activities in which they participate. Skills required are problem solving, brainstorming, data analysis, and communications. Third, management must respond by initiating the constructive ideas that people have.

An effective tool used to encourage participation is *quality circles*. A quality circle is a small group of people performing similar work, who form a team to meet on a regular basis to work on problems that are obstacles to quality and productivity. They propose solutions to management or resolve the obstacles. They need training in problem-solving techniques to enhance their effectiveness.

With appropriate planning, a culture can be established that will result in quality circles working on problems that are important to management. This way the quality circle participants feel better for having made a greater contribution. The attitude improvements gained by quality-circle participants play a meaningful role in the context of the total quality culture change.

Another method available for participation is a process that allows anyone in the organization to communicate to management those situations that deter the meeting of requirements. This process should be formalized to the degree that the problems and improvements are documented, communicated to the appropriate people, and appropriately addressed. The response to the initiators must be made in a timely manner so that the personnel maintain high confidence in the process.

Management must recognize that the most effective participation is the day-to-day interaction between managers and their subordinates. Effort should be directed toward making this relationship as open and participative as possible.[9]

With the basic recognition that the participation of people help achieve the goal of quality in software, it is germane to point out that there are common themes concerning people in excellent companies as reported in *In Search of Excellence*. The language in people-oriented institutions has a common flavor. Words and phrases like *Family Feeling, open door, Rally, Jubilee, Management by Wandering Around* create an aura about basic concern for people.

Many of the best companies really do view themselves as an extend-

Figure 11.3 "On the Fastrack".[11] (*Reprinted with special permission of King Features Syndicate, Inc.*)

ed family. It usually transcends the "family" of employees, it includes the employees' entire families.

For day-to-day communications, there is an apparent absence of a rigidly followed chain of command. People do wander about, top management keeps in touch with employees at the lowest level. Informality is usually delineated by Spartan settings, open doors, fewer walls, and fewer offices.[10]

THE POOR PERFORMER

With all the positive elements that people bring to achieving zero defect software, the reality that people made those defects brings us back to earth. This section concentrates on the individual responsibility of the poor performer and management response to the poor performer. A response such as shown in "On the Fastrack" (Fig. 11.3) is not the desirable goal of a zero defect software program, but some better suggestions follow.

From *Software Engineering Economics,* Figure 11.4 (relates project effort as a logarithm of actual work-months to cost drivers) shows that five cost drivers explain about 80 percent of variability in work-months-per-delivered-source instructions. Most of the variability is explained by these five drivers:

ADSI—Project size (Adjusted Delivered Source Instruction; is adjusted to account for reuse of some software)

RVOL—Volatility of Requirements

TURN—Turnaround time on development computer

PCAP—Programmer Capability

ACAP—Analyst Capability[12]

About 6 percent of the cost, then, is a function of the capability of the people on the job.

In recognition of the importance of the people doing the job, the

Department of Defense has imposed requirements for descriptions of those persons. In the *Software Development Plan* Data Item Description (DID), DI-MCCR-80030A, personnel requirements are discussed in a number of paragraphs. The number and skill levels of personnel for performing each of the activities is required. The personnel shall be described by title and minimum qualification for the position. The summary shall indicate the total number of personnel for project management, software engineering, formal software testing, software product evaluations, software configuration management, and many other functions identified in this plan. Each of these areas is discussed, with emphasis on the personnel requirements.[14]

Also, the personnel subparagraph of DI-QCIC-80572 *Software Quality Program Plan* DID requires the description of number and skill levels of personnel who will perform software quality program activities. These personnel, again, shall be described by title and minimum qualification for the position.[15]

A major reason for these DID requirements concerning personnel is because the differences among software workers, as shown in Fig. 11.5, are enormous. Expected variations in performance in all but the smallest project teams will be in the order of ten to one. These variations are not caused solely by the extreme cases; they apply across the entire spectrum of workers. Even if your workers are not at the

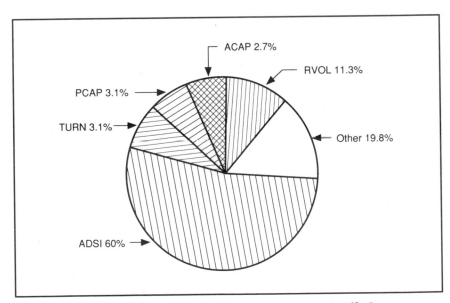

Figure 11.4 Productivity drivers (log of actual work-months).[13] (*Source: Boehm, 1981, Technion Int'l.*)

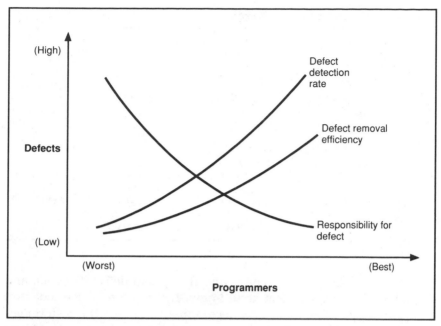

Figure 11.5   Individual differences among workers.[16]

extremes, you will see differences of three or four to one in your software project teams.

Using order of magnitude, poor performers are responsible for more defects than the best performer; lower-average performers are responsible for twice as many as upper-average. There are people on almost all projects who insert spoilage that exceeds the value of their production. *Taking a poor performer off your team can often be more productive than adding a good one.* In a software project team of ten, there are probably three people who produce enough defects to make them net-negative producers. The probability that there is not even one negative producer out of ten is negligible. A high-defect producing team (above 30 defects/thousand lines of executable code) may have fully half in the negative production category.

There are two reasons why not much is done about negative producers: defect-prone people *do not appear* to be bad developers, and the idea of measuring the individual is slightly repugnant to most people.

When we measure and allocate defects fairly and when we make the idea palatable to the people affected, we will find the worker who is defect prone. When we find defect prone workers, it does not mean they should be fired, but only that they should not be allowed to write code, or they need a better lead, or they need more training. If A

TABLE 11.1   Comparison of Two Workers Assigned the Same Task[17]

Item	Worker A	Worker B	A + B
Cost of Labor:			
Coding	$5,000.00	$5,000.00	$10,000.00
Testing	$5,000.00	$5,000.00	$10,000.00
Defect Insertion Rate	0.8 D/KLOEC	7.0 D/KLOEC	
Expected Defects	4.8	42	46.8
Defect Detection Rate	0.7	0.85	
Project Detected Defects	3.36	35.7	
Nominal Project Defect Cost	$1,200.00	$12,500.00	
Defect Removal Efficiency	50%	250%	
Actual Project Spoilage	$2,400.00	$5,000.00	$7,400.00
Residual Defects	1.44	6.3	
Product Spoilage	$4,032.00	$17,640.00	$21,672.00
Total Spoilage	$6,432.00	$23,640.00	$29,072.00

writes nearly defect-free products and B excels at defect detection and diagnosis, then assign them accordingly: Let A write all the code and B do all the testing. It is unconscionable to ignore the differences between A and B; assign them correctly and the differences in project results will be similar to those shown in Tables 11.1 and 11.2.

Switching roles as shown in Table 11.2 improves quality by more than 75 percent. Making these changes illustrate the difference in cost between removing defects ($18,000) and abstaining from them ($0). There were thirty-six more defects inserted when A and B were assigned tasks without regard to B's defect production.

If you collect accurate defect rates and efficiencies without upsetting the people involved, positive results are achieved. Not only is quality

TABLE 11.2   Comparison of Two Workers Assigned Different Tasks[18]

Item	Worker A	Worker B	A + B
Cost of Labor:			
Coding	$10,000.00	N/A	$10,000.00
Testing	N/A	$10,000.00	$10,000.00
Defect Insertion Rate	0.8 D/KLOEC	N/A	
Expected Defects	9.6	N/A	9.6
Defect Detection Rate	N/A	0.85	
Project Detected Defects	8.16	N/A	
Nominal Project Defect Cost	$2,850.00	N/A	
Defect Removal Efficiency	50%	250%	
Actual Project Spoilage	$2,850.00	$570.00	$3,420.00
Residual Defects	1.44	N/A	
Product Spoilage	$4,032.00	N/A	$4,032.00
Total Spoilage	$6,882.00	$570.00	$7,452.00

improved, but *each person's value to the project has increased.* No one need be embarrassed to have been assigned tasks that make optimal use of individual strengths. Even worker B, temporarily chastened to learn that all his testing and diagnostic skill barely made up for a high defect insertion rate, will know (once you have assigned him properly) that his prior low value to the project was due to *management failure,* rather than worker B failure.

A most important function of management is defaulted if the differences between people are ignored and they are assigned homogeneously. Measuring defect rates will prove that 25 percent or more of the staff should not be coding at all, and that some of the best coders should not be allowed to test.[19] Management must focus on those members whose performance is out of statistical control and not on those whose performance is merely low. Managers must understand variation; a team whose work is in statistical control has half its members performing below average.[20]

Management cannot afford to ignore the differences between people because entrance to the software field is too readily available for poor performers. There is a backlog of software development. The need for quality software professionals to tackle the development tasks exacerbates two serious problems. First, it acts as a brake on the achievement of productivity gains in other parts of the economy. It is estimated that roughly 20 percent of the productivity gains in the United States is achieved through automation and data processing. This lack of software professionals means that many nonsoftware personnel still have much tedious, repetitious content because software to eliminate that part of the job cannot be developed.

Second, and more serious, the backlog of development needs create a situation that results in the development of a great deal of bad software, with repercussions on our safety and quality of life. This backlog creates a personnel market in which *just about anybody can get a job whether he or she is capable or not.*[21]

John Gardner, in *No Easy Victories,* said, "An excellent plumber is infinitely more admirable than an incompetent philosopher." He went on to observe that if a society scorns excellence in plumbing because it is a humble activity and accepts shoddiness in philosophy because it is exalted, "neither its pipes nor its theories will hold water."[22] In the context under discussion, substitute "software professional" for "philosopher" and draw the conclusion that the computer program will not run.

The manager has a duty to see that there is excellence in the company's computer software. Historically, that excellence has been lacking, as indicated by (1) economic disasters in the systems development area; (2) users' dissatisfaction with the new systems that are built, or with the very long waiting time involved when changes to existing systems are being implemented; (3) the development of systems that consume large quantities of computer resources, or result in extremely slow response time; (4) inflexible systems that place demands on the user organization with which it is not comfortable; and (5) the escalation of a system's cost. The elimination of these expensive mistakes will provide dollar savings while simultaneously providing management confidence in computer software excellence.[23]

In 1985, Dr. David Parnas said, "How can it be that we have so much software that is reliable enough for us to use it? The answer is simple: programming is a trial and error craft. People write programs without any expectation that they will be right the first time. They spend at least as much time testing and correcting errors as they spent writing the initial program.

"Large concerns have separate groups of testers to do quality assurance. Programmers cannot be trusted to test their own programs adequately. Software is released for use, not when it is known to be correct, but when the rate of discovering new errors slows down to one that management considers acceptable. Users learn to expect errors and are often told how to avoid the bugs until the program is improved."[24]

Much has been said about "not trusting" programmers, anybody can get a software job whether "capable or not", and "poor performers"

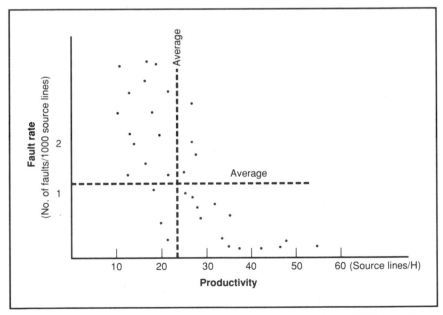

Figure 11.6   Programmer's personal spectrum.[28] (*Copyright © 1987, IEEE.*)

hurt a team. Even charts (Fig. 11.6) of a programmer's personal spectrum are being captured to provide personal defect rate production. Management must act on this information. However, since an individual could be hurt, a few words about the sociological impact of this type of situation are necessary.

If the concepts of egoless programming of Gerald Weinberg in *The Psychology of Computer Programming* are followed, then the individual should not claim possession of a program. Without individual possession, then the team carries the defect load so there is no individual to point to. Also, it removes the following fallacious logic. "This program is defective. This program is part of me, an extension of myself, even carrying my name. I am defective."[26]

But, in the case of individual responsibility for software production, management, given defect information, must act or not act on it. If management does not act, then the abrogation of an important function is made, as mentioned earlier. So, when management does act, does it hurt the individual? If handled as suggested above, the individual software developer does not have to be hurt. There can be a social consciousness and still help achieve project success when using negative information positively.

How to handle the reactions of poor performers to management's advice varies, of course, but managers must be prepared for the worst situation—an emotional outbreak. Anger or despondency would be the most likely reactions, and here are some comments for managers to help handle the situation.[27]*

Anger

1. Be firm, don't respond in anger. Allow a cooling off time.
2. Determine the reason for the anger by getting the facts. (You probably already know the facts—poor software performance.)
3. Listen to the complaint to help quiet matters.
4. If the employee regrets the outburst, let by-goings be by-goings.
5. If professional help is needed, don't say "See a psychiatrist". Seek help from the company doctor.

Despondency

1. Don't say "Anything wrong?", say "I'd like to help."
2. Don't stop crying, it may help.

3. Suggest getting together later.

4. Suggest, "You may want to talk things over with someone."

As part of these sessions, follow the suggestions for general counseling:

1. Know your organization's policy and limits on counseling.

2. Counsel only as needed, neither more or less. Let the limits be determined by the character of the worker and the nature of the problem.

3. Distinguish between directive and nondirective styles:

   • Directive—a preplanned line of questions to cover all relevant points

   • Nondirective—The manager takes few initiatives, leaves it to the worker to guide the talk and occasionally elicits clarifications

4. Show care and interest in the worker's feelings

5. Probe enough, not too much.

6. Offer options, not opinions.

7. Help the worker understand his or her problem and its solutions.

DISCIPLINED PROGRAMMING

One recommended method of improvement for programmers is disciplined programming. Disciplined programming brings software engineering more into line with other branches of engineering, where design is usually assisted by the use of mathematical tools. In system analysis, the types of inputs to be applied to a system are given, and we analyze the system to ensure that it gives the required relationship between input and output variables. Disciplined programming is directly analogous to system design. Techniques of system analysis are employed to assist in the process of system design, and, similarly, techniques of program analysis are used to assist in the program design process. Using this approach, the design stage requires most of the conceptual effort, and construction is relatively straightforward.

To implement disciplined programming requires programmers with a broader range of expertise than is usually encountered in a software group. It is increasingly accepted that the costs of providing the extra training required for implementation of disciplined programming are outweighed by the potential benefits.[28]

Much of what is known about the production of quality software can be summarized in one word—*discipline*. But we all know discipline requires enforcement. Software developers do not want to be regulated because they claim it would stifle their creativity and slow down technical progress. The appropriate response is to agree only if the software developer agrees to fly only on unregulated airlines and if a crash occurs, only be treated by volunteer medics rather than licensed physicians.[29]

In summary of this section, after the size of the software project, the next most significant influence on software cost is the selection, motivation, and management of the people doing software development. Employing the best people is usually a bargain, because the productivity range for people usually is much wider than the range of people's salaries.[30]

MANAGEMENT RESPONSIBILITY

A shift from individual responsibility to management responsibility for the zero defect software program is necessary. A fundamental tenet of management is that we do not actually manage reality, but models of reality. We manage budgets and schedules, rather than dollars and time; we manage markets and plans, rather than customers or the future. Models, therefore, are rightly our shorthand view of reality.[31] Similarly, we manage zero defect software programs, how then, do we manage to achieve zero defects software.

Management has a responsibility to question old methods and past performance in software. Software must be held to exacting standards, just as with every other business area. The software industry has little incentive to reform if management is willing to have sympathy for failures. Software development deserves serious management attention.[32]

Management functions have stages of individual action (Fig. 11.7) within a business organization:

- Volition is the choice to begin some new task or decision to increase profits.

- Policy is set by a desire to do a specific task in a specific way once volition has been invoked.

- Planning is done to give concrete shape to and development of policy. Ideal methods are devised and standard operations are put in place.

- Execution (programming) is when actual processes and operations are performed in accordance with plans.

- Control accompanies execution to ensure processes and operations adhere to standards.

- Monitoring checks the results of controlled execution.

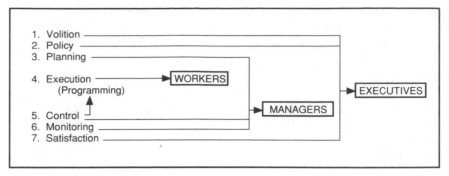

Figure 11.7   Seven stages of action.[33]

- Satisfaction is the comparison of results of monitoring with initial policy targets to establish percent (70 percent satisfaction). This will start off a new cycle with volition.

As seen in Fig. 11.7, each function has a complementary function to assure that the job gets done.

The Deming Circle (Fig. 11.8) consists of three elements: *plan, do,* and *check*. It is claimed that moving from circle to circle of *plan, do,* and *check* will achieve successively better management. This is because planning is done before doing and checking is done after doing. Section b. of Figure 11.8 ties these actions back to the management functions of Figure 11.7.

Shigeo Shingo suggests differences to the Deming Circle:

- The execution ("do") function exists independently of "management".

- Among management functions, the execution ("do") function is inseparable from the control function (how to do).

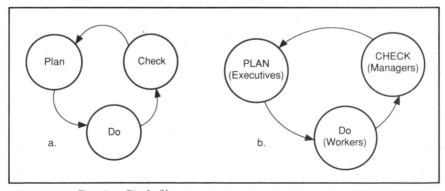

Figure 11.8   Deming Circle.[34]

The management cycle of Shigeo Shingo is shown in Figure 11.9. Usually, the control function is allotted primarily to managers, while the execution function is assigned mostly to workers. The execution function is constantly influenced by the control function. Sometimes the control function is assigned to the workers in charge of execution. But is the control function distinct from the execution function and does it belong among management functions? Recognizing the existence of this control function and making it more efficient is crucial to help eliminate defects.

Some argue that the Deming Circle does not recognize the control function. Many people tend to take Deming's "do" function at face value and overlook the existence of a control function.

At the stage of control and execution one should expect quality

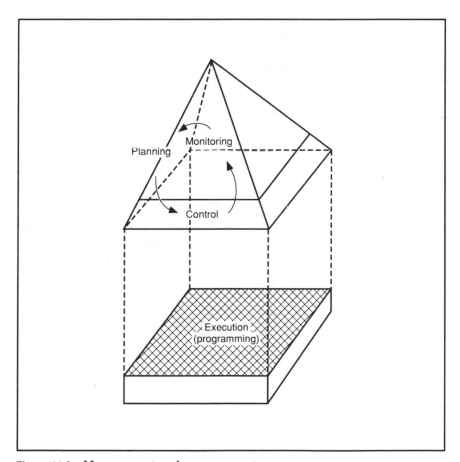

Figure 11.9 Management cycle.

maintenance, but not quality improvement. To improve quality, it has to be done at the planning stage.

This makes it easier to understand the significance of installing poka-yoke devices during control and execution. Poka-yoke techniques are effective means of regulating variations in quality, but that is a maintenance function. To improve quality, poka-yoke must be used at the planning stage.

Do is an execution function and never a management function. Planning functions are *plan, control,* and *check*—brainwork—while the "do" function refers to handwork and legwork. The control function has an overall effect on execution.

Managers exercise control when they show workers how to do their jobs. Workers control themselves by calibrating what they do versus the standard setup for the work.

Thus, because the Deming Circle views management functions and execution functions as the same and neglects control functions, the advance of quality control functions has probably been retarded. It must be understood that the control functions have tremendous impact on management activities.[35]

Management must maintain a sustained commitment to quality to make it successful. Too often good programs die a slow death due to lack of sustained management attention.

Key people required to make a quality program vibrant are: *program facilitator, manufacturing operations manager, quality assurance manager, divisions management,* and *employees.* The program facilitator is unique and must be totally dedicated full time to a program such as zero defect software. As a reminder, the responsibilities of the program facilitator are: strategic planning, development, implementation, communication, scheduling, reporting, coordination, and follow-up.[36] The characteristics of a program facilitator are to be articulate in engineering, factory, and management presentations; acceptable to all; to have necessary resources available; to show innovation for improvement areas; and to be self-motivated.

Management commitment to quality is manifest by:

- regular meetings dedicated to quality performance
- quality is a consistent topic of discussion
- consistent acceptance criteria, not compromised by schedule demands
- quality is an integral aspect of performance evaluations
- consistent, positive reinforcement is provided concerning quality
- establishing a team, win/win environment

■ participation in the objective setting process, expects the goals to be met, and provides recognition for success[37]

So, success in quality is a management issue. Management must recognize the weaknesses of the organization and see that quality applied correctly will eliminate them. Management establishes the organizational purpose, makes measurable objectives, and takes actions required to meet the objectives. Management sets the tone for the people in the organization. If people perceive management's indifference to quality, indifference will permeate the organization. On the other hand, when management is perceived to have a commitment to quality, quality will permeate the organization.[38]

Management must show patience in its commitment to quality, because the quality improvement culture change is a long-term process. There is usually short-term improvement, but the big payoffs occur in future years. Management must show the tenacity necessary to leave no doubt as to their long-term quality commitment. Management must focus the developers on serving the customers (internal and external) by continuously helping to improve the software development process.[39]

Management must eliminate all temptations to compromise conformance to requirements. It only takes one compromise to create doubt—forget that software unit test, ship that software design specification without software quality review. Once there is doubt, long-term consistent behavior on the part of (software) management is the only way to diffuse the doubt.

Management has the responsibility to educate, coach, and sell quality to the organization continually. Education provides the understanding, coaching defines the application, and selling establishes the desire.

The greater challenge usually involves those few people who do not believe in or resist getting involved in the quality process. They can be educated and they can be coached. The problem is usually getting them to participate in the quality process. Management may make them responsible for some important action or expose them to "nonquality" situations (such as irate customers). By doing this, management has a way to sell them on the movement.

Management makes the difference in those organizations that achieve outstanding success in quality improvement. Management's understanding of the magnitude of the opportunity, management's acceptance of leading the improvement effort, and management's willingness to drive the internal mechanisms are those items that make the quality difference.[40] Workers work IN a system. Managers work ON a system to improve it with workers help. Acceptance of this concept is a major cultural change (as discussed earlier) in an organization.[41]

Management must organize for quality. Simplicity with clear reporting enhances the ability to achieve quality. A clean, well-defined organizational structure and operation philosophy go together with process simplification. Process simplification, such as proposed in the software development process chart, leads to quality performance.

Many managers think they are committed to quality, while their subordinates perceive that they are not committed. This is the cause of the failure of many quality improvement programs. If it is perceived that quality is not a high management priority, then it will not be a high priority with the people. People must see management leading the quality improvement process and making it work on a continuing basis.

To achieve this commitment, management must understand quality and be involved in the process with active participation (Fig. 11.10). Each person in the organization must see participation by the level above him.

Management shows its commitment to quality by establishing a quality policy. The policy should set the expectations for quality and should apply to all departments and individuals in the organization. The policy needs to be simple, direct, and concise. With proper man-

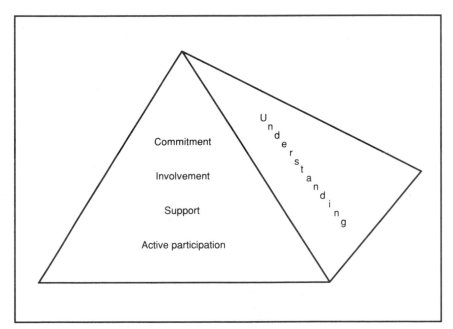

Figure 11.10   Management quality involvement.[42]

TABLE 11.3   Strategic Management Elements[45]

	Minimize defects	Minimize engineering effort and schedule	Maximize customer satisfaction
Major business factor	Hold/increase market share	Competitive pressures forcing new-product development or cost control	Attempt to capture market share
When least effective	When product features are not competitive or reasonable market is not held	When single product is primary source of revenue	Late in the life of a product
Characteristic features	Analysis and removal of sources of defects	Focus on balancing resources between maintenance and new development	Customer communication, quick response
Most visible metrics	Defect categorization by module, cause, type, and severity; size; branch coverage	Calendar time, engineering effort, defects	Product metrics, defects, time
Group most likely to drive strategy	Lab or quality organization; customer support as catalyst	Division or company management	Lab during initial development, customer support later
Potential drawbacks if focus is too restricted	Defects may be fixed that are not cost-effective; modules may not be rewritten that should be	Defect backlog can become unmanageable	Process of developing products may not improve

(Copyright © 1987 IEEE)

agement attention to establish the policy as the basis for quality performance, the policy becomes a rallying point for people to determine actions and priority.

The most resistance to quality usually comes from the middle-manager and supervisory levels. For many, management by quality seems a threat to their authority—if not their jobs. Shop-floor workers usually are eager to assume responsibility for the quality of their work. But it is a different from what they learned from observing middle managers. Middle managers must function less like bosses and more like coaches, relying on persuasion instead of directives to help overcome their perceived threat to their authority. It is by acting as coaches that middle managers can achieve management by quality.[43]

Three primary strategic elements appear to control the actions of managers (Table 11.3) involved in software. They are to:

- minimize defects
- minimize engineering effort and schedule
- maximize customer satisfaction[44]

For error cause removal, every employee is encouraged to identify the cause of any problem he or she may have that detracts from the quality of the product. Management must assure that every problem is given proper attention and that it is responded to in a timely manner.[46] For the general quality case, the zero defects program was instituted in 1961 by Philip Crosby. The United States industries thought it was impractical, and so it was degraded and ignored. The Japanese have been using zero defects to explain what management wants people to do. The United States companies have elaborate reporting systems to show improvement and advertising programs about how hard they are working on quality—they do not have error-free products.

Those quality professionals who believe zero defect products can be built are very often active in helping to reduce the effort of establishing programs. Too often, however, programs are established for workers, while top management is being told that zero defect software cannot be built.[47] Consultants well-known in the industry recognize this.

> "[middle and senior managers are] beginning to ask for more productivity and more quality" because "the top levels of the organization feel the threat" because "they're gradually beginning to see all their products and services depend on computer systems of some sort." "You've got to do a lot of work at senior levels to make them understand that they're building a product that will last 10 years, and quality has to be built into it."[48]*

As a way to summarize the points made about software managers and developers in this chapter, there are two traps to look out for as they will hinder the success of a zero defect software program. First is "let-the-quality-organization-do-it" trap. All the quality functions cannot be delegated to the software quality organization, with the software development team walking away. In a zero defect software program, software development management must accept the

---

*Reprinted with the permission of *Software Magazine,* February 1988, Sentry Publishing, Inc., Westborough, MA 01550.

Figure 11.11   The Born Loser® by Art & Chip Sansom.[50] (*Reprinted by permission of NEA, Inc.*)

responsibility for a sound and effective quality program, so that employees, too, will assume that software quality is important.

Second is "the-fox-guarding-the-hen-house" trap. This usually involves having the inspector report to the function responsible for the product. In the case of the zero defect software program, however, the inspector is the producer, the next person in the process (the internal customer), and software quality. By moving inspection immediately following production, repeating inspection with the next person in the process, and integrating quality reviews throughout the software development process, this trap is avoided.[49*]

Finally, a quick look at "The Born Loser" cartoon (Fig. 11.11) brings to mind that we in software (managers and developers) have "something in common", and that is to achieve zero defect software.

REFERENCES

1. Blanchard, Kenneth, Ph.D. and Spenser Johnson, M.D. *The One Minute Manager,* Copyright © 1981, 1982 by Blanchard Family Partnership and Candle Communication Corporation. Reprinted by permission of William Morrow & Co.
2. Shingo, Shigeo, *Zero Quality Control: Source Inspection and the Poka-yoke System,* Andrew P. Dillon, trans., Productivity Press, Cambridge, MA, 1986, p. 265.
3. Skrzycki, Cindy, "Making Quality a Priority," *The Washington Post,* October 1987, p. k1.
4. Guaspari, John, "You Want to Buy into Quality? Then You've Got to Sell It," *Management Review,* January 1988, Copyright © 1988 American Management Association, New York, pp. 23–25, Reprinted by permission.
5. Sargent, Terry R., "Psychological Consistency Breeds Quality," International Conference on Quality Control, Oct. 20–23, 1987, Tokyo, Copyright © 1987, Terry R. Sargent, p. 2, Reprinted by permission.
6. *Ibid.,* p. 2
7. Juran, J. M., *Managerial Breakthrough,* McGraw-Hill Book Company, (New York, 1964), pp. 266–269.
8. Shingo, Shigeo, *op. cit.,* pp. 73, 74.

*Reprinted from Ref. 49, pp. 231, 232, courtesy of Marcel Dekker, Inc.

9. Cooper, Alan D., *The Journey Toward Managing Quality Improvement*, Westinghouse Electric Corp., Orlando, 1987, pp. 39–41.

10. Peters, Thomas J. and Robert H. Waterman, Jr., *In Search of Excellence*, Harper & Row, Publishers, Inc., New York, 1982 by Thomas Peters and Robert H. Waterman, Jr. pp. 260–266, Reprinted by permission.

11. Holbrook, Bill, *"On the Fastrack," The Washington Post*, Nov. 19, 1988, Copyright © 1988, King Features Syndicate, Inc., New York.

12. Werling, Richard, *Data Collection System for Estimating Software Development Cost*, (U. S. Air Force Contract No. F33615-85-C-5123, 30 September 1986), Defense Technical Information Center, Alexandria, VA, pp. II-14, II-15.

13. *Ibid.*, p. II-15.

14. U.S. Dept. of Defense, DI-MCCR-80030A, *Data Item Description—Software Development Plan*, NAVMAT 09Y, Washington, DC, Feb. 29, 1988, pp. 4–12.

15. U.S. Dept. of Defense, DI-QCIC-80572 *Data Item Description—Software Quality Program Plan*, NAVMAT 09Y, Washington, DC, Apr. 29, 1988, p. 4.

16. DeMarco, Tom, *Controlling Software Projects*, Yourdon, Inc., New York, Copyright © 1982, p. 208, Adapted with permission of Prentice Hall Inc., Englewood Cliffs, NJ.

17. *Ibid.*, p. 209.

18. *Ibid.*, p. 210.

19. *Ibid.*, pp. 207–210.

20. Zultner, Richard, "The Deming Approach to Software Quality Engineering," *Quality Progress*, vol. XXI, no. 11, November 1988, Copyright © 1988, American Society for Quality Control, Inc., Milwaukee, WI., p. 61, Reprinted by permission.

21. Boehm, Barry W., "Understanding and Controlling Software Costs," private paper 1987, p. 3.

22. Longstreet, William, "Executive Exchange—Seize the Opportunity for 'Qualitivity'," Copyright © January 25, 1982, Penton Publishing, Inc., Cleveland, O, p. 13, Reprinted with permission from *Industry Week*.

23. Schulmeyer, G. Gordon, *Computer Concepts for Managers*, Van Nostrand Reinhold Co. Inc., New York, 1985, p. 133.

24. Parnas, David L., "Software Aspects of Strategic Defense Systems," *Communications of the ACM*, vol. 28, no. 12, December 1985, Copyright © 1985, Association of Computing Machinery, Inc., New York, p. 1330, Reprinted by permission.

25. Matsumoto, Yoshihiro, "A Software Factory: An Overall Approach to Software Production," *IEEE*, Copyright © 1987, IEEE, New York, p. 161, Reprinted by permission.

26. Weinberg, Gerald M., *The Psychology of Computing Programming*, Van Nostrand Reinhold Co., Inc., New York, 1971, p. 54.

27. Uris, Auren, *88 Mistakes Interviewers Make and How to Avoid Them*, Copyright © 1988, American Management Association, New York, pp. 123, 207, 208, Reprinted by permission.

28. Downs, T., "A Review of Some of the Reliability Issues in Software Engineering," *Journal of Electrical and Electronics Engineering, Australia*, vol. 5, no. 1, March, 1985, p. 42.

29. Shore, John, "Why I Never Met A Programmer I Could Trust," *Communication of the ACM*, vol. 31, no. 4, April 1988, Association for Computing Machinery, Inc., New York, Copyright © 1988, p. 373, Reprinted by permission.

30. Boehm, Barry W., *op. cit.*, p. 13.

31. Berglind, Bredford L. and Charles D. Scales, "White Collar Productivity," *Management Review*, vol. 76, no. 6, June 1987, American Management Association, New York, Copyright © 1987, p. 42, Reprinted by permission.

32. Mills, Harlan D. and J. H. Poore, "Bringing Software Under Statistical Quality Control," *Quality Progress*, vol. XXI, no. 11, November 1988, American Society for Quality Control, Inc., Milwaukee, WI, Copyright © 1988, p. 52, Reprinted by permission.

33. Shingo, Shigeo, *op. cit.*, p. 24.

34. *Ibid.*, p. 32.

35. *Ibid.,* pp. 23, 24, 31–33, 278, 279.
36. West, Andrew H., "Sustaining Top Management Commitment to Quality," *Quality Congress Transactions,* The American Society for Quality Control, Inc., Milwaukee, WI, Copyright © 1983, pp. 1, 2, Reprinted by permission.
37. West, Andrew H., *No Major Defects Program Overview* presentation at Westinghouse Electric Corp., Jan. 1987, pp. 1, 13.
38. Cooper, Alan D., *op. cit.,* p. 6.
39. Zultner, Richard, "The Deming Approach to Software Quality Engineering," *Quality Progress,* vol. XXI, no. 11, November 1988, American Society for Quality Control, Inc., Milwaukee, WI, Copyright © 1988, p. 58, Reprinted by permission.
40. Cooper, Alan D., *op. cit.,* pp. 17–20.
41. Stuelpnagel, Thomas R. "Total Quality Management," *National Defense,* vol. LXXII, no. 442, November 1988, American Defense Preparedness Association, Arlington, VA, Copyright © 1988, p. 59, Reprinted by permission.
42. Cooper, Alan D., *op. cit.,* p. 18.
43. "The Push for Quality" *Business Week,* No. 3002, June 8, 1987, McGraw-Hill, Inc., New York, p. 134.
44. Grady, Robert B., "Measuring and Managing Software Maintenance," *IEEE Software,* September 1987, IEEE, New York, Copyright © 1987, p. 35, Reprinted by permission.
45. *Ibid.,* p. 37.
46. West, Andrew H., *op. cit.,* p. 8.
47. Crosby, Philip B., *Quality Without Tears,* McGraw-Hill Book Company, New York, 1984, pp. 76, 77, 119.
48. Desmond, John, "The Friendly Master," *Software Magazine,* vol. 8, no. 2, February 1988, Westborough, MA, p. 43.
49. Schrock, Edward M. and Henry L. Lefevre, *The Good and The Bad News About Quality,* Marcel Dekker, Inc., New York, 1988, pp. 231, 232.
50. Sansom, Art, *The Born Loser,* April 25, 1988. Copyright © 1988 by NEA, Inc.

12

Critical Meetings

"Men's faults do seldom to themselves appear;
Their own transgressions partially they
smother."

SHAKESPEARE
The Rape of Lucrece

Because of the difficulties in establishing a zero defect software program, it is clear that changes in the way people think and act about software defects are required. Current industrial experience indicates that cultural and management change is harder to deploy than technical change[1]. This chapter is about the elements of that cultural and management change so that they may be recognized and manipulated to effect the technical change necessary to achieve zero defects software.

With change agents under control, some planning and training methods are provided relative to moving an organization toward zero defect software.

The progress of the actual meetings at Westinghouse ESG over the past few years is covered. Organization and participation for the meetings receive coverage. Although the meetings lost specific direction occasionally to support related software defect issues, in general, the objectives were met. A tabulation of the subjects of these critical meetings include: total quality, inspection/walkthrough, "Software Quality Indicators" pamphlet, software problem reports/software configuration control board, software activities checklist, management requested defect reports, presentation generation, and practical zero defect software implementation methods. These various subjects are discussed in relation to the meetings that moved toward implementation of the zero defect software program.

CHANGE METHODS

This book started with the cry that software development is in a crisis. This software development crisis may be perilous. The preparation necessary to capitalize on crisis creates achievement out of adversity, inspiration out of humiliation, opportunity out of danger. Any individual can play a crisis to his or her advantage. A crisis may strike at the heart of a corporation, but it is always the individual who must have the courage to respond.[2] Every software developer needs that courage because software is so error-prone and because programmers are fallible and the more complex the task, the more fallible they are. Programmers' frailty cannot explain all the degrees of fallibility. A major explanation lies in the fact that the design of software systems has not been subjected to the mathematical discipline imposed on other engineering design.[3]

Management and quality professionals try to devise methods to solve the software development crisis, but management and quality professionals are often interpreted by the workers as saying:

> We want you to work very hard at something that is a lot more important to us than it is to you. Your performance in this effort will be carefully measured and noted, and you are ultimately guaranteed to fail.[4]

Quality is conformance to requirements, and so there are only two possibilities for doing the software development job. Either the work conforms to requirements (quality), or it fails to conform to requirements (lack of quality).

The approach to achieving quality is one of prevention, initiated in advance to assure that requirements are met when work is *initially* performed. This "doing-the-right-thing-right-the-first-time" approach prevents nonconformances from happening in the first place.

Achieving quality then, harkens back to the individual's performance doing the work. Performance standards relate to expectations established for achieving quality. The question, "How often do you want to meet requirements?", should be asked. The answer is "always", with no exceptions.

CULTURAL CHANGE

Quality must become vital to running a business and be a top priority throughout the business. A *cultural change* must permeate the organization. Everyone must recognize the importance of quality, understand quality, and accept his or her responsibility for improving quality.

Changing the old habits and conventional ways of thinking about quality is the quality improvement effort. The successful organization undergoes a culture revolution because it is such a dramatic change. It is a process rather than a program. The quality improvement process is to make permanent improvements in habits, behavior, and style of all the people in the organization.[5]

This change may be brought about successfully through:

1. The people involved.

2. Reduction of high stress that results from low participation.

3. Having all understand the vision and reasons for the change.

4. Management consistency in word and deed.

5. Everyone taking responsibility for change—it is not just something someone else does.

The elements that make the quality improvement process change successful are:[6]

1. Vision
    - clear, positive, forceful, simple
    - measurable objective
    - stretch the normal bounds
2. Drivers
    - strong forces, such as survival
    - weak forces are negative
3. Leadership
    - usually a single person
    - an obstacle is management inconsistency
4. Participation
    - use teaming, cut across organizational boundaries
5. Communication
    - continuous and consistent
    - upward and downward rapidly

6. Training and Education

7. Reinforcement

   ▪ use banners and signs

   ▪ make the change process highly visible

   ▪ give recognition for accomplishments

With this change in the quality requirements, there is potential for some degree of negative psychological impact. The magnitude of the impact depends upon the reason for the change and how well that reason is communicated. If the change benefits the organization in the long term and is sufficiently explained to the workers, the negative impact will be minimized; in fact, there will be positive impact. The positive effect will happen by identifying and removing one of the frustrations workers deal with in trying to meet requirements. Whenever you remove an obstruction to success, and inform people you have done it, you will find a decrease in worker frustration level.

Communicating the reasons for the change is very important because people want to feel that they control their lives. If management makes seemingly random changes, the feeling of worker control is lost, and anxiety and frustration set in, thereby reducing performance. If management explains the reasons for long-term change, as in the case of the zero software defect program, the feeling of being in control is not threatened.[7]

Transition is the psychological response to change. Transitions are difficult times for people. Change can threaten an individual's identity in four ways:

1. Meaning: What is the significance of the change to the person?

2. Mastery: How can an individual regain control?

3. Merit: What is the new worth of the individual as a result of the change?

4. Morale: Does it make a difference whether a person tries to adapt?

It is normal for unconscious reactions to begin when personal identity is threatened.[8] For the zero defect software program, the reaction would be:

1. Meaning: They will resist the added time it may take to review the checklists and process chart. They may be threatened by the "impossible" goal of zero defect software.

2. Mastery: They will resent being checked by another (the internal customer) at every step in the development process. They may lose control of the choice of tools (poka-yoke) employed in the process.

3. Merit: When they hand over a product that they "self inspected", they will have pride when it is error free.

4. Morale: The difference achieved by customer acceptance of the defect-free product keeps the developers' morale positive.

QUALITY CIRCLES

A special program fostering quality awareness and involvement should be designed to overcome lethargy by leading employees through their first steps in quality improvement. Improvement of quality is foremost an effort to change the culture of any organization. Middle managers between top management and professionals are most likely to be threatened by the change. Special programs focusing on professional involvement play a part in this cultural change.[9] One of the most potent methods to help achieve these quality changes is the use of quality circles as described elsewhere. The quality circles can operate at two (or more) levels to smooth the change toward zero defect software.

The middle management leading the software developers can form one circle to provide change management as discussed earlier and be a support group for each other. This support group can help remove the threats that the middle managers perceive.

The second level quality circle is for the software developers themselves. By providing support and direction through a quality circle, it is possible to ease the change needed for process and inspection modification that leads to zero defect software. There is hardly a better way to get commitment except when the change agents (software developers) have a say in the implementation of the change.

The planning necessary for a zero defect software program that should flow into the quality circles to achieve effective results are:

1. Explain the concept and programs to all software supervisors; prepare software supervisors to explain it to their software developers.

2. Determine necessary material and ensure its preparation.

3. Decide how best to launch the program in your cultural environment.

4. Spell out the functions that will be accomplished.

5. Determine what recognition should be given for improved performance (rewards).

6. Set up the time schedule and rehearse those who will take part.

7. Identify the zero defect software program and make the plans for its execution.[10]

Do not forget, during this planning stage for a zero defect software program, the value of a facilitator. A full-time facilitator, if you recall, can provide eight functions: strategic planning, development, implementation, communication, scheduling, reporting, coordination, and follow-up.

Planning a zero defect software program requires a concomitant activity of training for a zero defect software program. This training needs to start with periodic training for software developers and software management on quality systems.[11]

Items such as those posited by Tom Poston for a one-day refresher course are appropriate if emphasis for the final item is given to zero defect software:

- Requirements are the starting point for all software and test-case design.

- A quality product depends on well-written requirements.

- Well-written requirements are testable, unambiguous, uniquely identifiable.

- A quality design contains separately testable building blocks.

- Well-designed tests will exercise all requirements for all input values that have a high probability of detecting failures.

- Early error detection is more cost-effective than waiting for testing and then having to do rework.

- *Error prevention is more cost-effective than early detection.*[12]

THE MEETINGS

Having set the stage for change, and how to manage it, and some planning and training ideas for a zero defect software program, attention is now given to the two years of meetings that have focused on this objective. The meetings are reviewed here to provide sufficient background as to the elements considered and how they resulted in a real program directed toward achieving zero defect software.

The kickoff meeting for the zero defect software program was May 13, 1986, and there have been over fifty meetings. As mentioned earlier, the zero defect software program was placed under the Transition Improvement Program (TIP), which is part of the total quality program at Westinghouse ESG. All TIP projects had to provide a project description at the outset, along with an implementation plan and the project's key objectives. This is shown in Fig. 12.1. The project description contained realistic goals which were achieved.

A major reason for many meetings was to bring together elements from various software development organizations and software quality and reliability. To be successful, it was necessary to involve all effected

PROJECT TITLE: Zero Software Defects

PROJECT DESCRIPTION:

A team made up of software engineering (representing the various software development activities within the organization), software quality, and reliability will be organized to define and implement a software error measurement system that will provide the following information on the software development process:

1. Nature and extent of the effectiveness of the software development methodology as it relates to defect identifiction and source of error.
2. Trend analysis of software errors during the development process to ascertain the improvement in the process over time.
3. Overall quality of the delivered product to the customer.
4. Identification of high error processes in the development cycle.
5. The cost of software defect removal.

IMPLEMENTATION PLAN:
1. Determine team membership.
2. Establish team action plan to include:
   a. Definition of terms
   b. Description of data base reporting system
   c. Twice a month meeting schedule
   d. Quarterly reports
3. Select an existing, full scale development project as a prototype to provide a baseline for future comparison.
4. Implementation of software defect measurement system on all major new projects upon sufficient, available definition.

KEY OBJECTIVES:
1. Establish viable software defect measurement system that encourages early error detection and correction within the product development cycle.
2. Establish system for evaluation of software development methodology and identification of processes that yield high error rates.
3. Identify actions to be taken to reduce the number of errors in the error prone processes.
4. Improve the delivered end product to the customer through quantifiable metrics.

Figure 12.1   Zero defect software project description.[14]

organizations. It took over fifty meetings because organizations involved had to understand and agree upon the concepts proffered.

The topics covered during the meetings, along with the number of meetings devoted to a topic, provide an idea of the timeline associated with the meetings. The topics covered in the various meetings are in Table 12.1

The initial meetings[13] were about the total quality programs at Westinghouse as described by the Westinghouse Quality and Productivity Center in Pittsburgh. The relevant material from those meetings has been previously covered in this book.

TABLE 12.1   Zero Defect Software Program Meetings

Topic	Number of Meetings
Total Quality	4
Inspections/Walkthroughs	3
Software Quality Indicators Pamphlet	11
Software Problem Reports/Software Configuration Control Board	10
Software activities checklist	3
Management requested defect reports	5
Presentation generation	2
Practical zero defect software implementation	20+

The meetings' direction quickly shifted to the software related issues facing us. Some definitions of interest from the minutes follow:

AUDIT   An activity to determine through investigation the adequacy of, and adherence to, established procedures, instructions, specifications, codes, and standards or other applicable contractual and licensing requirements, and the effectiveness of implementation (ANSI Std. N45.2.10-1973).

DESIGN REVIEW   The formal review of an existing or proposed design for the purpose of detection and remedy of design deficiencies that could affect fitness-for-use and environmental aspects of the product, process or service, and/or for identification of potential improvements of performance, safety and economic aspects (ANSI/ASQC Std. A3-1978).

INSPECTION   A formal evaluation technique in which software requirements, design, or code are examined in detail by a person or group other than the author to detect faults, violations of development standards, and other problems (IEEE Std. 729-1983).

WALKTHROUGH   A review process in which a designer or programmer leads one or more other members of the development team through a segment of design or code that he or she has written, while the other members ask questions and make comments about technique, style, possible errors, violation of development standards, and other problems (IEEE Std. 729-1983).[15]

These definitions were provided as a lead-in to a presentation for the meeting concerning inspections. The inspection process was explained, based upon the paper by Mike Fagan[16] introducing the concepts. A summation of the process is also given by Jim Dobbins in "Inspection as an Up-Front Quality Technique".[17] Of particular interest stressed for zero defect software from the Dobbins' paper are the defect types and definitions used in inspection summary logs:

Design defect—function description does not meet the requirements specification.

Logic defect—data is missing; wrong or extra information.

Syntax defect—does not adhere to the grammar of the design/code language defined.

Standards defect—does not meet the software standards requirements. This includes in-house standards, project standards, and military standards invoked in the contract.

Data defect—missing, extra, or wrong data definition or usage.

Interface defect—incompatible definition/format of information exchanged between two modules.

Return code/message defect—incorrect or missing values/messages sent.

Prologue/comment defect—the explanation accompanying the design/code language is incorrect, inexplicit, or missing.

Requirements change defect—change in the requirements specification which is the direct and proximate reason for the required change in the design or code.

Performance improvement defect—code will not perform in the amount of time/space/CPU allocated.

SOFTWARE QUALITY INDICATORS MEETINGS

Next, several meetings were devoted to discussion of the Air Force Systems Command Pamphlet (AFSCP) 800-14 entitled *Software Quality Indicators,* which is the entire subject of Chap. 4.

A review of all the items input to the software quality indicators were identified and discussed to determine ease and feasibility of capture.

Of all the various measures in AFSCP 800-14, the ones of greatest consequence to the zero defect software program are the defect density and fault density indicator. These indicators show errors during the development process with emphasis on errors uncovered during inspections, walkthroughs, and tests.[18]

PROBLEM REPORTING MEETINGS

In a series of meetings[19], the question of when to start counting Software Problem Reports (SPRs) was discussed. Several suggestions were given:

Defect Count for Software Projects

Software defect count is based upon a count of defects in software products delivered to the customer on a project. Defects forms could be called SPR (Software Problem Report), STR (Software Trouble Report), SCR (Software Change Request), etc. Herein SPR is used to encompass all alias names for defect forms. SPRs should also be counted for defects on every formal test against requirements not met for contractual items delivered to the customer, and for defects in documents that have been delivered to the customer. The defects should be accumulated on a project by project basis.

The defect count is against document defects delivered to the customer, not the action item count from formal design reviews.

When customers send formal contract letters with corrective action for documents, that corrective action is counted as one defect. Gather together all editing (readability, spelling, grammar, etc.) items under one defect. Questions or comments are not counted as defects unless they result in a document change.

Since AFPRO (Air Force Program Review Office) represents the customer, any official AFPRO difficiency form against software on a project will be counted as a defect.

The software program manager has the responsibility to provide the count in chart form quarterly to software quality engineering. A sample graph (Fig. 12.3) is attached showing the type of visibility to be provided. Any job with more than 30 person-months of software development effort shall comply with this reporting activity.

The project Software Configuration Control Board (SCCB) has the final responsibility to make the determination what to count as a defect. The SCCB will maintain a one defect per SPR count as the most desirable goal. Multiple defects on one SPR should be split up to a defect per SPR by the SCCB. When the SCCB closes a SPR, then it is counted as completed and fixed.

Figure 12.2   Defect count for software projects.

- To start counting defects, not errors, only after baseline for formal test would allow the possibility of achieving zero defect software.

- To count during all the phases of the development process would not help zero defect software, but trends of improvements in the development process which result in fewer defects may be shown from project to project.

- Count should be made of every SPR written for every formal test against requirements.

- Count should be made of every SPR written against documents delivered to the customer.

- Count should be made only at "sell-off".

The Software Configuration Control Board, SCCB, makes the determination what to count as a defect. The SCCB will see that one defect per SPR be maintained. Multiple ones on one SPR should be split up

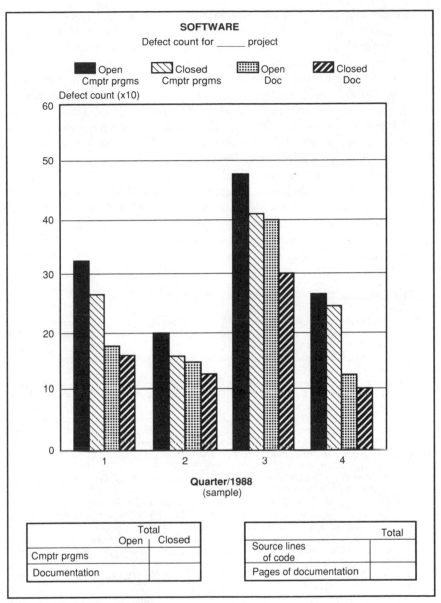

Figure 12.3 Defect count for projects (chart).

by the SCCB. When the SCCB closes SPRs, then the defects are counted as completed or fixed. If corrective action is taken, then the item requiring corrective action is a defect. All readability (spelling, grammar, etc.) items under one defect are gathered together.

An activities list detailing the software development activities was composed and has been under continual review. The results of this activity list is given in App. B. It is set to coincide with the software development process chart which was first distributed at the November 9, 1987, meeting.

Upper management requested the zero defect software meeting members to provide a method of getting defect visibility on software to upper management on a regular basis. The meetings devised a method of explaining defects as written in Fig. 12.2. Also a chart showing the defect count by project is given in Fig. 12.3. These were promulgated in early 1988, as a successful first step initiating the organization toward zero defect software.

The meetings to achieve practical implementation of the zero defect software program first focused on the theories proposed. A detailed look at those theories was taken to see how they could apply in a real-life software development project. The meetings focused on how to make a practical, usable zero defect program.

REFERENCES

1. Winner, Robert I., et al., *The Role of Concurrent Engineering in Weapons System Acquisition—IDA Report R-338*, Institute for Defense Analysis, Alexandria, VA, 1988, p. 37.
2. Fink, Steven, *Crisis Management, Planning for the Inevitable* AMACOM, New York, 1986, p. 1.
3. Downs, T., "A Review of Some of the Reliability Issues in Software Engineering," *Journal of Electrical and Electronics Engineering, Australia*, vol. 5, no. 1, March, 1985, p. 36.
4. Guaspari, John, "The Role of Human Resources in `Selling' Quality Improvements to Employees," *Management Review*, March 1987, American Management Association, New York, Copyright © 1987, p. 22, Reprinted by permission.
5. Cooper, Alan D., *The Journey Toward Managing Quality Improvement*, Westinghouse Electric Corp., Orlando, 1987, pp. 7–10.
6. Arendt, Carl H., "Change Management" presentation, E & AT Statistics Symposium III, Pittsburgh, PA, October 19 & 20, 1987.
7. Sargent, Terry R., "Psychological Consistency Breeds Quality," International Conference on Quality Control, October 20–23, 1987, Tokyo, Copyright © 1987, Terry R. Sargent, p. 3, reprinted by permission.
8. Grady, Robert B., and Deborah L. Caswell, *Software Metrics: Establishing a Company-wide Program*, Prentice Hall Inc., Englewood Cliffs, NJ, Copyright © 1987, p. 92, Adapted by permission.
9. Burrill, Claude W. and Leon W. Ellsworth, *Quality Data Processing*, Burrill-Ellsworth Associates, Inc., Tenafly, NJ, 1982, pp. 168, 170.
10. Crosby, Philip B., *Quality is Free*, New American Library, Inc., New York, 1979, pp. 198, 199.
11. West, Andrew H., *No Major Defects Program Overview* presentation at Westinghouse Electric Corp., Jan. 1987, p. 6.
12. Poston, Robert M. and Mark W. Bruen, "Counting Down to Zero Software Failures," *IEEE Software*, September 1987, IEEE, New York, Copyright © 1987, p. 57, Reprinted by permission.
13. Schulmeyer, G. Gordon, "Minutes of Zero Software Defects Meetings," unpublished meeting minutes, Westinghouse Electric Corp., March 16, 1987.
14. *Ibid.*, May 11, 1986.

15. Hollocker, Charles P., "The Standardization of Software Reviews and Audits," in *Handbook of Software Quality Assurance*, G. Gordon Schulmeyer and James I. McManus, eds., Van Nostrand Reinhold Co. Inc., New York, 1987, pp. 255, 256.
16. Fagan, Michael E., "Design and Code Inspections and Process Control in the Development of Programs," IBM-TR-00.73, June 1976.
17. Dobbins, James H., "Inspections as an Up-Front Quality Technique," in *Handbook of Software Quality Assurance*, G. Gordon Schulmeyer and James I. McManus, eds., Van Nostrand Reinhold Co. Inc., New York, 1987, pp. 138–149.
18. U. S. Air Force, AFSCP-800-14, *Software Quality Indicators* NAVMAT 09Y, Washington DC, 1987, pp. 3, 4.
19. Schulmeyer, G. Gordon, *op. cit.*, 6/11/87, 7/7/87, 7/23/87, 8/13/87, 9/10/87, 11/9/87, 1/15/88, 1/21/88, and 1/25/88.

13

Program Initiation Methods

"So on the top of his subduing tongue
All kind of arguments and question deep,
All replication prompt and reason strong"
SHAKESPEARE
A Lover's Complaint

Remember that the way to handle a crisis—the software crisis—is covered. Almost any individual on any rung of the management ladder, or even outside of the business environment, can play a crisis to his or her advantage. And the operative word here is "individual". No matter where the crisis strikes, it is always an individual who must have the mind—and the courage—to respond. For this software crisis that individual may be *you*.[1] You may be the one who must step forward and present a program leading to zero defect software.

A great way to set the stage for all the future quality programs is to take the advise of John Guaspari presented in his popular *Theory Why*. In new employee orientations, replace the word "employee" with the word "customer-server". Because quality is to be designed in at the beginning, and orientation is at the beginning, then the orientation is*

**Reprinted by permission of publisher, from *Theory Why,* pp. 92–95, Copyright © 1986, John Guaspari. Published by AMACON, a division of American Management Association, New York. All rights reserved.

the best place to provide the quality message of the company.

According to Guaspari, employees should understand they are customer-servers from the moment they walk in the door. New employees should be oriented with "Welcome to your first day serving customers of x company". The company will receive positive reinforcement from the new employees.

This focus of quality efforts on the customer, rather than on morale, has improved morale as a side issue.[2]

QUALITY IMPROVEMENT PROGRAMS

With proper orientation for quality with a customer mindset, the "customer-servers" should be given opportunities to participate in special programs for quality improvement, such as, zero defect software programs. These programs are all based on certain premises from Burrill and Ellsworth:

Analysis. Studies and analyses are required to uncover the causes of poor quality because the causes of many problems are not obvious.

Everything. Every job, standard, and procedure must be studied from a quality viewpoint. Management activities are the ones where the greatest, most likely improvements will occur.

Everyone. Everyone must work on quality improvement, especially the person doing the work because he or she has special job knowledge.

Involvement. People's natural inertia must be overcome by guiding them through the quality improvement experience. It is not enough just to say, "Quality is everyone's job."

Teamwork. Quality improvement programs should promote and utilize teamwork because modern organizations do work by teams.

Visibility. Quality improvement must be constantly brought to people's attention.

Education. People must be taught how to improve quality, and the teachers must learn how to present the message.

Commitment. Involvement in quality improvement generates commitment to solutions.

Also, these special quality improvement programs all have certain characteristics which are worth knowing prior to planning for a zero software defect program presentation:

Publicity. Widely publicize the program throughout the organization.

Structured involvement. Everyone is involved. Generally there is a kickoff meeting, progress is tracked openly, and results displayed publicly.

Prescription for action. Special programs tell what is needed to improve quality and provide a program for accomplishment. The points stressed are the importance of achieving quality objectives, the responsibility of the individual to identify and solve quality problems, and the solution of a practical problem relating to your job.

Deadline for action. Special programs establish a deadline for results.

Reward. Public recognition for outstanding achievement is provided in special programs.

Repetition. Special programs recognize that quality improvement is an ongoing activity, not a one-time effort.[3]

THE VALUE OF REPETITION

To keep a zero defect software program alive, it is necessary to continually reinforce concepts. This reinforcement strengthens the learning curve and dampens the forgetting curve. A brief look at these curves will reinforce, herein, the value of repetition.

There are three learning curves* (Fig. 13.1): equal returns, increasing returns, and S-shaped. For equal returns, progress moves at a steady rate; each trial produces an improvement. For increasing returns, progress is slow at first, then rapidly increases with more learning in each new trial than in many early trials. For S-shaped, progress is slow at first, then increases to a straight line, but later slows again.

A verbal and motor skills forgetting graph (Fig. 13.2) tells us that when we learn something new, we quickly forget much of it, but remember some for a long time. Learning most likely takes place when there are 1) distinctive stimulus, 2) attention to the stimulus, and 3) a unit of previously learned behavior to which the stimulus can be attached.[4] So, apply these principles to a zero defect software program by providing lectures, logos, posters, presentations, promotional materials, and pamphlets.

---

*Excerpt and Figs. 13.1 and 13.2 from *Psychology: An Introduction* by Jerome Kagan and Ernest Havemann, Copyright © 1968 by Harcourt Brace Jovanovich, Inc., reprinted by permission of the publisher.

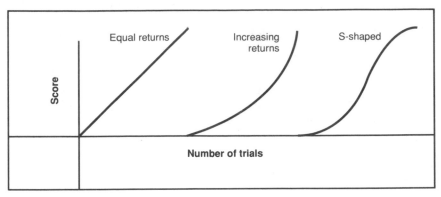

Figure 13.1 Three learning curves.[5]

INDIVIDUAL AND TEAM RECOGNITION

Individual and team contributions to success in quality should be recognized as part of a quality improvement program, such as the zero defect software program. This recognition contributes to the culture change needed in quality and enhances the participation effectiveness of the organization. The process should be flexible, but structured and formalized to the degree that recognition is consistently and fairly administered.

Recognition criteria should be established to define what performance qualifies for recognition. The criteria should require performance exceeding the satisfactory execution of job responsibilities.

An example the author is familiar with would help to define perfor-

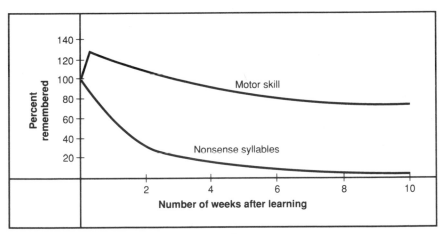

Figure 13.2 Verbal and motor forgetting.[6]

mance that exceeds the satisfactory. A well-defined team of thirteen software engineers were developing an embedded communications application CSCI (computer software configuration item) of about 55,000 LOC (lines of code). Over the course of two years, there were five different team leaders and a relatively inexperienced group of developers. This team was in crisis because it was functioning without an effective leader.

The embedded communications application team was lead by persons of varying experience levels of leadership—usually of limited experience. Eventually, a take-charge person assumed leadership responsibility and, by action, moved the team to positive results. This individual was promoted to a management position.

Two general social-psychological observations about group behavior are relevant to this crisis-ridden software development team. First, members of a group accept relatively strong leadership when in a crisis. But, the team becomes impatient if a leader does not produce effective results quickly. If there is constant reshuffling, a team, such as the one discussed above, will remain in crisis. However, that team will quickly follow a leader who can most effectively steer it.[7] It is the team leader who can turn around the communications CSCI development that deserves, and should receive, special recognition. However, once the team turns around, it also requires special recognition.

There should be enough "fanfare" associated with the recognition for it to be seen by the individuals being recognized as memorable events. The token given should not be money, but an item the recipient will want to keep because of its significance to the process, organization, or accomplishment. Publicity probably provides the greatest value of recognition to the individual and organization. It makes others aware of the activity and spurs them to similar, positive action. Recognition is a valuable tool that should become ingrained in the culture of the organization.[8]

A broad-based, United States-wide award is the Malcolm Baldrige National Quality Award which is the United States answer to the prestigious Deming Award given yearly in Japan. The first six awards were given in 1988. Motorola was one of three companies honored. The other winners were the commercial nuclear fuel division of Westinghouse Electric Corp. and Globe Metallurgical Inc., a 210-employee firm that makes special metal alloys. The three have trumpeted their achievement in advertisements and sales pitches to potential customers.[9] So, this quality recognition is certainly powerful and valuable at the national level.

At Westinghouse Electric Corp., there are two specific awards programs in place that meet the criteria just discussed. There is the

George Westinghouse Signature Award and the President's Quality Achievement Award. Each gathers much publicity and the highest-award winners receive trips and meetings with the highest company officials. The competition is keen, and the recognition is ingrained in the Westinghouse organization culture. The zero defect software program will use these existing methods to gain recognition and be ingrained into the corporate environment.

ZERO DEFECT SOFTWARE PROGRAM

Armed with methods and rewards for quality improvement programs, it is appropriate to move specifically toward the zero defect software program. Establish a committee to investigate the zero defect software concept and ways to implement the program in your organization. This committee can perform similar functions to those discussed in the previous chapter. Those committee meetings took a long time and were very productive. To be successful, these committee meetings must be success oriented.

Taking the lead in the committee, the quality manager must clearly state that zero defect software is *not* a motivation program. Its purpose is to communicate the literal meaning of the words "zero defect software" and that everyone should do things right the first time. All team members must be aware of this.

The committee must match the zero defect software program to the company's personality. This cannot be underestimated, because success can be determined by how implementation is accomplished in a particular environment. When the zero defect software program and the company's personality do not match, the clash will result in an unsuccessful program. How this is done is difficult to say without detailed knowledge of the company culture. That is why the committee in the company has such a significant effect on success at your company.

Formal orientation with all levels of management should be conducted prior to implementation. All managers must understand each step well enough to explain it to their people. The proof of understanding is the ability to explain it.[10]

The zero defect software commitment represents a major step in the software quality management process. Zero defect software day is a day to get software and other areas of management to stand up and make a commitment in front of everybody. It is time to show all that software management is serious. Zero defect software day should be taken seriously and with dignity, no hype. It needs to be different from other communications so that it can be recognized as special. Yearly anniversaries of zero defect software day are perfect times to rededicate to zero defect software.[11]

There are those who think zero defect software day is a time to get all employees together to sign a commitment to improve. That happens, but it is not what the day is about. Zero defect software day is coordinated with a presentation on what zero defect software is all about. Moving toward this process at Westinghouse ESG, various presentations have been conducted.

The kickoff presentation in App. D is a high-level overview of the zero defect software program. It is useful to present concepts for commitment at the higher levels and as an introduction with the software developers. The software developers need detail and extensive training in the principles and actualization of the zero defect software program.

The main points made by each chart are discussed below:

Chart 1: Zero software defects symbol

At Westinghouse ESG, the zero defect software program is specifically called "Zero Software Defects" to build upon prior programs called "No Major Defects" and "Zero Defects." The importance here is not specifically the name of the program, but that the program today is a real commitment, not just another motivation program.

An important part of the logo contains the words, "An Attitude of Excellence." These words ring out to the audience that this program focuses on excellence, which ultimately translates into zero defect software.

Chart 2: Pie chart of cost

The purpose of this chart is to explain to the audience the major benefit of the zero defect software program; and that is, a substantial cost reduction. It is proffered that only half of the total software development costs result in the actual production of the software product with zero defects. Of the remaining software development costs, 10 percent is spent on the price of prevention and an awesome 40 percent is wasted on the price of nonconformance.

In a 150,000 lines of code project costing $5 million, that translates into $2.5 million to actually build the software product, $0.5 million to pay for prevention measures, and $2 million on nonconformists.

When the zero defect software program is implemented the price of nonconformance will approach zero, but there may be an additional 10 percent as the price of prevention. This would change the pie chart to show the price of doing the software development to be 80 percent of the total cost, with the remaining 20 percent being spent on the price of prevention.

The 150,000 lines of code project would then cost $3.5 million when zero defect software is implemented, which translates into $2.8 million to actually build the software product and $0.7 million for the price of prevention.

The total cost of software development should be 30 percent less expensive with the implementation of the zero defect software program.

Chart 3: Elements of zero defect software program

These six elements listed form the outline of the rest of the presentation. They are also the key elements that make up the zero defect software program.

Chart 4: What is a customer?

Emphasis is made here on the idea of an internal customer, so that every employee knows that he or she has a "customer" to satisfy. The distinction between the internal and the external, or ultimate customer, is clearly delineated.

Because everyone has a customer, it is important that each software developer realizes that his or her work product is immediately saleable and meaningful to the next person in line. We are all in business to serve the customer.

Chart 5: Software Development Process Chart

The Software Development Process Chart (see App. A) gives the "big picture" of how to follow the phases and detailed steps of the development of software. There is a lot to do in software development, and this process chart details all of it from the perspective of the flow of a process through the office.

This particular segment of the Software Development Process Chart shows that there are source inspections and successive inspections for the computer software units (CSUs), which is indicative of these inspections occurring at this detailed level throughout the process. These types of inspections imbedded throughout the Software Development Process Chart leads to the elimination of errors before they have an opportunity to propagate.

Chart 6: Software activities checklist

The software activities checklist (see App. B) correlates directly with the Software Development Process Chart. It gives the details of the software activities for every phase of software development. Because there are so many activities to be done, they could not be fully drawn in the Software Development Process Chart; that is why the software activities checklist is needed.

This is provided to ensure that the software manager and the software developer do not forget anything. The development of scenarios for a large software system was forgotten in a project the author is familiar with. They were done, but because they were done untimely, they taxed the software development staff.

On the example in the chart, the fragment coincides with the prior fragment from the Software Development Process Chart for CSUs. The subsections under the activity column coordinate with the terminology on the Software Development Process Chart.

Chart 7: Source inspection/successive inspection

The workers themselves perform the source inspections. They ensure through the use of specific product or process checklists that their own product is correct (error-free).

The internal customer does the successive inspection. Using specific product or process checklists, the next person in the process ensures the product he or she receives is correct (error-free). When the delivery is to oneself, then the successive inspector is an independent software quality person.

These inspections imbedded in the Software Development Process Chart provide the way to achieve progressive elimination of errors during software development. The specific example on this chart is an automation of the Software Requirements Specification checklist to be used by the source inspector and/or successive inspector.

Chart 8:Checklists

Checklists, both generic and specific are the method used for the conduct of the inspections described in the prior chart.

The generic checklists provide itemized guides to many of the software products and processes and are generally available to all who want them.

The specific checklists are used for only specific software products and processes. For example, the customer may provide a computer programming standard (CPS), as shown in the picture on this chart, which must specifically be used on that computer program product.

Chart 9: Software tools (poka-yoke)

An example software tool of requirements traceability is given. This software tool is an automation method that helps eliminate the mistake of proceeding when some requirements are missed. This type of automation ensures product integrity.

Chart 10: Meet commitments

The zero defect software process is designed to allow the developers of software to meet their commitments. This meeting of commitments harkens back to Chart 1 defining the zero defect software program as an attitude of excellence.

Of importance to meeting commitments is the necessity to meet not only performance, but also the project's cost and schedule requirements.

Throughout this book, Richard Zultner's interpretation of some of Deming's fourteen points for software quality are discussed. Point 10 is of interest here. Deming says eliminate slogans, exhortations, and targets that ask for zero defects. Slogans do not build quality systems. Zultner suggests that software management should respond to worker suggestions to help improve quality. There is no substitute for knowledge of software quality development methods. Only management can change the culture and environment that dominate an individual's performance. Let the software developers put up their own signs and slogans.[12]

In the past, these targets of zero defects may have been ephemeral, but with a concrete program as proposed in this book, the reality of "how to" strive toward achieving zero defect software is provided. It is not a mere slogan, it is a target that must be achieved.

REFERENCES

1. Fink, Steven, *Crisis Management, Planning for the Inevitable,* AMACOM, New York, 1986, p. 1.
2. Guaspari, John, *Theory Why,* AMACOM, New York, Copyright © 1986, American Management Association, pp. 92–95, Reprinted by permission.
3. Burrill, Claude W. and Leon W. Ellsworth, *Quality Data Processing,* Burrill-Ellsworth Associates, Inc., Tenafly, 1982, pp. 170, 171.
4. Kagan, Jerome and Ernest Havemann, *Psychology: An Introduction,* Harcourt, Brace Jovanovich, Inc., Orlando, Copyright © 1968, pp. 88–99.
5. *Ibid.,* p. 89.
6. *Ibid.,* p. 92.
7. Weinberg, Gerald M., *The Psychology of Computing Programming,* Van Nostrand Reinhold Co., New York, 1971, p. 90.
8. Cooper, Alan D., *The Journey Toward Managing Quality Improvement,* Westinghouse Electric Corp., Orlando, 1987, pp. 41, 42.
9. Amerbach, Stuart, "U.S. Honors Three Firms for Quality," *The Washington Post,* November 15, 1988, p. D3.
10. Crosby, Philip B., *Quality is Free,* New American Library, Inc., New York, 1979, pp. 116, 117.
11. Crosby, Philip B., *Quality Without Tears,* McGraw-Hill Book Company, New York, 1984, pp. 114–116.
12. Schulmeyer, G. Gordon and Halsey B. Chenoweth, Ph.D., "The Trouble with Software Reliability," *IEEE COMPSAC Proceedings,* IEEE Press, Oct. 8–10, 1986, Copyright © 1986, IEEE, New York, p. 61, Reprinted by permission.

14

Zero Defect Software Implementation

"How use doth breed a habit in a man!"
SHAKESPEARE
The Two Gentlemen of Verona
Act V, Scene 4

There are specific elements that need to be considered in order to have a successful zero defect software program. This chapter consolidates these ideas. Options about how to portray defect and error ratios is given coverage. The software development process chart, its symbology and meaning are expanded from the initial comments about it earlier in the book. The software activities checklist relationship to the software development process chart is discussed. The importance of having all the 800+ activities necessary for large system software development listed in one place cannot be underestimated, because it is so easy to forget an element among so many.

The concepts of the internal and external customer are defined in relationship to the zero defect software program. The importance of how source inspections fit into the picture for an internal customer should not be forgotten. Then the entry/exit criteria so important to any inspection-based process is discussed.

TABLE 14.1   Software Documentation Deliveries

Delivery	Pages	Defects	Defects ratio options
1 0.05/page	1000	50	50/1000
2 0.05/page	1100	5	55/1100 or 5/1100 or 5/100
3 0.05/page	1250	10	65/1250 or 10/1250 or 10/150
4 0.07/page	1100	9	74/1100 or 9/1100 or 9/?

The checklists for the key elements of the zero defect software program are described. These include checklists for both products and activities processed along the way. The recording of data relevant to the zero defect software program and the appropriate responses to such data is covered.

There is discussion of how this program relates to incremental releases of software and the importance of consistency. The chapter concludes with how the CASE (computer-aided software engineering) environments permit the actualization of software tools into the zero defect software program.

COUNTING DEFECTS

What does one count as a defect? Essentially it is any failure or discrepancy that the customer is delivered. A further investigation of the possibilities and what they mean are elucidated here.

For a software development document, there are usually incremental deliveries to the customer, such as those shown in Table 14.1.

In Table 14.1, after each delivery, defects were found. The real choice of count for the final delivery included in possibilities shown under "defects ratio options" would be 74/1100 pages or 9/1100 pages making a difference of 0.07/page or 0.008/page. Since the customer saw all seventy-four defects, the choice made is to accumulate customer-delivered defects to seventy-four and use the final page count of the document, with a resultant defect ratio of 0.07/page, or more usually 7/100 pages. This is the preferred count as most representative of the quality of the document. The alternate is if the defects were removed between incremental deliveries and prior to final delivery, the defect ratio is 9/1100 = 0.008/page, or more usually 0.8/100 pages (final defect count to final page count).

For a new software development of any size, the code is developed and delivered incrementally (Table 14.2), where each increment has a

TABLE 14.2   Software Code Deliveries

Build	KLOC*	Defects	Defects ratio options	
1	10	50	50/10	5/KLOC
2(+5)	15	35	85/15 or 35/15 or 85/25 or 35/25	5.67/KLOC
3(+15)	30	70	155/30 or 70/30 or 155/30 or 70/55 or 155/55	5.16/KLOC
4(+10)	40	60	215/40 or 60/40 or 215/95 or 60/95	5.38/KLOC
(FQT) 5(+10)	50	25	240/50 or 25/50 or 240/145 or 25/145	4.8/KLOC
TOTALS	145	240		

*thousand lines of code

predefined functionality. These incremental deliveries have names such as *build, string,* or *block;* build is used here.

Again, in this example, after each build release to the customer, defects were found. The range of defects per KLOC for the final build from time of FQT (formal qualification test) includes 0.2, 0.5, 1.66, 4.8—quite a range. The ratio that makes the most sense is to count the defects the customer has seen (25), since FQT (Formal Qualification Test), as a ratio of total lines of code finally delivered (145K), resulted in a 0.2 defects/KLOC defect ratio for this example. The other important ratio deals with development errors/KLOC, which are those errors prior to FQT. In the example, the error ratio is 215/95, where 215 is the total number of errors made during development and 95 is the 95,000 lines of code developmentally tested. This leads to an error ratio of 2.3/KLOC.

Maybe a more interesting example involves enhancements to an existing code baseline, such shown in Table 14.3.

It seems logical to eliminate 115/30 and 115/50 because that number of defects applies to more than just the enhancements; it would include the baseline count of lines of code. Similarly, the 45/130 and 45/150 should be eliminated because the 45 defects apply only to the enhancement, not the original baseline count of lines of code. If the 115/130 or 115/150 ratio is used, that would bring the baseline into the defect ratio count which is not justified for a defect ratio on enhancements—this task. This only leaves the ratios 45/50 or 45/30 which translates to 0.9/KLOC or 1.5/KLOC. The total enhancement task involved 50KLOC, both addition and modification, so the ratio should

TABLE 14.3   Software Enhancements

	KLOC*	Defects	Defects ratio options	
BASELINE	100	70	70/100	0.7/KLOC
ENHANCEMENT: ADD	30	45	45/30 or 45/50 or 45/130 or 45/150 or 115/30 or 115/50 or 115/130 or 115/150	0.9/KLOC
MODIFY	20			
TOTAL	130 or 150	115		

*thousand lines of code

include both, resulting in 0.9 defects/KLOC. This count assures that the defect count is initiated from baseline for FQT onward. Otherwise, this would be an error ratio.

A cumulative defect count chart (Fig. 14.1) serves as an example of maintaining the defect count over the life of the delivered product. It will usually show a major amount of defects in the first year after

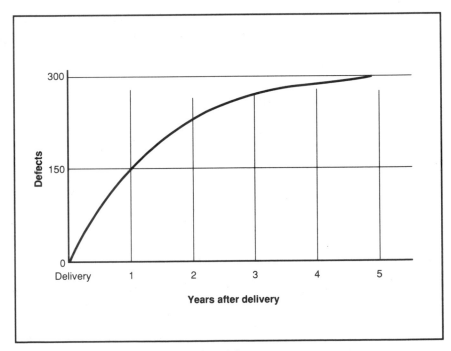

Figure 14.1   Cumulative defects after delivery.

release, with generally progressively less defects. The goal of this zero defect software program is to make the defect line coincident with the ordinate. This example shows 150 defects in year 1, 95 in year 2, 20 in year 3, 20 in year 4, and 15 in year 5, for a total of 300 defects over 5 years or 60 defects/year average.

SOFTWARE DEVELOPMENT PROCESS CHART

NASA's goal is zero defects. Flight software quality for the shuttle software is based on Mission Operations' Director Gene Krinz's philosophy that "you can't test quality into the software." He said it must be built into the design, development, and verification right from the start.

The NASA shuttle software emphasis is on early error detection using formal code inspection, audits and reviews, systematic discrepancy analysis, independent test and verification, and quality metrics and trend analysis.[1] This zero defect software thrust is an appropriate lead-in to the software development process chart.

To introduce the software development process chart (App. A) for the zero defect software program, it is necessary to define the symbology used. The symbology is modified from the procedure charting method used in value analysis primarily for forms flow,[2] and each symbol is defined on page 272. Of special mention about the symbology is that arrows flow back on the process when items are deemed OK (not acceptable). The square and the circle are used for multiple purposes in the software development process chart, and are combined to identify the major products and actions necessary for software development.

It has been shown in various company value analysis exercises that the creation of a process chart can lead to significant understanding of the process which, in turn, results in process improvement. It is a fundamental method in total quality activities also, to picture the process to achieve understanding and improvement. The software development process chart is provided for these reasons.

The flow on the Software Development Process Chart is based primarily on software development as outlined in DOD-STD-2167A, *Defense System Software Development.*

The terminology used on the Software Development Process Chart itself needs further explanation and expansion. The "review" of RFP (request for proposal), proposal, SOW (statement of work), customer standards, and internal standards should be interpreted as reading, internalizing, understanding, and note-taking from those documents. All software developers and managers are responsible to perform this "review".

The "source inspection" used throughout the Software Development Process Chart needs special emphasis and interpretation. Many parts of this book cover inspection concepts, so they are explained in detail elsewhere. The "source inspection" implies sanity checking by the generator of the document or code to check its integrity. This also takes place whenever a work product is updated, which happens frequently during software development. A method to carry out the source inspections for various activities is given later in this chapter where appropriate checklists and software tools are described. This is a keystone concept for the producer to conduct self inspection of the work product before passing the work on.

Also, whoever in the development process (the "internal customer" about whom more is said in the next section) receives this work product *must* conduct a detailed analysis of the work product (successive inspection). The receiver has a vested interest in what he or she is going to have to work with and so will be critically sure that this is a good product. Handover of interim products from one group of software developers to another offers a powerful method to ensure that planned development practices are followed.[3] So, the successive inspection called out in the Software Development Process Chart is the reuse of the checklists and software tools by someone other than the originator.

This point of handing off the product raises the question does the Software Development Process Chart move software development closer to the Japanese model of the specialized software factory. The implication being that each software developer becomes a specialist doing only one task in the software development process, and then handing off to the next specialist.

The difficulty with this specialization in the complex, embedded, real-time software development process with which the author is most familiar is that personnel would get bored; and there are too few software experts in this arena to specialize too minutely. Consequently, the Software Development Process Chart could be used in the "software factory" mode, but was not originally intended for that use.

The "quality review" noted in the Software Development Process Chart implies an independent evaluation of the product. Of course, this is after the worker has reviewed his or her own work. In Figs. 7.2 through 7.9, there are references to DOD-STD-2167A evaluation methods that would be appropriately applied at these points.

The primary responsibility rests with the systems organization to conduct the formal SRR (Software Specification Review) and SDR (System Design Review) reviews. It is up to the software development team to help with the software aspects of these reviews.

For the software formal reviews and audits, the word "internal" is used in the Software Development Process Chart. These "internal" reviews and audits are essentially dry runs of the actual formal reviews and audits so that when the real thing occurs, it will be done right. This dry run makes sure the customer sees only the results of the good work achieved thus far. The work product undergoing "internal" review has been through multiple reviews already, but not the viewgraphs explaining that work product.

Poka-yoke techniques do not show up as such in the chart. This does not imply that they should not be used. A discussion of how they could be used throughout the process is in Chap. 8, and the computer-aided software engineering (CASE) discussion concluding this chapter again emphasizes the importance of software tools to the success of a zero defect software program.

The other action words used on the Software Development Process Chart are self explanatory. Words, such as, "send to", "update", "retrieve", etc. are easily interpreted by the user of the chart. Of special importance is when there is a "not OK" condition telling the developer to go back. This implies revisiting earlier documents rather than redoing the various prior, formal, customer reviews.

The Software Development Process Chart deals with the computer program production and associated documentation. It has been noted by Dr. C. K. Cho in his various publications, that the "software" itself should be treated as a factory having inputs and producing a population of output data. By thinking this way, statistical methods may be applied to the "software" to produce a confidence level in the goodness of its output. This statistical quality control is another recommended poka-yoke method to help achieve zero defect software. In this sense, it is clear that the software development process chart is directed also to "software" (in the Cho sense) that produces a population of output data that is error free, culminating in zero defect software that is usable.[4]

SOFTWARE ACTIVITIES CHECKLIST

Using DOD-STD-2167A again as a guide and coordinating with the Software Development Process Chart, a Software Activities Checklist[5] was generated. This list is to be read in conjunction with the Software Development Process Chart to form a unified action checklist emphasizing inspections along the way.

Appendix B is the Software Activities Checklist. It purposely goes to very detailed levels because too often items are forgotten during the development pressures. Here is a technique available to help one remember all the items at each phase that need to be done.

The Software Activities Checklist provides the details behind the Software Development Process Chart. There is an indentation method used for readability. Each of the eight developmental phases are at the highest level. These eight major breakouts conform to the same eight breakouts on the Software Development Process Chart.

The next level starts to expand the activities required, but for consistency in all phases at this level, there are documentation, planning, reviews, and baselines. At this level, there are also specifics for each development phase:

Development Phase	Specific
System Requirements Analysis/Design	contract requirements
Software Requirements Analysis	software requirements
Preliminary Design	software design baseline
Detailed Design	software design baseline
Code and CSU Testing	code and test baseline
CSC Integration and Testing	test execution
CSCI Testing	formal CSCI tests
System Integration and Testing	configuration audits

The third level of indentation is the key connection point between the Software Activities Checklist and the Software Development Process Chart. The actions discussed below are shown on both of these parts of the zero defect software program to provide consistency between the two. Lower levels are given in the software activities checklist for completeness. To put all the detail on the Software Development Process Chart would have made it unreadable, and so unusable.

It is at the third level of indentation that a "O" is placed in the matrix. The "O" is for convenience if one wishes to check off the completed activity "O". The assumption is that all lower indented levels also have had their respective activity checked or performed. The actions associated with the "O" taken on the activities are:

Activity	Action
Generate	initial performance
Update	subsequent performance
Review	read, understand, ensure readiness
Source	perform a source inspection
Successive	perform a successive inspection
Quality	perform an independent quality audit
Customer	customer reviews for possible defects

To sum up this section, it should be clear that software can only be as good as the process that produces it. The software development process must start with an understanding of the users' needs. The most effective tools and techniques must be used and upgraded regularly. Effective feedback is required and should come from (1) inspection of specific work products, (2) analysis of the results from each development phase, and (3) measurement of the users' satisfaction with the software product.[6] The thrust of the Software Development Process Chart and the related Software Activities Checklist is on items 1 and 2, with item 3 returning a 100 percent.

DEFINING THE CUSTOMER

Customer satisfaction must be considered from two viewpoints. First from the viewpoint of the ultimate customer who is paying for the product or service; second, from the viewpoint of the internal customer (the next person in the chain of operations within an organization). Both must be satisfied for successful quality improvement.

The three major points to improve employee involvement with the ultimate customer are: (1) that every customer contact should be a quality interface, (2) responsiveness to the customer is important, and (3) customers are involved in activities (for example, design reviews) related to their work. Not only do these improve employee involvement, but they also help to build a team approach that results in openness and trust.

The concepts applied to the ultimate customer also apply to the internal customer—the next person in the process. Meeting the internal customer's requirements completely and timely usually contributes to the ultimate customer's satisfaction. Infrequently there is a conflict, and when that occurs, the ultimate customer must come first.

Everyone has customers and success comes from satisfying those customers. This is achieved by meeting customer expectations, which, of course, is meeting requirements. Customer satisfaction is an integral part of any quality improvement process. Goals, objectives, and action plans for internal and ultimate customer satisfaction must be established, measured, and managed.[7]

Successful companies are customer oriented. They work to please customers because *only customers can define quality*. Most companies in the United States are share-price oriented; they work to please the equity market—not the customers. For software, this may be changed when the educated customer demands a warranty on the software.

In order to be truly customer-oriented, every worker must find out what the next person in line needs in order to do a good job and, then, must provide it. In a well-managed business, each employee considers the next person in line as the customer (the internal customer) and works to help him or her to do a better job.[8] This is a vital concept in the Software Development Process Chart that can lead to zero defects software.

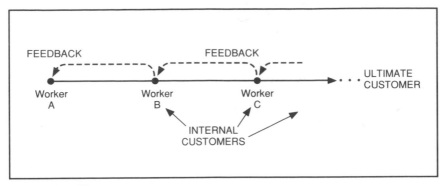

Figure 14.2   The customers.

Customer satisfaction is the core of the quality revolution. Every person on a production line is the customer of the preceding operation (called the internal customer above), so each worker's goal is to make sure that the quality of his work meets the requirements of the next person (Fig. 14.2). When that happens throughout the organization, the satisfaction of the ultimate customer should be assured. Realizing that they have a customer,[9] was a revolutionary concept to some workers.

Every worker and every team of workers must understand that it is both producer and customer. Each must receive and deliver products and services with no errors at each stage of the process until they reach the ultimate customer. Perfection is the goal.[10] This is a fundamental concept of the zero defect software program, as shown in the Software Development Process Chart, with its emphasis on source inspections.

ENTRY/EXIT CRITERIA

The inspection process used in the zero defect software program is verification that a product meets requirements. A source inspection is a 100 percent inspection of the work performed by the person doing the work. A successive inspection is a 100 percent inspection of the work performed in the prior task by the next person in the process. If the user (the next person in the process) is the same as the person doing the work, then the software quality person performs the successive inspection. The successive inspection can be a look at the objective evidence of the source inspection when that is appropriate.

When software tools are used in the zero defect software process, there is no need to be repetitious in a successive inspection of re-executing the tool. Instead, only a check that the tool was run is neces-

TABLE 14.4   Entry/Exit criteria

Elements	Entry criteria	Exit criteria

Requirements	a. Applicable documents from customer
	b. Dry run package for Systems Requirements Review (SRR)
		a. Place documents under control
		b. Complete checklist
		  ▪ all (source inspections)
		  ▪ review the checklist (successive inspection)
		c. Action items closed from SRR

Design	a. Applicable documents from requirements
	b. Dry run package for Preliminary and Critical Design Reviews (PDR, CDR)
	c. Evidence of prior (successive) inspection
		a. Place documents under control
		b. Complete checklist
		  ▪ all (source inspections)
		  ▪ review the checklist (successive inspections)
		c. Action items closed from PDR and CDR

Code	a. Applicable documents from design
	b. Source code
	c. Evidence of prior (successive) inspection
		a. Place code under control
		b. Complete checklist
		  ▪ all (source inspection)
		  ▪ review the checklist (successive inspection)
		c. Code Walkthroughs

Test	a. Compiled code
	b. Applicable test documents
	c. Evidence of prior (successive) inspection
	d. Test Readiness Review (for formal tests)
		a. Place test results under control
		b. Complete checklist
		  ▪ all (source inspections)
		  ▪ review the checklist (successive inspection)

Documentation	a. Draft document
	  ▪ typed
	  ▪ All sections
	b. Evidence of prior (successive) inspection—for updated documents
		a. Place documents under control
		b. Complete checklist
		  ▪ all (source inspections)
		  ▪ review the checklist (successive inspections)

Management visibility	a. Charts of development progress*
	b. Evidence of management reaction
		a. Place charts under management control
		b. Complete checklist
		  ▪ all (source inspection)
		  ▪ review the checklist (successive inspections)

Timing & sizing	a. Allocations of initial estimates
	b. Actuals
	c. Evidence of prior (successive) inspections
		a. Place T & S values under control
		b. Complete checklist
		  ▪ all (source inspections)
		  ▪ review the checklist (successive inspections)

* Defined in Software Activities Checklist (App. B)

TABLE 14.4   Entry/Exit criteria *(Continued)*

Elements	Entry criteria	Exit criteria
Configuration management	a. Identification of code unit or document b. For correction or update, a written record has been made	a. Release approved by SCCB b. A working system can be constructed from code units c. Correction or update adequately tested
Software Development File (SDF)	a. Source inspect before placing anything into SDF	a. Successive inspect before using anything retrieved from SDF
Reviews	a. Dry run package for formal reviews b. Dry run package for formal audits c. Prepare packages for peer inspections/walkthroughs	a. Complete checklist • all (source inspections) • review the checklist (successive inspections)

sary. Throughout the entire inspection process, it is the responsibility of software quality to ensure the integrity of the inspections.

Ten activities relevant to the zero defect software program are highlighted in Table 14.4. The entry criteria are applied to the zero defect software program (inspections and software tools) but not to the entry to that phase or element of software development. Similarly, the exit criteria given are for that phase or element to move forward in the zero defect software program.

The checklist referred to in the exit criteria of Table 14.4 are zero-defect-software-program specific and are covered for each element in the next section.

It is important for each element that closure be achieved. Conforming to the exit criteria helps to ensure that closure. But, someone must ensure that the steps leading to closure were done. It is the job of the software quality person to certify that the steps required have been completed. A simplified diagram (Fig. 14.3) of that process is given.

ZERO DEFECT SOFTWARE CHECKLISTS

The elements in Table 14.4 have a checklist associated with most of them. A documentation checklist specific to a Software Requirements Specification is included in App. E. This checklist is designed for use in the Westinghouse ESG software development environment, but is indicative of the detail required in such a checklist. The building of these checklists is a major activity necessary to make a zero defect software program successful in your environment. In this section, the checklists for each of those elements in Table 14.4 are elaborated upon.

There is a generic checklist that applies to all elements that use a checklist. The generic checklist includes the standards and procedures in the Software Development Plan (SDP) and traceability/flowdown of requirements for completeness and testability. If the project is government sponsored, it most likely will have DOD-STD-2167A which contains checklists that should be included as part of the generics. If your company has its own software development and/or software quality standards, they become part of generic checklist. So in summary, the generic checklist includes:

- Standards in SDP
- Traceability/Flowdown
- DOD-STD-2167A Checklists
- Company Standards

Table 14.5 gives the same elements as were given in Table 14.4, but in this case, the zero defect software checklist and related activities are provided along with a list of specific software tools (poka-yoke) for that element. It is through doing the inspections and poka-yoke that successful closure is accomplished for that element.

Some of the elements in Table 14.5 require special discussion of how

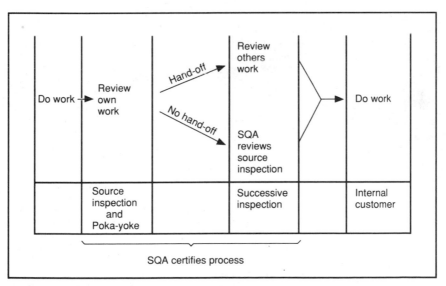

Figure 14.3 SQA certification.

TABLE 14.5   Zero defect software checklists

Element	Checklists	Tools (poka-yoke)
Requirements	a. Generics b. Hardware/Test bench Facilities checklists	a. Requirements tracking b. Templates for documents c. Structure analysis d. Data Flow Diagram (DFD) e. Data Dictionary (DD) f. Input, Processing, Output (IPO)
Design	a. Generics b. Coupling checklist c. Cohesion checklist	a. Requirements tracking b. Templates for documents c. PDL (Program Design Language) checker d. Hierarchy (CALL/CALLED) tree automation e. Automatic sizing from PDL f. Global software SYSGEN g. Flow diagram
Code	a. Generics	a. Requirements tracking b. Templates for code c. Compiler, assembler, linker d. Pretty printer e. Standards checker f. Automated sizing g. Automated line of code (LOC) counter h. Language sensitive editor
Test	a. Generics for CSU b. Generics for CSC c. Generics for CSCI/FQT—Dry run(s)	a. Requirements testability b. Templates for documents c. Cyclomatic complexity measurement d. Path analysis identification e. Unit test tool f. Automated systems test tool g. Automated test setup h. Simulators/emulators i. Test drivers j. Subsystem emulators
Documentation	a. Generics b. Use DID (Data Item Description) for table of contents—if contractually required c. Grammar correctness	a. Requirements traceability through documents b. Templates for documents c. Available "boilerplate" d. Spell checker and dictionary

TABLE 14.5   Zero defect software checklists *(Continued)*

Element	Checklists	Tools (poka-yoke)

Documentation *(Continued)*	d. Use MIL-STD-490 (Specification Practices)—if contractually required	e. Word Processing
		f. Grammar checker
		g. Automated generation of:
		    PDL—Program Design Language
		    DFD—Data Flow Diagram
		    DD—Data Dictionary
		    DBDD—Data Base Design Document
		    SDD (sections)—Software Design Document
		    IDD—Interface Design Document
		    Flow Diagram

Management visibility	a. Software activities list in App. C b. Use AFSCP 800-43—if contractually required c. Check accuracy of data	a. Automate chart generation for a and b b. PERT or CPM charts c. Page & line progress counts

Timing & sizing	a. Standards in SDP
	b. Software activities list in App. C
	c. Consider:
	    ▪ disk access time
	    ▪ interdependencies of tasks
	    ▪ latencies in system
		a. Trend analysis/extrapolation
		b. Automated page & line updates
		c. Automated execution time recording
		d. Automated sizing recording
		e. Logic analyzer/Timing analyzer
		f. Line of code (LOC) counter
		g. SLAM or similar timing & sizing models

Configuration management	a. Standards in SDP b. Standards in company manuals c. Use MIL-STD-483—if contractually required	a. Automated configuration control
Software Development File (SDF)	a. Generics	a. Requirements flowdown b. Automate the file entry and retrieval
Reviews	a. Generics b. MIL-STD-1521B—if contractually required c. Design, code, and walkthroughs or inspection list activities	a. Automated presentation material

to handle them. Management visibility must start with the individual software leads. It is at this lowest level of the projects' management that the most accurate data is collected. The source inspection using the checklists and tools of Table 14.5 is logically performed by that software lead. The successive inspection of management visibility could be done by the CSCI (Computer Software Configuration Item) manager on very large projects or by the software project managers.

On large government projects, there are periodic program management reviews (PMRs) where software visibility is discussed. The flow of software management visibility information for a PMR is from the software project manager to the project manager and other company management, then a quality review of the data through a dry run of the PMR material.

Timing and sizing shown in Table 14.5 moves through phases of crude estimates to actual measurements. This flow is traced as part of the management visibility package. In the initial requirements stage, sizing is based upon the lines of code estimates. Software timing is typically the product of number of instructions and execution time per instruction. The system timing is determined using the time slice diagram. As development progresses into design, use the methods described for requirements, plus use the PDL (program design language). For sizing, the expansion rate of the PDL is used. For timing where the PDL is executable, it should be executed with a timing analyzer.

At the coding stage to determine memory sizing, use the data from requirements and design plus the count of the actual code. For timing, the software should be executed with a timing analyzer. Finally, when in test, timing the software should be executed with maximum data rates to stress the system.

The configuration management process is an interesting activity to describe for the zero defect software program. Figure 14.4 pictorially displays this process with software quality playing an integral part. The main points of configuration management in relation to this program are the release concept and the change control (error handling) process.

The steps to be considered before a formal or informal release can be made are:

1. All units must be identified.

2. All prerequisite testing and SDF (software development file) actions must be completed for each unit.

3. SCCB must approve release.

4. The units must be consistent and clear so that a working software system may be developed.

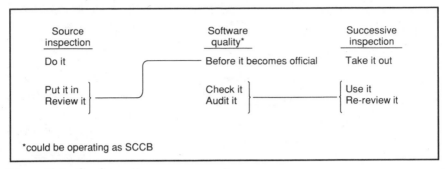

Figure 14.4 Configuration management process.

5. The scope of a change must be identified in a connectivity matrix so all affected units are covered.

The error identification is done through the use of problem reports. So the problem report activities are:

1. In writing the problem report, follow all the correct procedures.
2. Do a self-inspection of step 1.
3. The SCCB does a quality inspection of the problem report.
4. Worker performs correction of problem and fills in appropriate part of problem report. This is a successive inspection of the problem report.
5. The worker performing the correction completes the problem report.
6. Configuration personnel inspect the finished form for completion.
7. Software quality ensures the testing of the correction of the problem.
8. The SCCB signs off the problem report as closed.

The final special situation from Table 14.5 concerns the SDF (software development file). Before any item is placed into the SDF, a source inspection is required. The type of inspection is dependent on what item is being placed into the SDF. This inspection comes from the normal flow of the zero defect software process. Before using anything retrieved from the SDF, a successive inspection is required. Again, the type of inspection depends on the item that is being retrieved from the SDF. While in the SDF, the software quality person would inspect the material using the appropriate checklists and/or tools. This process is diagrammed in Fig. 14.5.

The double boxed item in Fig. 14.5 contains special case situations. For TRR (test readiness review), it is required to place on the table

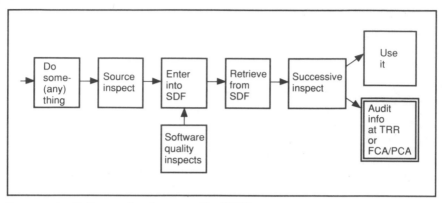

Figure 14.5   Software development file (SDF) process.

proof of the informal testing. That proof is contained in the SDF and is placed on the table for the TRR. For the FCA/PCA (Functional Configuration Audit/Physical Configuration Audit), the test and documents information must be placed on the table. Test report and documentation information is retrieved and made available for customer review at FCA/PCA.

INCREMENTAL RELEASES

Incremental releases, called "builds" previously, need some special commentary. It has been reported[11] that in several projects over half of the reported errors occurred during redesigns. Redesigns occur frequently after a build release because some problem is uncovered resulting in that redesign. During the redesign, the review mechanisms were typically not in place to ensure quality.

A software defect in a newly released air traffic control program used by the Boston Air Route Traffic Control Center (ARTCC) caused delays up to an hour for more than fifty flights on the East Coast. The new release (.1) replaced the earlier (.0) version. The defect discovered was in the code written to adapt the program for use in the Boston Center airspace. Updating software is a process of continual evolution, with the local adaptations to core programs being changed every fifty-six days to accommodate the current status of airways and navigation aids.[12]

Although not builds in the classical sense for a developmental environment, these regular releases contain similar indicia. Like the builds, the releases require a discipline of reinstituting the zero defect software process. These enhancements (additions, modifications) require the same detail as the original development.

CASE CONSIDERATIONS

CASE (computer-aided software engineering) consists of software tools tightly integrated throughout the software development process. Major elements include an object management system (OMS), a configuration management system (CMS), and a program management system (PMS). A key feature of CASE is that items captured early during development are available for use and evaluation later in the process.

The OMS will support any of the zero software defect tools mentioned in Table 14.2. Importantly, it is through the OMS that the user is able to interface with the zero defect software tools. It is the basic layer of a CASE system.

The CMS provides an automated method for proper document control. The handoff for reviews and inspections are controlled through the CMS. Also, all code controls are through the CMS.

The PMS provides the vehicle for management visibility. The project statistics are maintained through the PMS. In the zero defect software program, special emphasis is placed on error counts and related problem resolutions.

REFERENCES

1. Doherty, Richard, "The Shuttle's Software—NASA goal: software with zero defects," *Electronics Engineering Times,* Issue # 503, September 12, 1988, CMP Publications Inc., Manhasset, NY, Copyright © 1988, p. 88, Reprinted by permission.
2. Graham, Jr., Ben S., "Procedure Charting," prepared for Ben S. Graham Conferences, Copyright © 1977.
3. Dunn, Robert H., "The Quest for Software Reliability," in *Handbook of Software Quality Assurance,* G. Gordon Schulmeyer and James I. McManus, eds., Van Nostrand Reinhold Co. Inc., New York, 1987, p. 354.
4. Schulmeyer, G. Gordon, "Directions Toward Zero Software Defects," Proceedings of Software Quality Assurance, National Institute of Software Quality & Productivity, April 1988, p. 14.
5. Holden, James J., III, Westinghouse ESG software activities checklist, November 1987.
6. Zultner, Richard, "The Deming Approach to Software Quality Engineering," *Quality Progress,* vol. XXI, no. 11, November 1988, American Society for Quality Control, Inc., Milwaukee, WI, Copyright © 1988, p. 58, Reprinted by permission.
7. Cooper, Alan D., *The Journey Toward Managing Quality Improvement,* Westinghouse Electric Corp., Orlando, 1987, pp. 13–16.
8. Tribus, Myron, "The Quality Imperative," *The Bent of Tau Beta Pi,* vol. LXXVIII, no. 2, Spring 1987, p. 26.
9. "The Push for Quality" *Business Week,* No. 3002, June 8, 1987, McGraw-Hill, Inc., NY, p. 135.
10. Stuelpnagel, Thomas R., "Improved U.S. Defense, Total Quality Control," *National Defense,* vol. LXXIII, no. 438, May/June 1988, American Defense Preparedness Association, Arlington, VA, Copyright © 1988, p. 43, Reprinted by permission.
11. Grady, Robert B., and Deborah L. Caswell, *Software Metrics: Establishing a Company-Wide Program,* Prentice Hall, Inc., Englewood Cliffs, NJ, Copyright © 1987, p. 127, Adapted by permission.
12. "Boston ATC Center Software Error Causes East Coast Delays," Courtesy *Aviation Week & Space Technology,* vol. 129, no. 8, August 22, 1988, Copyright © 1988, McGraw-Hill, Inc., NY, All rights reserved, p. 107.

Expected Benefits

*"They say, best men are moulded out of faults,
And, for the most, become much more than better
For being a little bad"*
SHAKESPEARE
Measure for Measure, Act V, Scene 1

There are various socioeconomic benefits that accrue to a successful zero defect software program. This chapter centers on those various aspects beginning with the product, i.e., a software product that is defect free.

Some thoughts about the process and its benefits are discussed. The zero defect software process focuses the software development community on something the Japanese are very familiar with; viz., constantly improve the process.

A look at the cost versus benefits and, consequently, the payoff is covered. That payoff can translate into big money considering the size of the software development costs throughout the world.

Management benefits that accrue because of the zero defect software process include the reduction in the number of software managers that may be required. It may also provide expert knowledge allowing the use of less-knowledgeable software managers.

Employee benefits for the use of the zero defect software program are given. Especially pointed out is the return to pride in work, as well as returning a needed discipline to the software development process.

The chapter concludes with the all-important customer satisfaction. The notion that the customer deserves and expects software with zero defects.

THE PRODUCT

It was pointed out that we did not want to lose sight of the product by giving too much emphasis on the process. But it is only through controlled process that we achieve a correct product. After all, as already pointed out, the customer is not buying the process, nor the software itself, but the results (the output) that the software produces.

The goal of the zero defect software program is to produce a product that provides correct, usable output that the customer wants. So, an important element of the process is to adhere to requirements and then to produce a product that meets the requirements of the customer, which implies without defects.

THE PROCESS

Here, reference to the process means the zero defect software process. A major point I noticed as a former software quality manager was that software developers lacked discipline in following an engineering development process. The zero defect software process brings the discipline into the development of software. A key reason is that it involves the developer back into the process through the various inspections.

One of Deming's fourteen points for quality is to improve constantly. Applied to the software development process, it means never let it remain static, but constantly improve quality and productivity, thereby decreasing the development time and cost of the system. Improving quality is not a onetime effort, but everyone must constantly try to improve. This means the software development methodology, standards, and practices must be constantly revised[1], such as with the zero defect software program.

COST/BENEFIT ANALYSIS

Any costs incurred because something is not right the first time is the cost of poor quality. The costs can be categorized in four areas: prevention, appraisal, internal failure, and external failure.

Prevention costs include all activities for preventing nonconformities in systems, included are items such as, training and support materials (standards, job aids, etc.). The price of this book and its subsequent training program would be a prevention cost.

Appraisal costs include evaluation and auditing for conformance to standards, included are items such as, inspections, reviews, and walk-throughs. The zero defect software process increases the appraisal costs of a software development substantially through source and successive inspections.

Internal failure costs are the costs associated with the fixing of the software before the customer sees it. There will be a heightened consciousness about this with all the inspections taking place. It will result in higher costs for this activity, at least initially, until the errors are reduced through heightened quality consciousness.

External failure costs are the costs for fixing the software that is in production use, but excludes any enhancements to the software. With a successful zero defect software program where the customer receives zero defects, there should be no external failure costs.[2]

Considering that three of four of the cost components of quality cost rise with a zero defect software program, what then is the benefit? It turns out that the external failure costs can easily cost 100 times more than what it costs to correct the software in the earlier phases. So those external failure costs far outweigh the other, earlier costs of quality.

Would you invest the cost of setting up the zero defect software process to achieve a 10 percent savings in your overall software development costs? How about a 20 percent savings? Or, maybe a 30 percent to 40 percent savings? That translates into having a $3 million software development costing between $1.8 million and $2.7 million when using the zero defect software process.

A related cost benefit is that with greater emphasis on doing the job right the first time, less time will be spent on rework. That reduced rework will result in increased productivity for the software developer. Rework in the factory has been identified as 20 percent of the cost of production. For software development, rework costs are most likely similar. So much is done over so frequently that one tends to think that is the way it should be done. It is the wrong way to develop software.

MANAGEMENT BENEFITS

There is a lack of management talent available in software development. It shows by the inability of many software products to meet their performance, cost, and/or schedule requirements. The earlier discussions about the software crisis stem from this lack of software management personnel.

The zero defect software program has within it the expert knowledge base that helps prevent software developers from forgetting what needs to be done. With the various elements of the zero defect software program the detailed pieces are there and only need to be used.

A step that needs to be taken soon is an automation of the entire process. This automation would tie the elements together under a relational database system. When this is accomplished the inspections can act as automatic monitors that stop the process from continuing until the inspection is successful.

With an automated zero defect software process in place, the number of software managers may be reduced because the process will automatically perform some of their functions. Also, the knowledge-level of the software managers may be less than is required today with the expert knowledge built into the automated zero defect software process.

EMPLOYEE BENEFITS

It is clear that workers take pride in their work. That extra visibility they receive, such as in the Hawthorne effect, results in workers working better. The visibility the worker receives in the zero defect software program renews that pride in work. Each element of the process gets an inspection by the worker who produced the product. This allows the worker to make sure that his or her work is correct before passing it on. It is a content employee who knows that the job was well done.

Too many companies allow employees to sink or swim on the job. Some superior companies do superior training for their employees—IBM Corporation comes to mind. Those employees who do software development must be trained or taught how the company develops software. It is largely because of this lack of training attention that I made previous observations that software developers lack discipline. They do not know the discipline of software development—it was never taught to them!

It is through the zero defect software process that a discipline is established or overlaid on a company's environment for software development. With this methodology in place the software developer can again be assured of pride in a job well done.

CUSTOMER SATISFACTION

It is appropriate that this book ends with a focus on the customer. Throughout the book much was said about the importance of the customer. It is for the customer that the software is being developed, so without the customer, it is meaningless.

In some of the earlier chapters, the concept is supplied that there is always another defect left in the delivered software. This supports the attitude of software providers who deliver known defect(s) to the customer. These points come directly to the heart of the opinion that any sizable software with zero defects is impossible.

Today, a software defect may easily cause death, injury, or other disaster, such as financial ruin. The damage wrought by a returned sale—a software defect—is so great now that it cannot be tolerated. An attitude of delivering known defect(s) to the customer is no longer acceptable. The direction to turn to get there is by implementation of the zero defect software process.

In business, we are continually concerned with our customer image, and for software, the way to heighten our customer image is to deliver software with zero defects.

REFERENCES

1. Zultner, Richard, "The Deming Approach to Software Quality Engineering," *Quality Progress,* vol. XXI, no. 11, November 1988, American Society for Quality Control, Inc., Milwaukee, WI, Copyright © 1988, p. 60, Reprinted by permission.
2. *Ibid.,* pp. 59, 60.

Software Development
Process Chart

A.1   Symbol Definitions

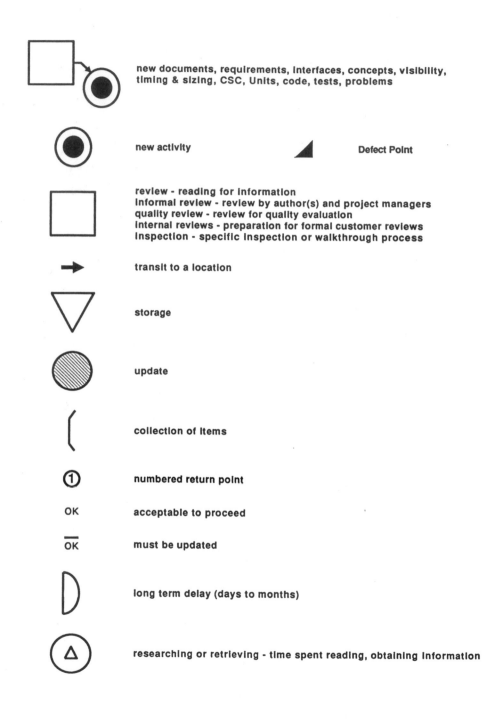

new documents, requirements, interfaces, concepts, visibility, timing & sizing, CSC, Units, code, tests, problems

new activity   Defect Point

review - reading for information
informal review - review by author(s) and project managers
quality review - review for quality evaluation
internal reviews - preparation for formal customer reviews
inspection - specific inspection or walkthrough process

transit to a location

storage

update

collection of items

numbered return point

OK   acceptable to proceed

$\overline{OK}$ must be updated

long term delay (days to months)

researching or retrieving - time spent reading, obtaining information

A.2   Software Development Process Chart

System Requirements Analysis/Design

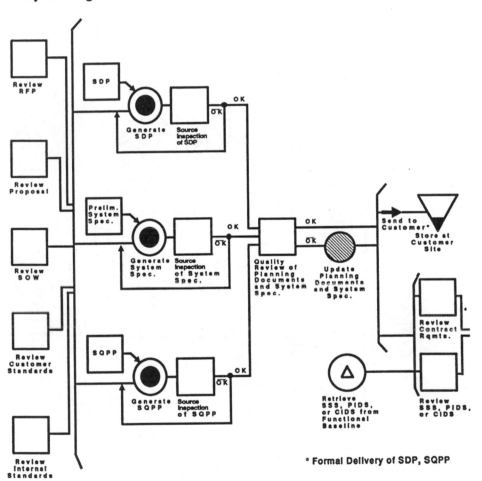

° Formal Delivery of SDP, SQPP

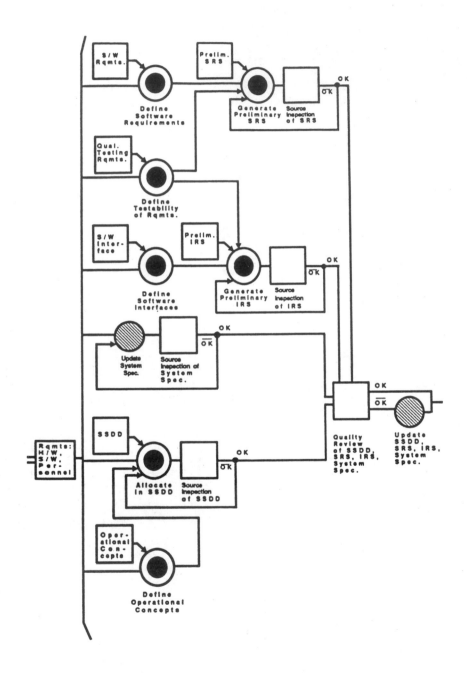

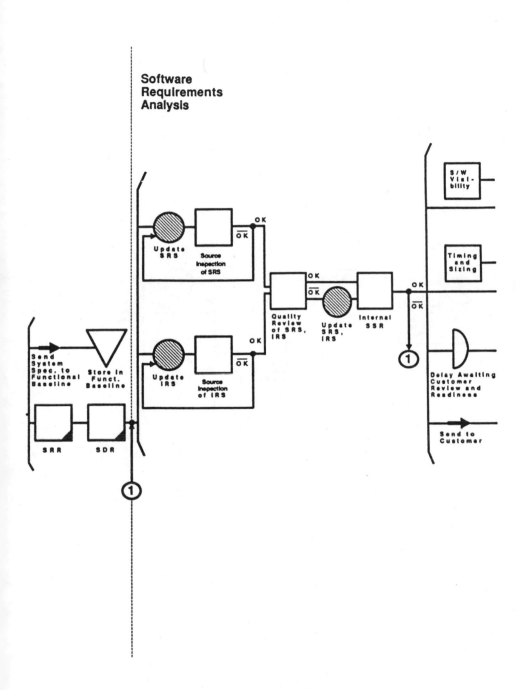

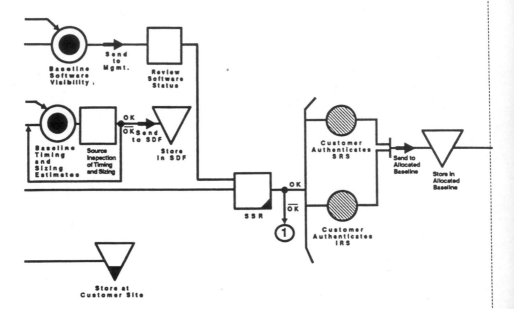

**Preliminary
Design**

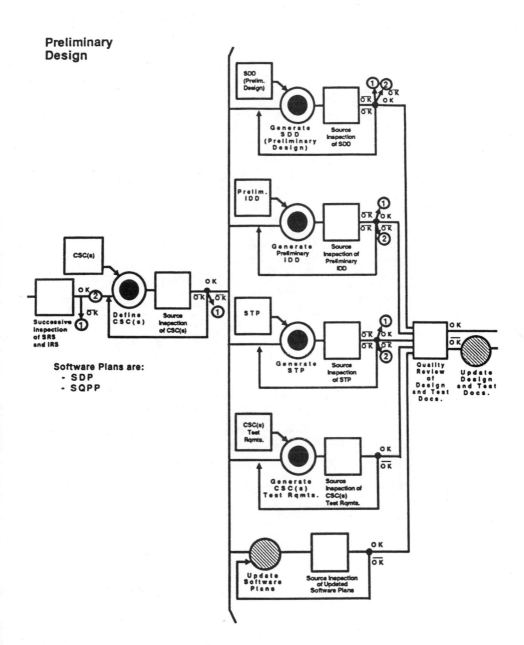

Software Plans are:
- SDP
- SQPP

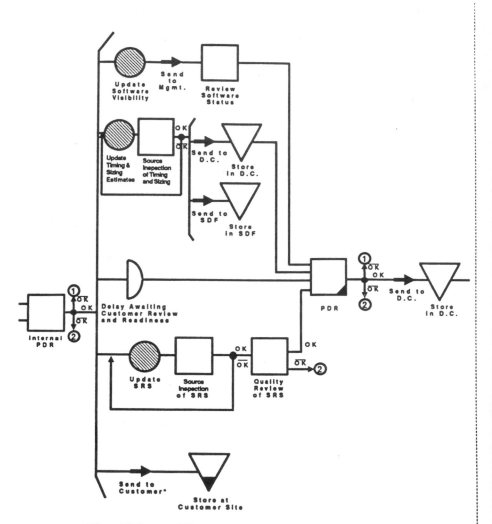

* Formal Delivery of STP and Preliminary SDD and IDD

Detailed Design

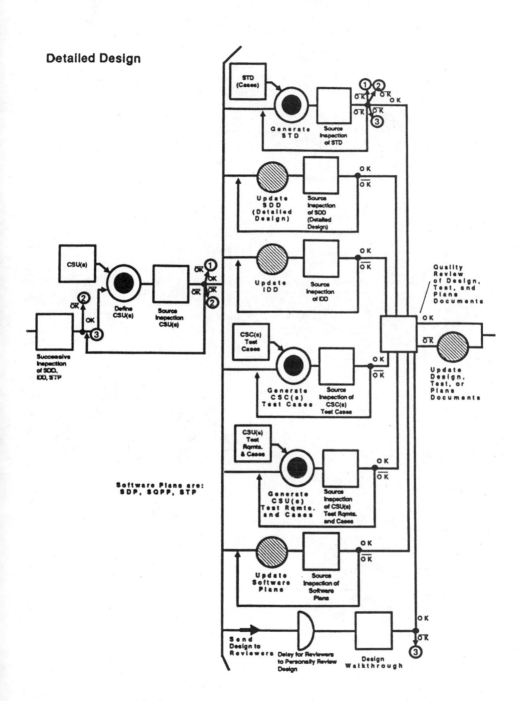

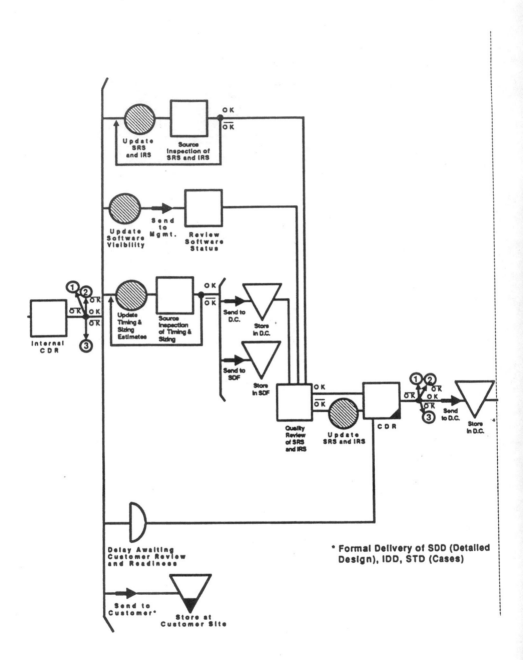

* Formal Delivery of SDD (Detailed Design), IDD, STD (Cases)

Coding and CSU Testing

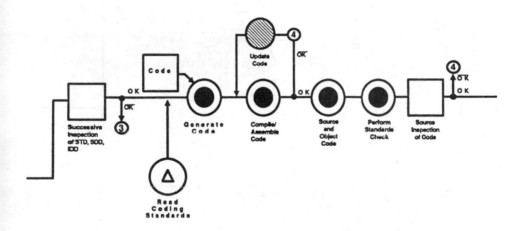

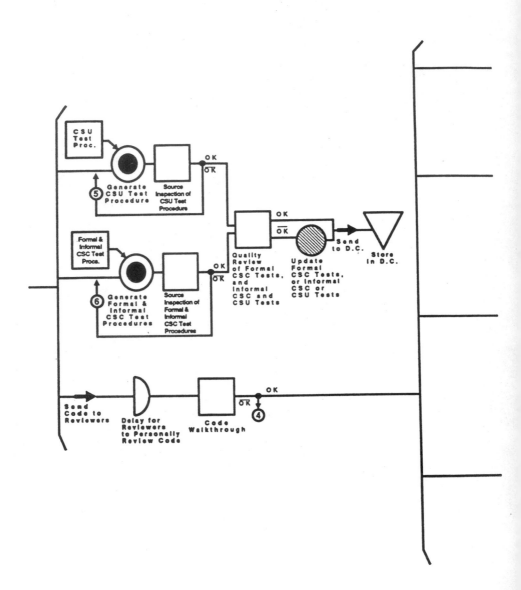

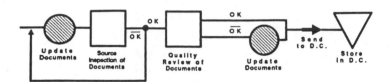

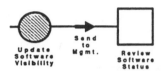

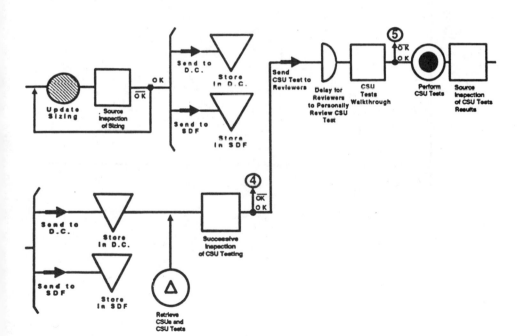

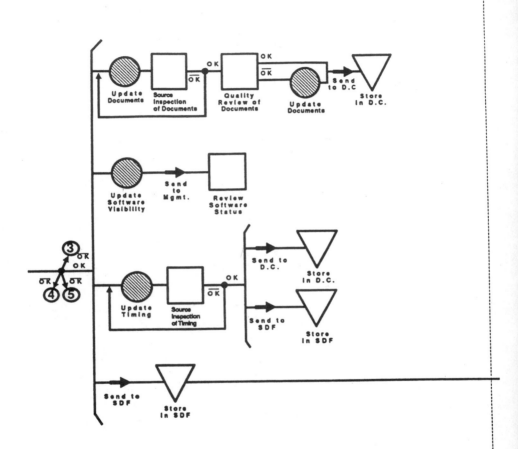

CSC Integration
and Testing

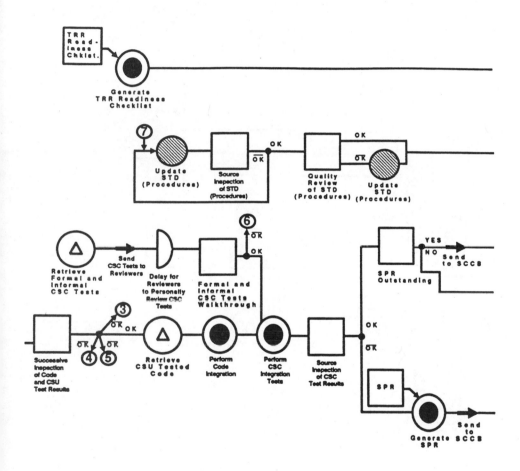

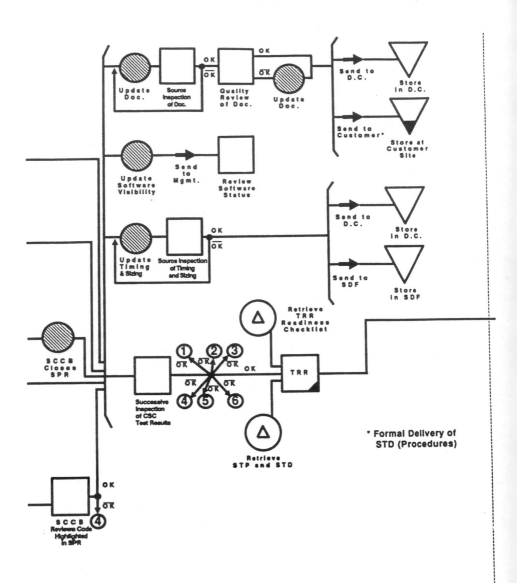

* Formal Delivery of
STD (Procedures)

CSCI Testing

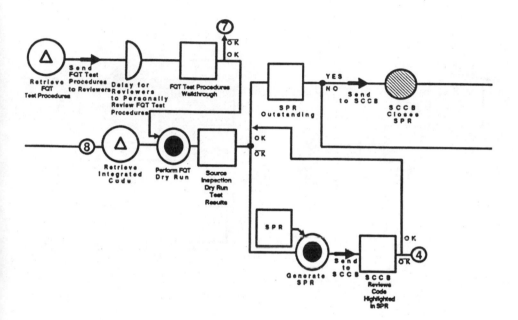

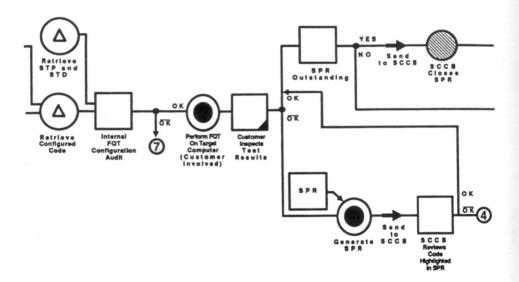

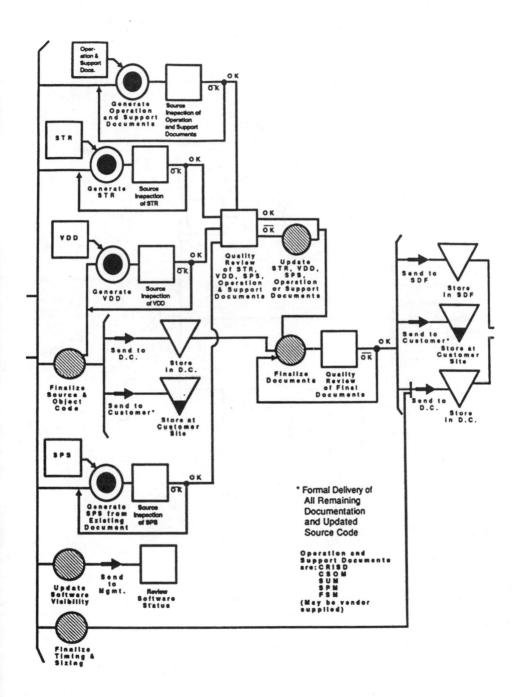

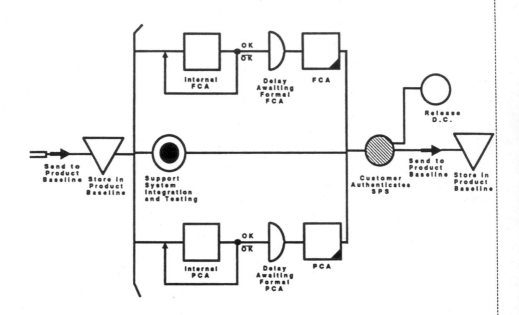

Software Activities Checklist

Zero Software Defects Software Activities Checklist

	Activity	Inspection
Activity Description	Generate / Update / Review / Source	Successive / Quality / Customer

System Requirements Analysis/Design

Contract Requirements

Internal & Customer Standards ————————————O————————————————
  Software Development
  Standards
    Requirements Definition Standards
    Design Flowdown
    Test Flowdown
    Enumeration of Requirements
    Matrices and Crossreference
    Design Standards
    Design Methodology
      Object Oriented
      Linear
      Top-Down
      Cohesion
      Coupling
    Design Representation
      Program Design Language (PDL)
        Constructs
        Form and Format
        Level of Detail
      Database
      Critical Timing and Interrupts
    Hierarchical Representation
    Coding Standards
    Banners
    Size of Units
    Form and Format
    Indentation
    Nesting Levels
    Naming Conventions
    Level of Commenting
  Testing Standards
    Unit Testing
    Methodology
      Statistical Quality Control
      Cyclomatic Complexity
      Path Analysis
      Executable Line Testing
      Boundary Checking
      Out of Bounds Verification
    Automation
    Repeatability
    Database

Zero Software Defects Software Activities Checklist *(Continued)*

Activity Description	Generate	Update	Review	Source	Successive	Quality	Customer
		Activity			Inspection		

Component Level Testing
  Methodology
    Task Oriented
    Functional Composition
    Incremental Interface
  Automation
    Repeatability
    Database
End-Item Level Testing
  Methodology
    Inspection
    Analysis
    Demonstration
    Test
  Formal Testing
    Procedure Form and Format
    Testing Type
      Engineering
      Computer Program Test & Evaluation (CPT&E)
      Preliminary Qualification Test (PQT)
      Formal Qualification Test (FQT)
      System Test & Evaluation (ST&E)
      Installation & Checkout (I&CO)
  Test Tools and Database
    Certification
    Configuration
    Structure
    Data Injection Method
Procedures
 Requirements Procedures
  Reviews and Audits
    Attendees
    Notification
    Presentation
    Action Items and Closure
    Sign-off
  Inspections
    Checklists
    Audit Trail
    Sign-off
 Design Procedures
    Attendees
    Notification
    Presentation
    Action Items and Closure
    Sign-off
  Inspections

Zero Software Defects Software Activities Checklist *(Continued)*

	Activity			Inspection		
Activity Description	Generate	Update	Review	Source	Successive	Quality	Customer
Checklists							
Audit Trail							
Sign-off							
Administrative							
PDL Statement Accounting							
Automation of Timing & Sizing							
Coding Procedures							
Reviews and Audits							
Attendees							
Notification							
Presentation							
Action Items and Closure							
Sign-off							
Inspections							
Checklists							
Automated Auditors							
Audit Trail							
Sign-off							
Files and Structures							
File Names							
Compilation/Assembly Instructions							
Job Control Stream							
Automatic Generation							
Authorization							
Administrative							
Lines-of-Code Accounting							
Automation of Timing & Sizing							
Software Configuration Management							
Library Controls							
Documentation Controls							
Source/Executable Controls							
Configuration Management Systems							
Automated Access Control							
Privilege							
Verification							
Vault System							
Storage Media							
Drawing Number System							
Software Quality							
Audits							
Frequency							
Coverage							
Accountability							
Documentation Reviews							
Acceptance Criteria							
Release to Customer							
Procedures							

Zero Software Defects Software Activities Checklist *(Continued)*

	Activity			Inspection		
Activity Description	Generate	Update	Review	Source	Successive	Quality	Customer

Checklists
  Role in Inspection Process
Software Documentation
 Deliverable End Items
 Form and Format
 Internal Notebooks
  Design
  Test
 Review and Approval
  Sign-off Responsibility
  Number of Reviews
  Source Inspections
   Checklists
   Objective Evidence
  Successive Inspections
   Checklists
   Objective Evidence
Statement of Work (SOW) ———————————————O————————————
 Task Definitions
 Contractual Clauses
  Overtime
  Acquisition of Material
  Lease vs Buy Requirements
 Schedule for Performance of Tasks
  Critical Program Milestones
  Lead Time for Reviews
 Deliverable End Items
  Review and Approval
  Cycle Times for Customer Reviews
 Number of Copies of Deliverable
 Shipping and Packing Requirements
  Media for Delivery
  Markings and Labeling
 Work Breakdown Structure
 Contract Type
  Firm Fixed Price
  Fixed Price Incentive Price
  Cost Plus
  Time and Materials
 Administration/Program Control
  Management Indicators
   Required Metrics
   Reporting Format
  Meetings and Design Reviews
   Number of Technical Interchange Meetings
   Number and Type of Formal Reviews
  Program Management Controls

Zero Software Defects Software Activities Checklist *(Continued)*

Activity Description	Generate	Update	Review	Source	Successive	Quality	Customer
Cost/Schedule Control							
Level of Accountability							
Mechanism for Cost Performance Tracking							
Mechanism for Schedule Performance Tracking							
Status Reporting							
Request for Proposal				O			
Requirements Document/Systems Specification				O			
Top-Level Performance Requirements							
Top-Level Requirements							
Inspection							
Analysis							
Demonstration							
Test							
Recording and Formality							
Level of Sell-off of Requirements							
Database							
Scenarios							
Drivers							
Timing & Sizing Envelopes							
Proposal				O			
Cost Rationale for Basis of Work Effort							
Technical Trade-offs and Design Decisions							
Operational Concepts							
Operability and Maintainability							
User System Interface							
System Safety Requirements							
Documentation							
Software Development Plan (SDP)	O			O	O	O	
System/Segment Design Document (SSDD)	O			O	O		
Software Quality Program Plan (SQPP)	O			O	O	O	
Software Requirements Specification (SRS)	O			O	O		
Interface Requirements Specification (IRS)	O			O	O		
Planning							
Funding Allocation			O				
Allocation to Tasks							
Reserves							
Software Visibility Approach			O	O			
Project Plan							
Functional Software Schedule							
Build/Block Plan							
Spend Plan							
Staffing Plan							
PERT Chart							

Zero Software Defects Software Activities Checklist *(Continued)*

Activity Description	Generate	Update	Review	Source	Successive	Quality	Customer
		Activity			*Inspection*		

Detailed Software Schedule
Lowest Level Software Detailed Schedules
Progress Tracking Charts
Documentation Delivery List and Schedule
Costing Estimate to Complete
Performance vs Spending Chart
Weekly Status Report
Action List/Problem Plan
Timing & Sizing Plan
Requirements Tracking Report
Formal Test Generation Plan
Developmental Checklists for Critical Events
Staffing Stability Chart
Computer Resource Utilization
Requirements Stability Chart
Software Test Readiness Chart
Software Tools Availability
Software Facilities Loading
Software Personnel Loading
Management Reaction Curves
Zero Software Defects Program ——————O————————
  Training Program
   Management
   Engineering
  Management Process
  Management Reaction Curves
   Criteria for Management Action
   Action Plan
  Procedures
   Source Inspection Requirements
    Responsibility
    Scheduling
    Storage and Retrieval
   Successive Inspection Requirements
    Responsibility
    Scheduling
    Storage and Retrieval
   Checklists
   Reporting Responsibility

Reviews

System Requirements Review (SRR) ——————O———————O————
  Prepare Package
  Checklist for SRR
  Presentation Material
  Action Items

Zero Software Defects Software Activities Checklist *(Continued)*

		Activity			Inspection		
Activity Description	Generate	Update	Review	Source	Successive	Quality	Customer
Closure Criteria							
System Design Review (SDR)			O			O	
Prepare Package							
Checklist for SDR							
Presentation Material							
Action Items							
Closure Criteria							
Baselines							
Functional	O						
Configuration Control							
Informal	O						
Software Requirements Specification (SRS)							
Interface Requirements Specification (IRS)							
Formal	O						
Software Development Plan (SDP)							
Software Quality Program Plan (SQPP)							
System/Segment Design Document (SSDD)							
Problem Reports	O						
Documents							
Development							

Zero Software Defects Software Activities Checklist *(Continued)*

	Activity			Inspection			
Activity Description	Generate	Update	Review	Source	Successive	Quality	Customer
Software Requirements Analysis							
Software Requirements							
Timing & Sizing Baseline	O		O				
Timing Allocations							
Component Level							
Critical Path/Reaction Points							
Sizing Allocations							
Component Level							
ROM/RAM Utilization							
Traceability Matrix	O		O				
Design Flowdown from System Level Specifications							
Test Flowdown from System Level Specifications							
Test to Design Correlation							
Documentation							
Software Development Plan (SDP)	O		O			O	O
Software Quality Program Plan (SQPP)	O		O			O	O
Software Requirements Specification (SRS)	O		O			O	O
Interface Requirements Specification (IRS)	O		O			O	O
Planning							
Baseline Software Visibility Package	O		O				
Reviews							
Software Specification Review (SSR)			O			O	
Prepare Package							
Checklist for SSR							
Presentation Material							
Action Items							
Closure Criteria							
Baselines							
Functional			O				
Allocated		O					
Software Requirements Specification (SRS)							
Interface Requirements Specification (IRS)							
Developmental Configuration		O					
Timing & Sizing Estimates							
Software Development File (SDF)		O					
Timing & Sizing Estimates							

Zero Software Defects Software Activities Checklist *(Continued)*

Activity Description	Activity			Inspection		
	Generate	Update	Review	Source	Successive	Quality	Customer

Configuration Control

Activity Description							
Informal			O				
Formal			O				
Software Development Plan (SDP)							
Software Quality Program Plan (SQPP)							
System/Segment Design Document (SSDD)							
Software Requirements Specification (SRS)							
Interface Requirements Specification (IRS)							
Problem Reports		O					
Documents							
Development							

Zero Software Defects Software Activities Checklist *(Continued)*

	Activity			Inspection			
Activity Description	Generate	Update	Review	Source	Successive	Quality	Customer

Preliminary Design

Software Design Baseline

Activity Description	Generate	Update	Review	Source	Successive	Quality	Customer
Computer Software Components	O		O				
Hierarchy Chart							
Data-Flow Diagram							
System-Level Functional Flow							
Logical to Physical Transformation							
Functional Description							
Data Base	O						
High-Level Interface							
IPO Definition							
Definition Language							
Naming Conventions							
Access and Control							
Local							
Global							
Read Only							
Write/Read							
Organization							
Memory Allocation							
Storage Devices							
Timing							
Semaphors							
Structures							
Test (reference Code and CSU Testing for details)	O						
Organization							
Requirements Flowdown							
Traceability Matrix							
Scope of Work							
Verification Levels							
Independency of Testing							
Timing & Sizing	O		O				

Documentation

Activity Description	Generate	Update	Review	Source	Successive	Quality	Customer
Software Development Plan (SDP)	O		O		O	O	
Software Quality Program Plan (SQPP)	O		O		O	O	
Software Requirements Specification (SRS)				O			
Interface Requirements Specification (IRS)				O			
Preliminary Software Design Document (SDD)	O		O		O	O	
Preliminary Interface Design Document (IDD)	O		O		O	O	
Software Test Plan (STP)	O		O		O	O	

Planning

Activity Description	Generate	Update	Review	Source	Successive	Quality	Customer
Software Visibility Package	O	O					

Zero Software Defects Software Activities Checklist *(Continued)*

Activity Description	Activity			Inspection			
	Generate	Update	Review	Source	Successive	Quality	Customer
Reviews							
Preliminary Design Review (PDR)	O	O				O	
Prepare Package							
Checklist for PDR							
Presentation Material							
Action Items							
Closure Criteria							
Baselines							
Functional			O				
Allocated			O				
Developmental Configuration			O				
Timing & Sizing Estimates							
Updated Documents							
PDR Minutes							
Software Development File (SDF)			O				
Timing & Sizing Estimates							
Configuration Control							
Informal			O				
Formal			O				
Software Development Plan (SDP)							
Software Quality Program Plan (SQPP)							
System/Segment Design Document (SSDD)							
Software Requirements Specification (SRS)							
Interface Requirements Specification (IRS)							
Preliminary Software Design Document (SDD)							
Preliminary Interface Design Document (IDD)							
Software Test Plan (STP)							
Problem Reports			O				
Documents							
Development							

Zero Software Defects Software Activities Checklist *(Continued)*

Activity Description	Activity			Inspection			
	Generate	Update	Review	Source	Successive	Quality	Customer

Detailed Design

Software Design Baseline

Activity Description	Generate	Update	Review	Source	Successive	Quality	Customer
Computer Software Units (CSU)	O		O				
Functional Descriptions							
Purpose							
Abstract							
Functional Flows/PDL							
Audit for Compliance to Standards							
Record Results							
Interfaces							
Input/Output							
Other CSUs							
Database							
Record/File Structures							
Format for Automated Database Description							
Limitations							
Critical Time Functions							
Interrupts							
Cycle Times							
Critical Parameter Limits							
Maximum Number of Parameters							
Boundary Conditions							
Testing	O		O				
Methodology							
Statistical Quality Control							
Cyclomatic Complexity							
Path Analysis							
Executable Line Testing							
CSC Level							
CSC Test Concept							
Definition of Cases							
CSU Level							
CSU Test Concept							
Definition of Cases							
Test Description							
Definition of Input/Output							
Boundary Checking							
Success Criteria							
Timing & Sizing		O	O				

Documentation

Activity Description	Generate	Update	Review	Source	Successive	Quality	Customer
Software Development Plan (SDP)		O	O		O	O	
Software Quality Program Plan (SQPP)		O	O		O	O	
Software Requirements Specification (SRS)		O	O		O	O	

Zero Software Defects Software Activities Checklist *(Continued)*

	Activity			Inspection			
Activity Description	Generate	Update	Review	Source	Successive	Quality	Customer
Interface Requirements Specification (IRS)	O		O		O	O	
Software Design Document (SDD)	O		O	O	O	O	
Interface Design Document (IDD)	O		O	O	O	O	
Software Test Plan (STP)	O		O	O	O	O	
Software Test Description (STD)							
Planning							
Software Visibility Package	O	O					
Reviews							
Design Walkthroughs			O	O			
Schedule							
Documentation							
Action Item Closure							
Sign-off							
Critical Design Review (CDR)			O	O		O	
Prepare Package							
Checklist for CDR							
Presentation Material							
Action Items							
Closure Criteria							
Baselines							
Functional	O						
Allocated	O						
Developmental Configuration	O						
Timing & Sizing Estimates							
Software Design Document (SDD)							
Interface Design Document (IDD)							
CDR Minutes							
Software Development File (SDF)	O						
Timing & Sizing Estimates							
CSU Listings							
Configuration Control							
Informal	O						
Formal	O						
Software Development Plan (SDP)							
Software Quality Program Plan (SQPP)							
System/Segment Design Document (SSDD)							
Software Requirements Specification (SRS)							
Interface Requirements Specification (IRS)							
Preliminary Software Design Document (SDD)							
Preliminary Interface Design Document (IDD)							

Zero Software Defects Software Activities Checklist *(Continued)*

Activity Description	Generate	Update	Review	Source	Successive	Quality	Customer
Software Test Plan (STP)							
Software Test Description (STD)							
Problem Reports ———————————O———————							
Documents							
Development							
PDL							

Zero Software Defects Software Activities Checklist *(Continued)*

	Activity			Inspection		
Activity Description	Generate	Update	Review	Source	Successive	Quality	Customer

Code and CSU Test

Coding and Test Baseline

Source Code ——————————————— O—— O———— O———— O —————
  Allocation to Resources
  Working File Structure
  Working File Protection
  Lines-of-Code (LOC) Estimate Update
  Coding Standards Verified
  Growth Trend Analysis for LOC
  Generate Object Code
  Automated Job Control Stream
  Version Control
  Sizing Measurement (Actual)
Testing ——————————————— O———————— O—— O—— O —————
  Formal CSCI Tests
   Tools
   Database
   Data Definition
   Data Entry
   Data Verification
   Automation
   Regression Capability
   Form and Format
   Allocation to Resources
   Detailed Implementation Plan
   Procedures
  Formal CSC Tests
   Tools
   Database
   Data Definition
   Data Entry
   Data Verification
   Automation
   Regression Capability
   Form and Format
   Allocation to Resources
   Detailed Implementation Plan
   Procedures
  Informal CSC Tests
   Tools
   Database
   Data Definition
   Data Entry
   Data Verification
   Automation

Zero Software Defects Software Activities Checklist (Continued)

Activity Description	Activity — Generate	Activity — Update	Activity — Review	Inspection — Source	Inspection — Successive	Inspection — Quality	Inspection — Customer
Regression Capability							
Form and Format							
Allocation to Resources							
Detailed Implementation Plan							
Procedures							
Informal CSU Tests							
Generate Detailed Data and Procedures							
Execute Test							
Timing Measurement (Actual)							
Requirements Checkoff							
Configuration Control	O						
CSU Source Code							
CSU Test Results							
Timing & Sizing	O		O				
Actual Sizing from Compile/Link							
Actual Timing of Units from Unit Test							

Documentation

Activity Description	Activity — Generate	Activity — Update	Activity — Review	Inspection — Source	Inspection — Successive	Inspection — Quality	Inspection — Customer
Software Development Plan (SDP)	O		O		O		
Software Quality Program Plan (SQPP)	O		O		O		
Software Design Document (SDD)	O		O	O	O		
Interface Design Document (IDD)	O		O	O	O		
Software Test Plan (STP)	O		O		O		
Software Test Description (STD)	O		O	O	O		

Planning

Activity Description	Activity — Generate	Activity — Update	Activity — Review	Inspection — Source	Inspection — Successive	Inspection — Quality	Inspection — Customer
Software Visibility Package	O	O					

Reviews

Activity Description	Activity — Generate	Activity — Update	Activity — Review	Inspection — Source	Inspection — Successive	Inspection — Quality	Inspection — Customer
Code Walkthroughs		O	O				
Schedule							
Documentation							
Action Item Closure							
Sign-off							
CSU Test Walkthroughs		O	O				
Schedule							
Documentation							
Action Item Closure							
Sign-off							

Baselines

Activity Description	Activity — Generate	Activity — Update	Activity — Review	Inspection — Source	Inspection — Successive	Inspection — Quality	Inspection — Customer
Functional	O						
Allocated	O						
Developmental Configuration	O						

Zero Software Defects Software Activities Checklist *(Continued)*

	Activity				Inspection		
Activity Description	Generate	Update	Review	Source	Successive	Quality	Customer
Software Design Document (SDD)							
Interface Design Document (IDD)							
CSU Listings							
CSU Test Procedures							
CSU Test Results							
Software Development File (SDF)			O				
Timing & Sizing Estimates							
CSU Listings							
Configuration Control							
Informal			O				
CSU Source Code							
CSU Test Procedures							
CSU Test Results							
Formal			O				
Software Development Plan (SDP)							
Software Quality Program Plan (SQPP)							
System/Segment Design Document (SSDD)							
Software Requirements Specification (SRS)							
Interface Requirements Specification (IRS)							
Preliminary Software Design Document (SDD)							
Preliminary Interface Design Document (IDD)							
Software Test Plan (STP)							
Software Test Description (STD)							
Problem Reports			O				
Documents							
Development							
PDL							
Code Complete Unit Test							

Zero Software Defects Software Activities Checklist *(Continued)*

| | Activity | | | Inspection | | | |
Activity Description	Generate	Update	Review	Source	Successive	Quality	Customer
CSC Integration and Testing							
Test Execution							
Informal CSC Test			O				
Detailed Data							
Execute Test							
Timing Measurement for CSC (Actual)							
Requirements Checkoff							
Testing	O		O	O	O	O	
Formal CSCI Tests							
Tools							
Database							
Data Definition							
Data Entry							
Data Verification							
Engineering Execution							
Formal CSC Tests							
Tools							
Database							
Data Definition							
Data Entry							
Data Verification							
Engineering Execution							
Timing & Sizing	O		O				
Actual Sizing from Compile/Link							
Actual Timing of CSCs from CSC Test							
Source Code				O			
Documentation							
Software Development Plan (SDP)	O		O		O		
Software Quality Program Plan (SQPP)	O		O		O		
Software Design Document (SDD)	O		O		O		
Interface Design Document (IDD)	O		O		O		
Software Test Plan (STP)	O		O		O		
Software Test Description (STD)	O		O		O		
Planning							
Software Visibility Package	O	O					
Reviews							
Test Procedure Walkthroughs			O	O			
Schedule							
Documentation							

Zero Software Defects Software Activities Checklist *(Continued)*

Activity Description	Generate	Update	Review	Source	Successive	Quality	Customer
Action Item Closure							
Sign-off							
CSC Test Results					O	O	
Documentation							
Record Errors							
Sign-off							
Test Readiness Review (TRR)				O			
Prepare Package							
Checklist for TRR							
Presentation Material							
Action Items							
Closure Criteria							
Baselines							
Functional			O				
Allocated			O				
Developmental Configuration			O				
Software Design Document (SDD)							
Interface Design Document (IDD)							
CSU Listings							
CSC Test Results							
Software Development File (SDF)			O			O	
Timing & Sizing Estimates							
CSU Listings							
Engineering Dry Run Results							
Configuration Control							
Informal			O				
CSU Source Code							
CSU Test Procedures							
CSU Test Results							
CSC Test Procedures							
CSC Test Results							
CSCI Test Procedures							
Formal			O				
Software Development Plan (SDP)							
Software Quality Program Plan (SQPP)							
System/Segment Design Document (SSDD)							
Software Requirements Specification (SRS)							
Interface Requirements Specification (IRS)							
Preliminary Software Design Document (SDD)							
Preliminary Interface Design Document (IDD)							
Software Test Plan (STP)							
Software Test Description (STD)							
Problem Reports			O				

Zero Software Defects Software Activities Checklist *(Continued)*

Activity Description	Generate	Update	Review	Source	Successive	Quality	Customer
Documents							
Development							
PDL							
Code Complete Unit Test (SCCB)							
Closure							
Define Open Problems for TRR							
Define Closure Plan							
Categorize Open Problems							

Zero Software Defects Software Activities Checklist *(Continued)*

Activity Description	Generate	Update	Review	Source	Successive	Quality	Customer
			Activity			Inspection	
CSCI Testing							
Formal CSCI Tests							
Test Preparation	O						
Master Book Available							
Test Log Available							
Test Personnel Identified							
Test Schedule Detailed							
Formal Qualification Test (FQT) Dry Run	O		O				
Execution							
Problem Closure							
Record Errors							
SQA Witness of Closure							
Procedure Redlines Incorporated							
Record Errors							
SQA Witness of Closure							
All Pass							
Formal Qualification Test (FQT)	O			O	O		
Notification to Customer							
Pretest Meeting							
Daily Review Meeting							
Execute on Target Computer							
Complete Log Book							
Document Discrepancies							
SQA Sign-off							
Customer Sign-off							
Documentation							
Software Development Plan (SDP)		O		O		O	O
Software Quality Program Plan (SQPP)		O		O		O	O
Software Design Document (SDD)		O		O		O	
Interface Design Document (IDD)		O		O		O	
Software Test Plan (STP)		O		O		O	O
Software Test Description (STD)		O		O		O	O
Version Description Document (VDD)	O			O		O	O
Software Test Report (STR)	O			O		O	O
Software Product Specification (SPS)	O			O		O	O
Operations and Support Document	O			O		O	O
Planning							
Software Visibility Package	O	O					
Reviews							
FQT Test Procedures Walkthrough			O	O	O		

Zero Software Defects Software Activities Checklist *(Continued)*

Activity Description	Activity				Inspection		
	Generate	Update	Review	Source	Successive	Quality	Customer
Identify Updates via Redlines							
Action Items							
Documentation Updated							
SQA Sign-off							
Customer Sign-off							
Internal FQT Configuration Audit			O		O	O	
Review FQT Test Procedure Updates							
Review FQT Dry Run Results							
Code Configured							
Software Test Tools Certified							
Hardware Test Tools Configured and Calibrated							
Quality Audits Closed							
Software Problem Reports Closed							
FQT Post-Test Review			O		O	O	
Regression Test Required							
Action Items							
Documentation Compiled							
SQA Sign-off							
Customer Sign-off							
Baselines							
Functional		O					
Allocated		O					
Developmental Configuration		O					
All Design Documentation							
All Test Documentation							
Listings							
Software Development File (SDF)		O			O		
Timing & Sizing Final							
CSU Listings							
FQT Results							
Product	O						
Configuration Control							
Informal		O					
CSU Test Procedures							
CSU Test Results							
CSC Test Procedures							
CSC Test Results							
CSCI Test Procedures							
CSCI Test Results							
Formal		O					
Software Development Plan (SDP)							
Software Quality Program Plan (SQPP)							
System/Segment Design Document (SSDD)							

Zero Software Defects Software Activities Checklist *(Continued)*

	Activity			Inspection		
Activity Description	Generate	Update	Review	Source	Successive	Quality	Customer
Software Requirements Specification (SRS)							
Interface Requirements Specification (IRS)							
Preliminary Software Design Document (SDD)							
Preliminary Interface Design Document (IDD)							
Software Test Plan (STP)							
Software Test Description (STD)							
Version Description Document (VDD)							
Software Test Report (STR)							
Software Product Specification (SPS)							
Operations and Support Document							
Source Code							
Object Code							
Configuration Inventory Number							
Problem Reports				O		O	
Documents							
Development							
PDL							
Code (SCCB)							
Close All Problems							

Zero Software Defects Software Activities Checklist *(Continued)*

Activity Description	Activity			Inspection			
	Generate	Update	Review	Source	Successive	Quality	Customer
System Integration and Testing							
Configuration Audits							
Internal Functional Configuration Audit (FCA)		O	O		O		
Compliance Matrix							
Software Documentation							
Test Documentation							
Internal Physical Configuration Audit (PCA)		O	O		O		
Compliance Matrix							
Software Documentation							
Test Documentation							
Documentation							
Software Design Documents	O				O	O	
Software Test Documents	O				O	O	
Software Configuration Documents	O				O	O	
Planning							
Software Visibility Package	O	O					
Reviews							
Functional Configuration Audit (FCA)		O			O	O	
Prepare Package							
Checklist for FCA							
Presentation Material							
Action Items							
Closure Criteria							
Physical Configuration Audit (PCA)		O			O	O	
Prepare Package							
Checklist for PCA							
Presentation Material							
Action Items							
Closure Criteria							
Baselines							
Functional		O					
Allocated		O					
Developmental Configuration		O					
Software Development File (SDF)		O			O		
Product		O			O	O	
All Design Documentation							
All Test Documentation							
Listing							

Software Quality Indicators

COMPLETENESS

The inputs for completeness indicator are obtained as the software specifications, requirements, and design mature. However, the inputs should initially be available by the identified development milestones shown in parentheses. For purposes of this indicator, functions and requirements may be considered equivalent. The inputs are:

a. P_1 – Number of functions not adequately defined or specified (Software Specification Review—SSR)

b. P_2 – Total number of functions (SSR)

c. P_3 – Number of data items not defined (Preliminary Design Review—PDR)

d. P_4 – Total number of data items (PDR)

e. P_5 – Number of defined functions not used (PDR)

f. P_6 – Total number of defined functions (SSR) ($P_6 = P_2 - P_1$)

g. P_7 – Number of functions referenced by defined functions but not defined (PDR)

h. P_8 – Total number of functions referenced by defined functions (PDR)

i. P_9 – Number of decision points not using all conditions or options (PDR)

j. P_{10} – Total number of decision points (PDR)

k. P_{11} – Number of condition options without processing (PDR)

l. P_{12} – Total number of condition options (PDR)

m. P_{13} – Number of calling routines with calling parameters that do not agree with defined parameters (PDR)

n. P_{14} – Total number of calling routines (PDR)

o. P_{15} – Number of condition options that are not set (PDR)

p. P_{16} – Number of condition options that are set but have no processing associated with the option (PDR)

q. P_{17} – Number of set condition options (PDR) ($P_{17} = P_{12} - P_{15}$)

r. P_{18} – Number of data references having no destination (PDR)

The metric used by this indicator is the weighted sum of ten components defined by the relationship:

$$COMPLETENESS = \sum_{i=1}^{10} w_i C_i$$

Where w_i is the weight associated with each component (a value between 0 and 1), the sum of the weights equals 1, and each component (C_i) also has a value between 0 and 1. The components are defined as follows:

a. Functions satisfactorily defined (C_1)

$$C_1 = (P_2 - P_1)/P_2$$

b. Defined data item (C_2)

$$C_2 = (P_4 - P_3)/P_4$$

c. Defined functions used (C_3)

$$C_3 = (P_6 - P_5)/P_6$$

d. Defined references functions (C_4)

$$C_4 = (P_8 - P_7)/P_8$$

e. All condition options are used at decision points (C_5)

$$C_5 = (P_{10} - P_9)/P_{10}$$

f. All condition options with processing are used at decision points (C_6)

$$C_6 = (P_{12} - P_{11})/P_{12}$$

g. All calling routine parameters agree with the called routine's defined parameters (C_7)

$$C_7 = (P_{14} - P_{13})/P_{14}$$

h. All condition options are set (C_8)

$$C_8 = (P_{12} - P_{15})/P_{12}$$

i. All processing follows set condition options (C_9)

$$C_9 = (P_{17} - P_{16})/P_{17}$$

j. All data items have a destination (C_{10})

$$C_{10} = (P_4 - P_{18})/P_4$$

DESIGN STRUCTURE

The inputs for the Design Structure indicator are:

a. S_1 – Software size expressed in terms of units
b. S_2 – Number of units dependent on the source of input data (a result of prior processing or calling sequence) or destination of output data (post-processing or display)
c. S_3 – Number of units dependent on prior processing

d. S_4 – Number of database items. This is the same input as used for completeness indicator.

e. S_5 – Total number of unique database items, including local and global databases.

f. S_6 – Number of data base segments

g. S_7 – Number of units with a single entrance/single exit. Branch on error detection is not considered as a multiple exit condition.

The metric used to support this indicator is defined as:

$$\text{DESIGN STRUCTURE} = \sum_{i=1}^{6} w_i D_i$$

Where w_i is the weight associated with each component (a value between 0 and 1), the sum of the weights equals 1, and each component (D_i) also has a value between 0 and 1. The components are defined as follows:

a. Design organized top-down, bottom-up, or object-oriented as applicable, and structured (D_1)

$$D_1 = (1 = \text{Yes}, 0 = \text{No})$$

b. Unit independence (D_2)

$$D_2 = 1 - (S_2/S_1)$$

c. Units not dependent on prior processing (D_3)

$$D_3 = 1 - (S_3/S_1)$$

d. Database size (D_4)

$$D_4 = 1 - (S_5/S_4)$$

e. Database compartmentalization (D_5)

$$D_5 = 1 - (S_6/S_4)$$

f. Unit single entrance/single exit (D_6)

$$D_6 = (S_7/S_1)$$

TEST SUFFICIENCY

The inputs for the Test Sufficiency indicator are:

a. Total number of faults predicted in the software (PF)

b. Number of faults detected before software integration testing (FP)

c. Number of units integrated (UI)

d. Total number of units in the CSCI (UT)

e. Total number of faults detected to date during test (FD)

The metrics used by this indicator are:

Remaining Faults $(FR) = (PF - FP) \times (UI/UT)$

Maximum Tolerance $(MAXT) = c_1 \times FR$

Minimum Tolerance $(MINT) = c_2 \times FR$

Where c_1 and c_2 are the maximum and minimum tolerance coefficients. The remaining faults (FR) are really time, integration, and level of test-dependent number of faults that should be expected to be encountered up to a specified point during integration and test.

DOCUMENTATION

The metric used for the Documentation indicator is the combined average of the weighted averages for the documentation and source listings expressed as:

$$\text{DOCUMENTATION INDEX (DI)} = \frac{\displaystyle\sum_{i=1}^{6} \frac{w1_i D_i}{6} \quad \sum_{i=1}^{6} \frac{w2_i S_i}{6}}{2}$$

Where $w1_i$ and $w2_i$ are the weights associated with the assessments of the documentation and source listings, respectively. The sums of $w1_i$ and $w2_i$ are both equal to 1.

Zero Defect Software
Kickoff Presentation

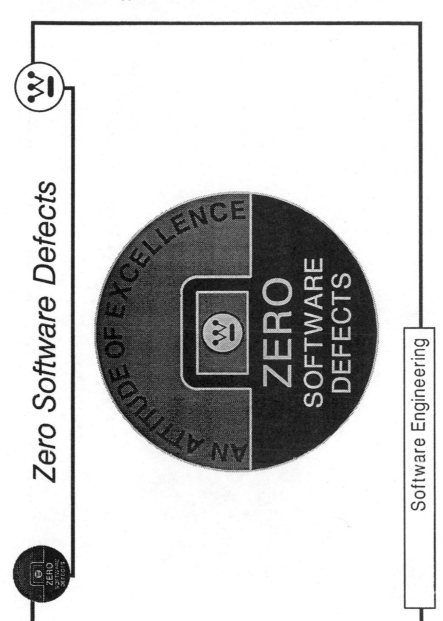

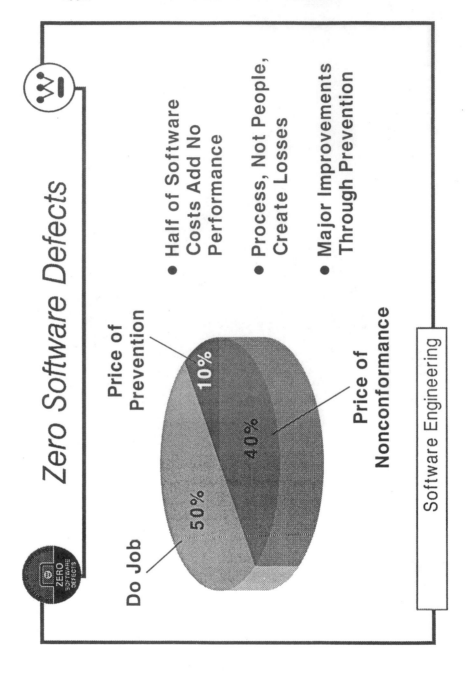

Zero Software Defects

Elements

- What Is a Customer?

- Software Development Process Chart

- Software Activities List

- Source Inspections/Successive Inspections

- Checklists

- Software Tools (Poka-Yoke)

Software Engineering

Zero Software Defects

What Is a Customer?

- All Employees Have a Customer

- Next Person in Process Is the Internal Customer

Software Engineering

Zero Software Defects

Software Development Process Chart

- The 'Big Picture'

- All Development Steps Detailed

- Every Step Is Inspected

- Eliminate Errors Before They Propogate

CSU(s)

Define CSU(s)

Source Inspection CSU(s)

Successive Inspection of SDD, IDD, STP

OK

OK

OK

OK

OK

OK

Software Engineering

Zero Software Defects

Software Activities List

- The 'Job Details'

- Know One's Job Requirements

- Do Not Forget Any Element of the Software Development Process

Activity Description	Generate	Update	Review	Sou
Detailed Design				
Software Design Baseline				
Computer Software Units (CSU)	0			0
Functional Descriptions				
Purpose				
Abstract				
Functional Flows / PDL				
Audit for Compliance to Standards				
Record Results				
Interfaces				
Other CSUs				
Data Base				
Record / File Structures				
Format for Automated Data Base Description				
Limitations				
Critical Time Functions				

Activity

Software Engineering

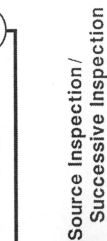

Zero Software Defects

Source Inspection/
Successive Inspection

- Progressive Inspection
  Via Checklists

- Progressive Elimination
  of Errors

- Worker Performs
  Source Inspection

- User Performs
  Successive Inspection

Software Engineering

Zero Software Defects

Checklists

- **Generic Checklists**

- **Specific Checklists**

SPECIFICS

CUSTOMER CPS

TIMING & SIZING BUDGET

GENERICS

DOD-STD-2167A

SQA PROCEDURES

SOFTWARE MANUAL

ZERO
SOFTWARE
DEFECTS

Software Engineering

Zero Software Defects

Software Tools (Poka-Yoke)

- **Mistake Proofing**

- **Automation To Ensure Product Integrity**

THIS REPORT CONTAINS REQUIREMENTS WHICH HAVE NOT BEEN ALLOCATED TO ALLOCATION OBJECTS

22-MAY-1989 11:30:58

UNALLOCATED REQUIREMENTS REPORT

3.4.6.1.1 Ambient Temperature
3.4.6.1.4.005

Because equipment located in the pedestal maintenance rooms, such as the...

Software Engineering

Sample Checklist for Software Requirements Specification

ZSDSRS-8/4'89   09/12/89

* * * * * * * * *   SOURCE INSPECTION CHECKLIST FOR SOFTWARE REQUIREMENTS SPECIFICATION   * * * * * * * * * * *

THIS DOCUMENT IS THE ZERO-SOFTWARE-DEFECTS INSPECTION-CHECKLIST TO BE USED FOR PREPARATION AND
INTERNAL ACCEPTANCE OF THE SOFTWARE REQUIREMENTS SPECIFICATION (SRS). THE CHECKLIST IS DIVIDED
INTO THREE AREAS:

> o   GENERIC CHECKLIST - GENERAL REQUIREMENTS,
> o   GENERIC CHECKLIST - SPECIFIC REQUIREMENTS,
> o   UNIQUE CHECKLIST - TAILORED REQUIREMENTS.

INSTRUCTIONS:
> o   COMPLETE EACH LINE ENTRY: (REFER TO COLUMN LABELLED "CHECK-OFF:)
>   FOR EACH REQUIREMENT LISTED, PLACE AN "X" IN THE APPROPRIATE COLUMN
>   AS FOLLOWS;
>
>   o   PLACE "X" IN COLUMN C IF REQUIREMENT HAS BEEN MET.
>   o   PLACE "X" IN COLUMN N IF REQUIREMENT HAS NOT BEEN MET.
>   o   PLACE "X" IN COLUMN W IF REQUIREMENT HAS BEEN WAIVED.

NOTES:
> o   THE "CHECKLIST ITEM NO." IS THE UNIQUE IDENTIFIER NUMBER ASSIGNED TO THE REQ.
> o   THE "SOURCE & PARA. NO." COLUMN STATES THE SOURCE DOCUMENT AND THE PARA. REF.
> o   THE "REQUIREMENTS DESCRIPTION" COLUMN IS A BRIEF STATEMENT OF THE REQ. TO BE MET.
> o   THE "NOTES" COLUMN IS RESERVED FOR THE INSPECTOR TO PROVIDE COMMENTS.

SOURCES/REFERENCES FOR REQUIREMENTS:

1) DOD-STD-2167A   DEFENSE SYSTEM SOFTWARE DEVELOPMENT, FEB 29,'89.
2) DI-MCCR-80025M   SOFTWARE REQUIREMENTS SPECIFICATION DID, NOV 19,'89.
3) DOD 5220.22-M   INDUSTRIAL SECURITY MANUAL, JULY '85.
4) AC 2120 REV. G   SOFTWARE QUALITY ASSURANCE MANUAL, REVISION J, RELEASE 7,
                         (AUDIT CHECKLIST - 2120 REVISION G.).
5) ESD-TR-88-337   B5 (SRS/IRS) SPECIFICATION GUIDELINES, MITRE, DEC '88.
6) STATEMENT OF WORK   CONTRACT F19628-89-C-0138, JULY 14,'89.
7)   U.S. GOV'T PRINTING OFFICE STYLE MANUAL
8) MIL-STD-12   LIST OF ABBREVIATIONS
9)   PROJECT SYSTEM SPEC (SSS/PIDS/CIDS)
10)   PROJECT I/F SPECS
11)   PROJECT CONTRACT, S/W QUALITY FACTORS
12)   PROJECT SYSTEM/SEGMENT DESIGN DOCUMENT

ELECTRONIC RECORDS:

> o   THIS CHECKLIST MUST BE (electronically) SIGNED ON THE LINE BELOW;
>   BOTH DATE AND SIGNATURE SPACES ARE PROVIDED FOR
>   SOURCE AND SUCCESSIVE INSPECTORS.

DATE: _____ SOURCE INSPECTOR: _____
        (mm / day / yr)   (signature)

DATE: _____ SUCCESSIVE INSPCT:_____
        (mm / day / yr)   (signature)

C = CHECK OK; N = NOT OK; W = REQUIREMENT WAIVED   1/11

```
ZSDSRS-8/4'89                                                                    09/12/89


* * * * * * * * *    SOURCE INSPECTION CHECKLIST FOR SOFTWARE REQUIREMENTS SPECIFICATION    * * * * * * * * * * *
------------------------------------------------------------------------------------------------------------
CHECK-OFF: CHECKLIST      SOURCE AND        REQUIREMENTS DESCRIPTION                                  NOTES
C  N  W ITEM NO.          PARAGRAPH REF.
============================================================================================================
              1.3         DOD-STD-2167A     INTERNAL CONSISTENCY
                          10.2.1 APP-D
( )( )( )     1.3.1                         STATEMENTS DON'T CONTRADICT EACH OTHER
( )( )( )     1.3.2                         TERMS, ACRONYMS, ETC MEAN THE SAME THING
( )( )( )     1.3.3                         ITEMS REFERRED TO BY SAME NAME/DESCRIPTION
------------------------------------------------------------------------------------------------------------
                          DOD-STD-2167A
              1.4         10.2.2 APP-D       UNDERSTANDABILITY
( )( )( )     1.4.1       USGPOSM            CAPITALS, PUNCTUATION, SYMBOLS & NOTATION CONSISTENT
                                               WITH US GOVN'T PRINTING OFFICE STYLE MANUAL
( )( )( )     1.4.2       USGPOSM            DEFINE ALL TERMS NOT IN USGPOSM OR MERRIAM
                          MWNID                WEBSTER'S NEW INTERNATIONAL DICTIONARY
( )( )( )     1.4.3       MIL-STD-12         STANDARD ABBREVIATIONS USED PER MIL-STD-12
( )( )( )     1.4.3.1        "              DEFINE ALL ACRONYMS/ABBREVIATIONS NOT IN MIL-STD-12
( )( )( )     1.4.3.2        "              SPELL OUT ACRONYMS/ABBREVIATIONS AT FIRST OCCURRENCE
( )( )( )     1.4.3.3        "              TABLES/FIGURES CALLED OUT IN TEXT PRIOR TO APPEARANCE
( )( )( ) 1.4.3.3.1          "              TABLES/FIGURES CALLED OUT IN ORDER OF APPEARANCE
------------------------------------------------------------------------------------------------------------

                          DOD-STD-2167A
              1.5         10.2.3 APP-D       TRACEABILITY TO SYSTEM SPEC (SSS/PIDS/CIDS)
( )( )( )     1.5.1                         SRS IMPLEMENTS ALL STIPULATIONS OF SYS SPEC
( )( )( )     1.5.2                         TERMS/ACRONYMS/ABBREV IN SRS SAME AS IN SYS SPEC
( )( )( )     1.5.3                         ITEMS/CONCEPTS IN SRS SAME AS IN SYS SPEC
( )( )( )     1.5.4                         BASIS FOR SRS IS IN SYS SPEC
( )( )( )     1.5.5                         SRS & SYS SPEC NOT CONTRADICTORY
------------------------------------------------------------------------------------------------------------
                          DOD-STD-2167A
              1.6         FIG.4 OF 5.1.4     CONSISTENCY WITH IRS (& OTHER INTERFACE SPECS)
( )( )( )     1.6.1       & 10.2.4 APP-D     NO CONTRADICTORY STATEMENTS FROM SRS TO IRS (& OTHER I/F SPECS)
( )( )( )     1.6.2                         TERMS/ACRONYMS/ABBREV IN SRS SAME AS IN IRS (& OTHER I/F SPECS)
( )( )( )     1.6.3                         TERMS/CONCEPTS REFERRED TO BY SAME NAME/DESCRIPTION

------------------------------------------------------------------------------------------------------------

              2           DOD 5220.22-M      SECURITY PRACTICES
( )( )( )     2.1                           IS COVER PAGE MARKED (TOP & BOTTOM) AT THE HIGHEST
                                              LEVEL OF CLASSIFICATION WITHIN THE DOCUMENT
( )( )( )     2.2                           ARE FIRST TWO PAGES & OUTSIDE OF BACK PAGE MARKED
                                              (TOP & BOTTOM) AT HIGHEST LEVEL OF CLASSIFICATION
                                              WITHIN DOCUMENT
( )( )( )     2.3                           ARE TOP & BOTTOM OF EVERY PAGE MARKED AT HIGHEST
                                              LEVEL OF CLASSIFICATION ON THAT PAGE




C = CHECK OK; N = NOT OK; W = REQUIREMENT WAIVED                                          2/11
```

```
* * * * * * * * *     SOURCE INSPECTION CHECKLIST FOR SOFTWARE REQUIREMENTS SPECIFICATION    * * * * * * * * * * * *
--------------------------------------------------------------------------------------------------------------------
   CHECK-OFF: CHECKLIST      SOURCE AND       REQUIREMENTS DESCRIPTION                                        NOTES
   C   N   W ITEM NO.        PARAGRAPH REF.
====================================================================================================================

  ( ) ( ) ( )     2.4                        IS EACH PARA. MARKED AT ITS BEGINNING AT THE
                                             LEVEL OF CLASSIFIED INFO CONTAINED IN THE PARAGRAPH
                                             (c) Confidential, (s) Secret, (ts) Top Secret,
                                             (u) Unclassified, (rd) Restricted Data, (frd) Formerly RD
  ( ) ( ) ( )     2.5                        IS UPPER LEFT CORNER OF PAGE MARKED AT THE REQUIRED
                                             LEVEL WHEN TEXT CONTINUES FROM PREVIOUS PAGE
                  2.6                        DOES COVER PAGE CONTAIN;
  ( ) ( ) ( )     2.6.1                        - AUTHORITY/SOURCE OF CLASSIFICATION INFORMATION
  ( ) ( ) ( )     2.6.2                        - OADR INFORMATION
  ( ) ( ) ( )     2.6.3                        - DOWNGRADING INFORMATION

  ( ) ( ) ( )     2.7                        DOES 1st OR 2nd PAGE CONTAIN SECURITY AUTHORIZATION
                                             SIGNATURE TO ASSURE DOCUMENT OK PRIOR TO RELEASE

  ( ) ( ) ( )     2.8          DD-254        CHECK DD-254 FOR ADDITIONAL SECURITY REQUIREMENTS

  --------------------------------------------------------------------------------------------------------------
                  3            P. C. UTILITIES  SPELLCHECKER
  ( ) ( ) ( )     3.1                           - RUN SPELL CHECKER
  ( ) ( ) ( )     3.2                           - CORRECTIONS MADE
  ( ) ( ) ( )     3.3                           - RERUN SPELL CHECKER

  --------------------------------------------------------------------------------------------------------------
          PART I.  GENERIC CHECKLIST - SPECIFIC REQUIREMENTS:

                               DI-MCCR-80025A
                  6            10.2.1         TITLE PAGE
  ( ) ( ) ( )     6.1                         TITLE PAGE TEMPLATE USED (SEE DID PARA. 10.2.1)
  ( ) ( ) ( )     6.1.1                       DOCUMENT NUMBER ASSIGNED (CP-204-####-#)
  ( ) ( ) ( )     6.1.2                       ALL CAPITALS
  --------------------------------------------------------------------------------------------------------------
                  7            DI-MCCR-80025A TABLE OF CONTENTS
  ( ) ( ) ( )     7.1          10.2.2         ALL PARAGRAPH TITLES & PAGE NUMBERS LISTED
  ( ) ( ) ( )     7.2                         ALL FIGURES & PAGE NUMBERS LISTED
  ( ) ( ) ( )     7.3                         ALL TABLES & PAGE NUMBERS LISTED
  ( ) ( ) ( )     7.4                         ALL APPENDICES & PAGE NUMBERS LISTED
  ( ) ( ) ( )
  --------------------------------------------------------------------------------------------------------------
                  8            DI-MCCR-80025A 1  SCOPE
                               10.2.3
  ( ) ( ) ( )     8.1          10.2.3.1       1.1  IDENTIFICATION
  ( ) ( ) ( )     8.1.1        10.2.3.1       APPROVED ID NUMBER, TITLE, & ABBREVIATION OF SYSTEM
                                             (CP-204-####-#, E3 AWACS RSIP)
  ( ) ( ) ( )     8.1.2        10.2.3.1       APPROVED ID NUMBER, TITLE, & ABBREVIATION OF CSCI
```

```
* * * * * * * * * *    SOURCE INSPECTION CHECKLIST FOR SOFTWARE REQUIREMENTS SPECIFICATION    * * * * * * * * * * *
----------------------------------------------------------------------------------------------------------------
  CHECK-OFF: CHECKLIST      SOURCE AND        REQUIREMENTS DESCRIPTION                              NOTES
  C   N   W  ITEM NO.       PARAGRAPH REF.
================================================================================================================
                           SQAM BWI 3.8.4
 ( ) ( ) ( )    8.1.3      AC 2120 REV.G #3   REPRESENTATIVE NAME/MNEMONIC FOR CSCI PROVIDED
----------------------------------------------------------------------------------------------------------------
 ( ) ( ) ( )    8.2        10.2.3.2           1.2 CSCI OVERVIEW
 ( ) ( ) ( )    8.2.1                         PURPOSE OF SYSTEM
 ( ) ( ) ( )    8.2.2                         FUNCTIONAL ROLE OF CSCI WITHIN SYSTEM
----------------------------------------------------------------------------------------------------------------
 ( ) ( ) ( )    8.3        10.2.3.3           1.3 DOCUMENT OVERVIEW
 ( ) ( ) ( )    8.3.1                         PURPOSE OF DOCUMENT
 ( ) ( ) ( )    8.3.2                         CONTENT OF DOCUMENT
 ( ) ( ) ( )    8.3.2.1                       PURPOSE OF EACH MAJOR SECTION
 ( ) ( ) ( )    8.3.2.2                       CONTENT OF EACH MAJOR SECTION
----------------------------------------------------------------------------------------------------------------
                9          DI-MCCR-80025A     2 APPLICABLE DOCUMENTS
                           10.2.4
 ( ) ( ) ( )    9.1        10.2.4.1           2.1 GOV'T DOCUMENTS, AS STATED BELOW.
                           "This paragraph shall be numbered 2.1 and shall begin with one of the
                           following paragraphs: 1) The following documents of the exact issue
                           shown form a part of this specification to the extent specified herin.
                           in the event of conflict between the documents referenced herein and the
                           contents of this specification, the contents of this specification shall be
                           considered a superseding requirement." 2) "The following documents of the
                           exact issue shown form a part of this specification to the extent specified
                           herein. In the event of conflict between the documents referenced herein and the
                           contents of this specification, the contents of this specification shall be considered
                           a superseding requirement, except for (spec. no.) listed below."

 ( ) ( ) ( )    9.1.1      SPECIFICATIONS;
 ( ) ( ) ( )    9.1.1.1      GROUP UNDER  FEDERAL, MILITARY, OTHER GOV'T AGENCY
 ( ) ( ) ( )    9.1.2      STANDARDS;
 ( ) ( ) ( )    9.1.2.1      GROUP UNDER  FEDERAL, MILITARY, OTHER GOV'T AGENCY
 ( ) ( ) ( )    9.1.3      DRAWINGS. Where detailed drawings referred to in a spec. are listed on an
                           assembly drawing, it is only necessary to list the assembly drawing.
 ( ) ( ) ( )    9.1.4      OTHER PUBLICATIONS;
 ( ) ( ) ( )    9.1.4.1      MANUALS,REGULATIONS,HANDBOOKS,BULLETINS..
 ( ) ( ) ( )    9.2        10.2.4.2  2.2 NONGOV'T DOCUMENTS. Same as 9.1...9.1.4.1 above.
----------------------------------------------------------------------------------------------------------------
                10         DI-MCCR-80025A     3 ENGINEERING REQUIREMENT
                           10.2.5             (INCLUDES ALLOCATTED/DERIVED REQUIREMENTS PER SSS)
                10.1       10.2.5.1           3.1 CSCI EXTERNAL INTERFACES IDENTIFIED
                                             (may use diagram)
 ( ) ( ) ( )    10.1.1                        All I/F names included.
 ( ) ( ) ( )    10.1.2                        Unique Project Identifier for each I/F.
 ( ) ( ) ( )    10.1.3                        Brief description for each I/F
 ( ) ( ) ( )    10.1.4                        ICD or IRS referenced for each I/F.
----------------------------------------------------------------------------------------------------------------
```

ZSDSRS-8/4'8   09/12/89

```
* * * * * * * * *    SOURCE INSPECTION CHECKLIST FOR SOFTWARE REQUIREMENTS SPECIFICATION   * * * * * * * * * *
-----------------------------------------------------------------------------------------------------
CHECK-OFF: CHECKLIST     SOURCE AND       REQUIREMENTS DESCRIPTION                              NOTES
C   N   W ITEM NO.       PARAGRAPH REF.
=====================================================================================================
                         DI-MCCR-80025A
            10.2          10.2.5.2         3.2  CSCI CAPABILITY REQUIREMENTS
( )( )( )   10.2.1        10.2.5.2   &     IDENTIFY CSCI CAPABILITY REQUIREMENTS
                         SQAM BWI 3.8.4
                         AC 2120 REV.G #5
( )( )( )   10.2.2        10.2.5.2         CORRELATE EACH CSCI CAPABILITY TO THE SYSTEM STATES
( )( )( )   10.2.3                         CORRELATE EACH CSCI CAPABILITY TO THE SYSTEM MODES
-----------------------------------------------------------------------------------------------------
                         DI-MCCR-80025A
            10.3          10.2.5.2.1       3.2.X  CAPABILITY NAME & PROJECT ID
( )( )( )   10.3.1        10.2.5.2.1  &    IDENTIFY CAPABILITY BY NAME & PROJECT ID
                         AC 2120 REV.G #3
( )( )( )   10.3.2        10.2.5.2.1  &    STATE PURPOSE OF CAPABILITY
                         AC 2120 REV.G #6
( )( )( )   10.3.3        10.2.5.2.1  &    STATE PERFORMANCE IN MEASURABLE TERMS
                         AC 2120 REV.G #6
( )( )( )   10.3.4        10.2.5.2.1  &    STATE PURPOSE OF EACH INPUT & OUTPUT
                         AC 2120 REV.G #6
( )( )( )   10.3.5        10.2.5.2.1       IDENTIFY ALLOCATED & DERIVED REQUIREMENTS SATISFIED BY THE CAPABILITY
( )( )( )   10.3.6                         IS CAPABILITY DECOMPOSED
( )( )( ) 10.3.6.1                         GIVE BRIEF PARAGRAPH FOR EACH DECOMPOSED REQUIREMENT
( )( )( ) 10.3.6.2                         ASSIGN PROJECT ID FROM PARENT CAPABILITY
                         SQAM BWI 3.8.4
( )( )( )   10.3.7        AC 2120 REV.G #10 DESCRIBE OPERATING SYSTEM & EXECUTIVE SYSTEM REQUIREMENTS
( )( )( )   10.3.8        AC 2120 REV.G #11 DESCRIBE SUPPORT & UTILITY SOFTWARE REQUIREMENTS
-----------------------------------------------------------------------------------------------------
                         DI-MCCR-80025A
            10.4          10.2.5.3         3.3  CSCI INTERNAL INTERFACES
( )( )( )   10.4.1                         I/Fs BETWEEN CAPABILITIES (3.2.X ABOVE) IDENTIFIED
( )( )( )   10.4.2                         I/Fs IDENTIFIED BY NAME & PROJECT ID
( )( )( )   10.4.3                         I/Fs BRIEFLY DESCRIBED
( )( )( )   10.4.4                         SUMMARIZE INFORMATION TRANSMITTED OVER I/Fs
-----------------------------------------------------------------------------------------------------
                         DI-MCCR-80025A
            10.5          10.2.5.4         3.4  CSCI DATA ELEMENT REQUIREMENTS
( )( )( )   10.5.1                         For each internal data element in the CSCI:
( )( )( ) 10.5.1.1                         - DATA ELEMENT PROJECT IDENTIFIER ASSIGNED
( )( )( ) 10.5.1.2                         - DATA ELEMENT BRIEFLY DESCRIBED
( )( )( ) 10.5.1.3                         - UNITS OF MEASURE IDENTIFIED
( )( )( ) 10.5.1.4                         - LIMIT/RANGE OF VALUES IDENTIFIED
( )( )( ) 10.5.1.5                         - ACCURACY DEFINED
( )( )( ) 10.5.1.6                         - PRECISION/RESOLUTION DEFINED (SIGNIFICANT DIGITS)
```

C = CHECK OK; N = NOT OK; W = REQUIREMENT WAIVED

```
* * * * * * * * * *   SOURCE INSPECTION CHECKLIST FOR SOFTWARE REQUIREMENTS SPECIFICATION   * * * * * * * * * * *
----------------------------------------------------------------------------------------------------------------
  CHECK-OFF: CHECKLIST      SOURCE AND       REQUIREMENTS DESCRIPTION                                       NOTES
  C  N  W ITEM NO.         PARAGRAPH REF.
================================================================================================================
                          DI-MCCR-80025A    3.4 CSCI DATA ELEMENT REQUIREMENTS (cont'd)
 ( ) ( ) ( )   10.5.2     10.2.5.4 (cont'd) FOR DATA ELEMENTS OF CSCI's INTERNAL I/Fs;
 ( ) ( ) ( )   10.5.2.1                       - DATA ELEMENT'S I/F NAME & PROJECT ID DEFINED
 ( ) ( ) ( )   10.5.2.2                       - NAME DATA ELEMENT SOURCE CAPABILITY
 ( ) ( ) ( )   10.5.2.3                       - NAME DATA ELEMENT DESTINATION CAPABILITY
 ( ) ( ) ( )   10.5.3                       For each external I/F data element in the CSCI:
 ( ) ( ) ( )   10.5.3.1                       - DATA ELEMENTS IDENTIFIED BY PROJECT ID
 ( ) ( ) ( )   10.5.3.2                       - I/F IDENTIFIED BY NAME & PROJECT ID
 ( ) ( ) ( )   10.5.3.3                       - SOURCE OR DESTINATION CAPABILITY IDENTIFIED
                                                BY NAME & PROJECT ID
 ( ) ( ) ( )   10.5.3.4                       - IS IRS REFERENCED WHERE I/Fs ARE SPECIFIED
----------------------------------------------------------------------------------------------------------------
                          DI-MCCR-80025A
                          10.2.5.5            3.5  ADAPTATION REQUIREMENTS

               10.6       10.2.5.5.1          3.5.1  INSTALLATION DEPENDENT DATA
 ( ) ( ) ( )   10.6.1                         REQUIRED SITE UNIQUE DATA IDENTIFIED
                                                FOR EACH INSTALLATION
 ( ) ( ) ( )   10.6.2                         CSCI CAPABILITIES, USING SITE UNIQUE DATA, IDENTIFIED
                          SQAM BWI 3.8.4
 ( ) ( ) ( )   10.6.3     AC2120 REV.G #8     IF CSCI IS RESIDENT OR EMBEDDED, DESCRIBE ENVIRONMENTAL CONSTRAINTS
                          DI-MCCR-80025A
----------------------------------------------------------------------------------------------------------------
               10.7       10.2.5.5.2          3.5.2  OPERATIONAL PARAMETERS
 ( ) ( ) ( )   10.7.1                         VARIABLE CSCI PARAMETERS DESCRIBED
 ( ) ( ) ( )   10.7.2                         IDENTIFY CSCI CAPABILITIES USING VARIABLE PARAMETERS
----------------------------------------------------------------------------------------------------------------
                          DI-MCCR-80025A
               10.8       10.2.5.6 OF DID     3.6  SIZING & TIMING
 ( ) ( ) ( )   10.8.1     10.2.5.6  &         INTERNAL MEMORY ALLOCATED TO CSCI
                          AC 2120 REV.G #9&4
                          DOD-STD-2167A
               1.1.2      4.2.10
 ( ) ( ) ( )   10.8.2     10.2.5.6  &         AUXILIARY MEMORY ALLOCATED TO CSCI
                          AC 2120 REV.G #9
 ( ) ( ) ( )   10.8.3     10.2.5.6 OF DID     LOCATION OF CSCI INTERNAL MEMORY IDENTIFIED IF APPLICABLE PER SOW
 ( ) ( ) ( )   10.8.4     10.2.5.6 OF DID     LOCATION OF CSCI AUXILIARY MEMORY IDENTIFIED IF APPLICABLE PER SOW
 ( ) ( ) ( )   10.8.5     10.2.5.6 OF DID     TIMING RESOURCES ALLOCATED TO CSCI ARE IDENTIFIED.
                          AC 2120 REV.G #4
               1.1.1      DOD-STD-2167A
                          4.2.10
                          DOD-STD-2167A
 ( ) ( ) ( )   1.1.1.1    10.2.6 APP-D        ALLOCATED & DOCUMENTED TIMING LIMITS NOT EXCEEDED
 ( ) ( ) ( )   10.8.6     10.2.5.6 OF DID     CSCI MEMORY RESERVE CAPACITY SPECIFIED
 ( ) ( ) ( )   10.8.7     10.2.5.6 OF DID     CSCI CPU RESERVE CAPACITY SPECIFIED
```

C = CHECK OK; N = NOT OK; W = REQUIREMENT WAIVED   6/11

```
* * * * * * * * *     SOURCE INSPECTION CHECKLIST FOR SOFTWARE REQUIREMENTS SPECIFICATION   * * * * * * * * *
--------------------------------------------------------------------------------------------------------
 CHECK-OFF: CHECKLIST      SOURCE AND        REQUIREMENTS DESCRIPTION                              NOTES
 C   N   W  ITEM NO.       PARAGRAPH REF.
========================================================================================================
                          DOD-STD-2167A
( ) ( ) ( )   1.1.2.1      10.2.6 APP-D   &  ALLOCATED & DOCUMENTED MEMORY LIMITS NOT EXCEEDED
                          AC 2120 REV.G #9

                          DOD-STD-2167A
( ) ( ) ( )      1.1       4.2.10            PROCESSING RESOURCES ALLOCATED TO CSCI
( ) ( ) ( )      1.1.3     4.2.10       &    I/O CHANNEL UTILIZATION ALLOCATED TO CSCI
                          AC 2120 REV.G #4
( ) ( ) ( )      1.1.3.1   10.2.6 APP-D   &  I/O CHANNEL UTILIZATION LIMITS NOT EXCEEDED
                          AC 2120 REV.G #4
( ) ( ) ( )      1.1.4     10.2.6 APP-D      SUM OF ELEMENTS' ALLOCATIONS < OVERALL CONSTRAINT
--------------------------------------------------------------------------------------------------------
                10.9       DI-MCCR-80025A   3.7  SAFETY REQUIREMENTS
( ) ( ) ( )     10.9.1     10.2.5.7     &   CSCI DESIGN RELATED SAFETY REQUIREMENTS SPECIFIED
                          AC 2120 REV.G #8
( ) ( ) ( )   10.9.1.1                           FOR POTENTIAL PERSONNEL HAZARDS
( ) ( ) ( )   10.9.1.2                           FOR POTENTIAL PROPERTY HAZARDS
( ) ( ) ( )   10.9.1.3                           FOR POTENTIAL PHYSICAL ENVIRONMENTAL HAZARDS
--------------------------------------------------------------------------------------------------------
                10.10      DI-MCCR-80025A   3.8  SECURITY REQUIREMENTS
(.) ( ) ( )     10.10.1    10.2.5.8         SPECIFY SECURITY REQUIREMENTS IMPACTING THE DESIGN
                                            OF THE CSCI TO AVOID COMPROMISING SENSITIVE DATA
--------------------------------------------------------------------------------------------------------
                10.11      DI-MCCR-80025A   3.9  DESIGN CONSTRAINTS
( ) ( ) ( )     10.11.1    10.2.5.9         ARE REQUIREMENTS SPECIFIED THAT CONSTRAIN DESIGN
                                                 SUCH AS USE OF PROCESSING CONFIGURATION
                                                 OR USE OF SPECIAL INTERFACE CAPABILITY
                          SQAM BWI 3.8.4
( ) ( ) ( )     10.11.2    AC 2120 REV.G #8  IF VEHICLE AND/OR EQUIPMENT SUPPORT CONSTRAINTS APPLY,
                                             THEN DESCRIBE FACILITIES & DEGREE OF INVOLVEMENT
--------------------------------------------------------------------------------------------------------
                10.12      DI-MCCR-80025A   3.10  SOFTWARE QUALITY FACTORS (SQF)
( ) ( ) ( )     10.12.1    10.2.5.10        SPECIFY EACH SOFTWARE QUALITY FACTOR
                                                 IDENTIFIED IN THE CONTRACT
( ) ( ) ( )     10.12.2                     SPECIFY EACH SOFTWARE QUALITY FACTOR
                                                 DERIVED FROM HIGHER LEVEL SPECIFICATIONS
                                                 (POSSIBILITIES INCLUE; RELIABILITY, MAINTAINABILITY, EFFICIENCY,
                                                 INTEGRITY, USABILITY, TESTABILITY, FLEXIBILITY, PORTABILITY,
                                                 REUSABILITY & INTEROPERABILITY)
( ) ( ) ( )     10.12.3                     USE A SEPARATE PARAGRAPH FOR EACH SQF
( ) ( ) ( )     10.12.4                     SPECIFY METHOD OF COMPLIANCE FOR EACH SQF
```

```
* * * * * * * * * *    SOURCE INSPECTION CHECKLIST FOR SOFTWARE REQUIREMENTS SPECIFICATION    * * * * * * * * * *
---------------------------------------------------------------------------------------------------------------
CHECK-OFF: CHECKLIST      SOURCE  AND         REQUIREMENTS DESCRIPTION                                    NOTES
C   N   W  ITEM NO.       PARAGRAPH REF.
===============================================================================================================
( ) ( ) ( )   10.12.5                         SPECIFY REQUIREMENTS FOR EACH SQF

                          DOD-STD-2167A
              1.8         !0.3.1 APP-D         ADEQUACY OF QUALITY FACTORS
( ) ( ) ( )   1.8.1                            Tradeoffs between Quality factors have been documented.
( ) ( ) ( )   1.8.2                            FEASIBLE METHOD DEFINED TO EVALUATE COMPLIANCE OF QUALITY FACTORS.
              10.13       DI-MCCR-80025A       3.11  HUMAN PERFORMANCE/HUMAN ENGINEERING
( ) ( ) ( )   10.13.1     10.2.5.11  &         SPECIFY HUMAN FACTORS ENGINEERING RQMTS FOR CSCI
                          SQAM BWI 3.8.4
                          AC 2120 REV.G #12
( ) ( ) ( )   10.13.2     10.2.5.11            SPECIFY HUMAN INFORMATION PROCESSING CAPABILITIES
( ) ( ) ( )   10.13.3                          SPECIFY HUMAN INFORMATION PROCESSING LIMITATIONS
( ) ( ) ( )   10.13.4                          SPECIFY FORESEEABLE HUMAN ERRORS FOR NORMAL CONDNS
( ) ( ) ( )   10.13.5                          SPECIFY FORESEEABLE HUMAN ERRORS FOR EXTREME CONDNS
( ) ( ) ( )   10.13.6                          SPECIFY HUMAN FACTORS REQUIREMENTS FOR TRAINING
( ) ( ) ( )   10.13.7                          SPECIFY HUMAN FACTORS REQUIREMENTS FOR SUPPORT
( ) ( ) ( )   10.13.8                          SPECIFY HUMAN FACTORS REQUIREMENTS FOR OPERATIONAL ENV.
---------------------------------------------------------------------------------------------------------------

              10.14       DI-MCCR-80025A       3.12  REQUIREMENTS TRACEABILITY
                          10.2.5.12
( ) ( ) ( )   10.14.1                          MAP SRS REQUIREMENTS TO CSCI REQUIREMENTS IN SYS SPEC
( ) ( ) ( )   10.14.2                          MAP ALLOCATED CSCI REQUIREMENTS IN SYSTEM SPEC TO SRS

              1.2         DOD-STD-2167A        REQUIREMENTS ALLOCATION
( ) ( ) ( )   1.2.1       5.1.2.1              CSCI REQUIREMENTS CONSISTENT WITH SSDD ALLOCATIONS FOR THIS CSCI
---------------------------------------------------------------------------------------------------------------

                          10.2.6
              11.1        10.2.6.1  &          4.1  QUALIFICATION METHODS
                          AC 2120 REV.G #13
( ) ( ) ( )   11.1.1                           SPECIFY QUALIFICATION METHODS USED TO ENSURE CSCI
                                               REQUIREMENTS OF SECTIONS 3 & 5 WILL BE SATISFIED
( ) ( ) ( )   11.1.1.1                         (A TABLE MAY BE USED; SEE TABLE-1 OF DID)
( ) ( ) ( )   11.1.1.2                         SPECIFY QUALIFICATION METHODS FROM INSPECTION,
                                               ANALYSIS, AND/OR DEMONSTRATION.

              1.2         DOD-STD-2167A        REQUIREMENTS ALLOCATION
( ) ( ) ( )   1.2.2       5.1.3                CSCI QUALIFICATION REQUIREMENTS DEFINED
( ) ( ) ( )   1.2.3       5.1.3                QUAL. REQUIREMENTS CONSISTENT WITH SYS SPEC
              11.2        10.2.6.1             4.2  SPECIAL QUALIFICATION METHODS
( ) ( ) ( )   11.2.1                           SPECIFY ANY SPECIAL RQMTS NEEDED TO QUALIFY THE CSCI
( ) ( ) ( )   11.2.2                           USE SEPARATE SUBPARAGRAPHS FOR EACH REQUIREMENT
( ) ( ) ( )   11.2.3                           SPECIFY SPECIAL TOOLS
( ) ( ) ( )   11.2.3.1                         SPECIFY TECHNIQUES (TEST FORMULAS, ALGORITHMS)
```

```
* * * * * * * * *   SOURCE INSPECTION CHECKLIST FOR SOFTWARE REQUIREMENTS SPECIFICATION   * * * * * * * * * *
------------------------------------------------------------------------------------------------------
 CHECK-OFF: CHECKLIST    SOURCE AND      REQUIREMENTS DESCRIPTION                              NOTES
 C   N   W  ITEM NO.     PARAGRAPH REF.
======================================================================================================
( )( )( )  11.2.3.2                      SPECIFY PROCEDURES
( )( )( )  11.2.3.3                      SPECIFY FACILITIES
( )( )( )  11.2.3.4                      SPECIFY ACCEPTANCE LIMITS
           11.2.4                        FOR EACH SPECIAL TEST:
( )( )( )  11.2.4.1                        SPECIFY PARAGRAPH NOS. REFERENCING THE CSCI
( )( )( )  11.2.4.2                        SPECIFY PARA. NOS. REFERENCING THE CSCI CAPABILITY REQ. TO WHICH
                                             THE TEST APPLIES
( )( )( )  11.2.4.3                        TEST DESCRIBED.
( )( )( )  11.2.4.4                        LEVEL OF TEST DESCRIBED (CSU,CSC,CSI,SEGMENT..)
                        DOD-STD-2167A
            1.7         10.2.7 APP-D     ADEQUATE TEST COVERAGE OF REQUIREMENTS
( )( )( )   1.7.1          "             EACH REQUIREMENT ADDRESSED BY A TEST
            1.9.2         10.3.2 APP-D   (I.E.,  FEASIBILITY TEST DESIGNED FOR EACH REQUIREMENT)
( )( )( )   1.7.2         10.2.7 APP-D   TEST CASES FOR AVERAGE SITUATION
( )( )( )   1.7.3          "             TEST CASES FOR BOUNDARY SITUATIONS
( )( )( )   1.7.4          "             STRESS TEST CASES SELECTED
( )( )( )   1.7.5          "             TEST CASES FOR COMBINED FUNCTIONS
                        DOD-STD-2167A
            1.9         10.3.2 APP-D     TESTABILITY OF REQUIREMENTS
( )( )( )   1.9.1          "             TEST OBJECTIVE STATED FOR EACH REQUIREMENT
------------------------------------------------------------------------------------------------------
                        DI-MCCR-80025A
            12          10.2.7           5  PREPARATION FOR DELIVERY
( )( )( )   12.1                         SPECIFY TYPE & CHARACTERISTICS OF CSCI DELIVERY MEDIA
( )( )( )   12.2                         SPECIFY REQUIREMENTS FOR THE MEDIA;
( )( )( )   12.2.1                         - LABELLING
( )( )( )   12.2.2                         - PACKAGING
( )( )( )   12.2.3                         - HANDLING
( )( )( )   12.2.4                         - CLASSIFICATION MARKING
( )( )( )   12.3                         SPECIFY CSCI NAME & PROJECT UNIQUE ID
( )( )( )   12.4                         SPECIFY ANY UNIQUE DELIVERY REQUIREMENTS
------------------------------------------------------------------------------------------------------
                        DI-MCCR-80025A
            13          10.2.8           6  NOTES
( )( )( )   13.1                         PROVIDE GENERAL INFO TO AID UNDERSTANDABILITY
( )( )( )   13.2                         INCLUDE ALPHABETICAL LISTING(s) OF ALL;
( )( )( )   13.2.1                         - ACRONYMS,
( )( )( )   13.2.2                         - ABBREVIATIONS,
( )( )( )   13.2.3                         - MEANINGS
------------------------------------------------------------------------------------------------------
                        DI-MCCR-80025A
            14          10.2.9           10  APPENDICES
( )( )( )   14.1                         USE FOR INFORMATION PUBLISHED SEPARATELY SUCH AS
( )( )( )   14.1.1                         - CHARTS, OR
( )( )( )   14.1.2                         - CLASSIFIED DATA
```

C = CHECK OK; N = NOT OK; W = REQUIREMENT WAIVED   9/11

```
* * * * * * * * *   SOURCE INSPECTION CHECKLIST FOR SOFTWARE REQUIREMENTS SPECIFICATION   * * * * * * * * * *
----------------------------------------------------------------------------------------------------------
 CHECK-OFF: CHECKLIST      SOURCE  AND       REQUIREMENTS DESCRIPTION                          NOTES
 C   N   W  ITEM NO.       PARAGRAPH REF.
==========================================================================================================
( ) ( ) ( )    14.2                          REF. IN MAIN BODY WHERE DATA WOULD NORMALLY OCCUR.
( ) ( ) ( )    14.3                          LETTER APPENDICES  A,  B,  ...
( ) ( ) ( )    14.4                          NUMBER PARAGRAPHS AS MULTIPLES OF 10
                                             -   APP-A;   PARA. 10.1, 10.2,  ...
                                             -   APP-B;   PARA. 20.1, 20.2,  ...
( ) ( ) ( )    14.5                          NUMBER PAGES ALPHANUMERICALLY
                                             -   APP-A;   A-1,  A-2,  ...
                                             -   APP-B;   B-1,  B-2,  ...

         PART II.  UNIQUE CHECKLIST - TAILORED REQUIREMENTS:

               U2                            SHARED RESOURCES
( ) ( ) ( )    U2.2                          COORDINATE SHARED SOURCE REQUIREMENTS BETWEEN CSCIs AT REVIEWS
( ) ( ) ( )    U2.2                          COORDINATE SHARED I/F DATA ELEMENTS BETWEEN CSCIs AT REVIEWS
( ) ( ) ( )    U2.3                          COORDINATE SHARED DATABASE DATA ELEMENTS BETWEEN CSCIs AT REVIEWS
( ) ( ) ( )    U2.4                          COORDINATE SHARED COMPUTER RESOURCES BETWEEN CSCIs AT REVIEWS

               U3                            REQUIREMENTS
( ) ( ) ( )    U3.1                          INDIVIDUAL REQUIREMENTS UNIQUELY IDENTIFIED (USE PARAGRAPH NUMBERS)
( ) ( ) ( )    U3.2                          ALL HIGHER LEVEL ALLOCATED TO SOFTWARE, HARDWARE, PEOPLE
( ) ( ) ( )    U3.3                          ONLY CSCI REQUIREMENTS ALLOCATED TO CSCI
( ) ( ) ( )    U3.4                          SPECIFY CSCI FUNCTIONS BY INPUT, PROCESSING, OUTPUT

               U4                            INTERFACES
( ) ( ) ( )    U4.1                          MAINTAIN INTERFACE SIMPLICITY WITH OTHER CSCIs

               U5                            IMPLEMENTATION
( ) ( ) ( )    U5.1                          NO IMPLEMENTATION DETAILS IN CSCI UNLESS PER SOW

               U6                            QUALIFICATION
( ) ( ) ( )    U6.1                          SPECIFY HOW EACH REQUIREMENT SHALL BE QUALIFIED

               U7                            TEST
( ) ( ) ( )    U7.1                          DEFINE A TEST METHOD FOR EACH REQUIREMENT EQUAL TO ITS COMPLEXITY
( ) ( ) ( )    U7.2                          ALLOCATE CSCI REQUIREMENTS TO A CSCI LEVEL OF TEST
( ) ( ) ( )    U7.3                          DO NOT DEFER CSCI TESTS TO HIGHER LEVELS OF TEST
```

C = CHECK OK; N = NOT OK; W = REQUIREMENT WAIVED

Index

ABOUT THE AUTHOR

G. Gordon Schulmeyer is Manager of Software Engineering for land based radars and systems at Westinghouse Electronic Systems Group, where he was previously Manager of Software Quality Engineering. He has written extensively on the subject of software quality control for a number of professional journals, and is the author of two books on the subject: *Handbook of Software Quality Assurance* and *Computer Concepts for Managers*. Mr. Schulmeyer is a member of the American Management Association and the Association for Computing Machinery and was the Vice-Chairman of the Aircraft Industries Association's Software Quality Subcommittee.